County boundaries of
England & Wales
after April 1974

D0636845

A guide to the Dark Age Remains in Britain

In the same series

A guide to the Prehistoric Remains in Britain
(South and East)
Richard Wainwright
A guide to the Roman Remains in Britain
Roger J. A. Wilson

Lloyd and Jennifer Laing

A guide to the

Dark Age
Remains
in Britain

Constable London

First published in Great Britain 1979
by Constable and Company Limited
10 Orange Street London WC2H 7EG
Copyright © 1979 Lloyd and Jennifer Laing

ISBN 0 09 462230 2

Set in Monophoto Times New Roman 9 pt and
printed in Great Britain by
BAS Printers Limited, Over Wallop, Hampshire

British Library CIP data

Laing, Lloyd Robert
  A guide to the Dark Age remains in Britain.
  1. Great Britain – Antiquities
  I. Title   II. Laing, Jennifer
  914.1′04′857   DA155

ISBN 0-09-462230-2

Acknowledgements

For their help in checking descriptions of sites for us, we would like to thank Misses Nichola Baxter, Sally Caswell, Nicole Dunn, Gwyneth Davies, Klaarje Koomans, Susan Kite, Caroline Rochester, Bernadette Singleton and Eileen White, and Messrs. Alan Harnasz, David Longley, John Oxley, Phil Wearne and David Wilson, and others who helped after the book was written.

Figures 21, 57(b), 83, 87, 90(a) and 93 are reproduced from L. R. Laing's *Archaeology of Late Celtic Britain*, by courtesy of Methuen.

Figures 29(b) and 30 are reproduced by permission of the Controller of Her Majesty's Stationery Office.

Contents

1 Gaut's Cross,
Kirk Michael,
Isle of Man

Illustrations

Introduction

Purpose
This book covers roughly the period from the early fifth century, when the Romans left, to the mid-eleventh, when the Normans arrived, which is commonly known as the Dark Ages. It is a period that has left superb jewellery and sculpture, magnificent manuscripts and glittering warrior graves. It has, moreover, left the oldest standing British buildings still capable of functioning. This is a guide to those earthworks and fortifications, towns, hill settlements, farms, churches, chapels and shrines that have visible remains. One of the features of the period is that much of artistic merit was displayed not inside buildings, as today, but outside where everyone could see it. Accordingly some of the finest artistic creations of the sculptor are still to be seen standing where they were erected over a millennium ago.

The structures of Dark Age Britain are not impressive for their grandeur nor their intricacy. However, the majority have the advantages over those of other periods in being readily accessible, easy to recognize and of readily understandable function. They have, too, an unspoilt charm and simplicity particularly refreshing today. The search will take you to some enchanting parts of the country. You can choose villages or towns, moorland, woodland or seaside, for, unlike the remains of the Roman period which have too long overshadowed those of the Dark Ages, there are things to see in almost every area from the Orkneys to Cornwall, from Yorkshire to Pembroke.

The remains cannot rival those of the later medieval period with its castles and churches, cathedrals and houses (many are, after all, twice as old). But they speak not of barbarian chaos as might be expected but of people striving for and indeed achieving the beginnings of civilization and a unified Britain. They are the forerunners of the later masterpieces, and interesting simply for this reason alone. Nor are they divorced from the people who created

PICTS

SCOTS

BERNICIA

BRITONS

NORTHUMBRIA

DEIRA

MERCIA

LINDSEY

GWYNEDD

POWYS

MIDDLE
ANGLES

EAST
ANGLES

DYFED

GWENT

EAST
SAXONS

WEST
SAXONS

KENT

SOUTH
SAXONS

them. Indeed, at no other period do the personalities of the builders and sculptors seem so vitally close. Some Dark Age monuments are connected with people whose careers are known to history – people who were important figures in their own time. Others are themselves the monuments to otherwise forgotten Celts, Saxons or Scandinavians.

The Dark Ages have left more marks than might be imagined for the twentieth century to enjoy. The term 'Dark Age' is usually used colloquially to mean a lack of civilization in the most derogatory sense. A picture of unmentionable squalor, of reed huts with peasants dressed in sacking, of savage raiders intent on rape, pillage and arson, immediately enters the mind. The reason for this is that Victorian and later historians looked on the period as an interval between the civilization of Rome and the civilization of feudal Europe, as a confusing hiatus for which documentary evidence was sparse, uninformative and chaotic. It was seen to begin in the early fifth century and to continue until 800 on the Continent and until 1066 in Britain. Research during the past century, using modern methods of evaluating historical records and above all archaeological studies, has radically changed the picture. For modern historians and archaeologists the period is not dark, but a fascinating saga of social change that was to shape the future of Europe politically and culturally and which left a great artistic legacy for future generations. True, the period was indeed uncertain politically, and the results of research are still not always clear. In addition to this the most popular material for everyday objects and for buildings was wood, which had naturally perished. A lack of remains should not however be allowed to suggest a low standard of living. It is salutary to consider that some of the most magnificent homes in Britain today are half-timbered and that they reflect the standards of living far from squalid, yet these in the fullness of time will crumble with no more traces than the halls of Anglo-Saxon or Celtic Britain.

This book has been written primarily for the non-specialist to help him find the abundant remains of Dark Age Britain, both *in situ* and in museums. It is not a comprehensive guide to Dark Age British archaeology, but a guide to the things that remain, and what should be made of them. To this end the first chapter provides general information about the historical and archaeological background of Britain between AD 400 and 1100 so far as it is known. We discuss the main types of visible remains both in the field and in museums.

Chapters

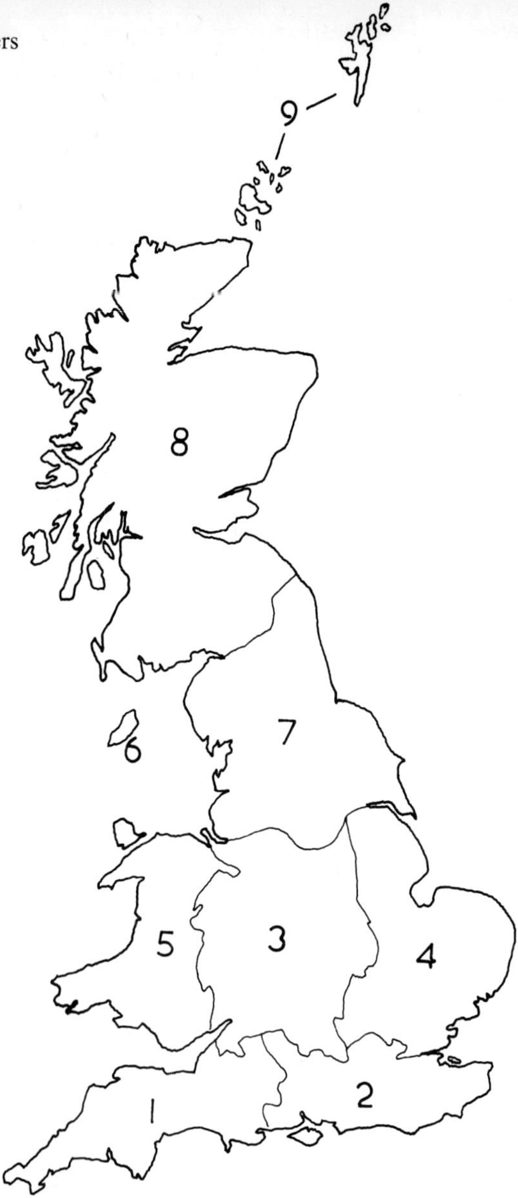

In this section we have assumed that the reader will have little or no
knowledge of Dark Age archaeology or history, but we hope that
having read it he or she will understand the remains better.

   Some technical terms are inevitable in a book which draws upon
the results of specialist research, and those that we have used are
explained in a Glossary. The main body of the text is a
comprehensive guide to the visible remains of the Dark Ages in
Britain – those not included in this part of the book are mostly to be
found in the Gazetteer provided in Appendix One.

   Unlike the companion volume to this, R J A Wilson, *A Guide to
the Roman Remains in Britain* (1975), it has not been possible in this
book to describe all the visible remains of the Dark Ages in Britain.
There are over 400 churches in England that display some work of
the period, and there are a comparable number of inscribed stones
of Dark Age date in Wales. As for Anglo-Saxon sculptures, there
are approximately 500 in Yorkshire alone, 210 in Co. Durham, 135
in Northumberland, 115 in Cumberland, 90 in Lincolnshire, 60 in
Cheshire, 55 in Derbyshire, and up to 50 in the other counties. If we
had included all the remains of certain or probable Dark Age date
in Britain the list would run to thousands of items, and to get them
into the compass of this book would mean producing no more than
an annotated list. We have therefore been forced to be very selective,
including only those sites where the visible remains seem sufficiently
interesting to be worth a trip: in borderline cases we have taken into
consideration general interest and accessibility. This immediately
rules out hundreds of sites which are familiar names in
archaeological literature, but which are now no more than a few
slight bumps or hollows in a field, visible only to the eye of the
informed. Not a single Anglo-Saxon village appears in the main text
of the book, nor do the Anglo-Saxon palace complexes uncovered in
excavation at Yeavering and Cheddar, though arguably they are
among the most interesting sites in Anglo-Saxon archaeology. The
same applies to cemeteries – there are few sites less impressive than
those of Anglo-Saxon cemeteries – though it is from the finds in
pagan Saxon cemeteries that most of our knowledge of this phase of
Anglo-Saxon archaeology is derived. Because of their exceptional
importance we have included a couple of barrows of pagan Saxon
date, and a list of the most important excavations will be found in
Appendix Two.

How to use this book

We have followed the formula successfully employed in *A Guide to the Roman Remains in Britain*, and avoided setting out the sites in accordance with a strict itinerary, as we assume that most people will not be making a special tour of the remains of the Dark Ages but will wish to combine a visit to some of these with visits to other sites in the same area, or will wish to stop to look at a few sites on their way from one place to another.

We have had to assume that potential visitors will equip themselves with an adequate road map. We have found the best for the purpose is the *AA Great Britain Road Atlas*, which incorporates the National Grid, and on which the majority of remains are marked. Any comparable atlas based on Bartholomew's $\frac{1}{2}''$ map will probably suffice. Ordnance Survey 1" maps will seldom prove necessary, except possibly in the Isle of Man and perhaps for some of the more remote sites in Wales and Scotland. We have given (in brackets) the 4-figure National Grid reference for each site which will enable it to be located on the map, together with general information about its location and the roads that lead there to facilitate its being planned into the itinerary. Where sites are particularly difficult to reach for any reason we have given detailed access information and a 6-figure grid reference, but where the site is signposted or happens to be the parish church of a village we have not considered such detailed information necessary.

Access

Some of the major monuments of Dark Age Britain are maintained by the Department of the Environment. These have been marked in the text by the letters 'AM' (Ancient Monument) in square brackets after the name of the site, and for these sites there is ready access and usually parking facilities. Some have free admission, others require a fee to be paid. Those indicated A are open at any reasonable time; those marked S are open during standard hours, which are as follows:

	Weekdays	*Sundays*
March–April	9.30–5.00	2.00–5.30
May–September	9.30–7.00	2.00–7.00
October	9.30–5.30	2.00–5.30
November–February	9.30–4.00	2.00–4.00

A great many of the sites are either churches or sculptures contained in churches. We have not said whether they are open, except in certain instances, because this varies constantly, and a church which has always in the past been open may be closed following black magic activities or vandalism, or simply because the policy has changed with a new incumbent. However, there is seldom any difficulty about obtaining the key to a locked church. Some churches of course are best seen from the outside – this should be apparent from our descriptions.

Some sites are on private land, and before visiting them every effort should be made to obtain the permission of the landowner, which is seldom witheld – the inclusion of a site in this book does not mean the public has a right to visit it, though nearly all have been visited during 1977 by the authors, students of Liverpool University and some of their very kind parents. Having obtained permission, you should remember the country code.

Historical outline

England
The Dark Ages in England were dominated by Germanic tribes from the Continent. Saxons entered Roman Britain either unofficially or with permission as early as the second century AD. Subsequently they were drafted into the Roman army as auxiliaries, with the result that Britain was no stranger to the tribesmen from Germania when the Roman forces were withdrawn in the early fifth century. From this point on increasing numbers of Germanic settlers entered Britain, particularly after 450. The incomers, now known collectively as Anglo-Saxons, were pagans, and goods from their cemeteries fill museum cases. Many different groups of people were represented in the Anglo-Saxon settlements. The Angles who settled predominantly to the north of the Thames, came mainly from Denmark, as did the Jutes who settled in Kent. The Saxons hailed from the North German Plain, and mainly colonized the region south of the Thames. There were other, smaller groups such as the Franks (who lived to the south of the Saxons on the Continent) and the Frisians (from the Low Countries). South of the Thames the incomers buried their dead in *inhumation cemeteries*, with few cremations, but to the north of the river, *cremation* was predominant, the ashes being placed in hand-made urns. This period is known as the *Pagan Saxon Period*.

From the outset Kent was one of the most important areas, and particularly rich finds have been discovered in cemeteries such as those at Kingston Down, Chartham Lines, Faversham, Crudale and Fairford. In Sussex the seventh-century barrow at Taplow represents the extension of Kentish culture.

Side by side with the new settlers, and often in conflict with them, lived the Romano-Britons who tried, well into the fifth century, to maintain the trappings of civilisation. They swept their town streets and kept their magistrates until at least the end of the fifth century. The Romano-Britons kept alive their Christian faith and enjoyed several missionary visits from spiritual leaders from the Roman world, but their remains belong to the last phases of Roman Britain and have little place in a book on the Dark Ages; their valiant attempts to keep up the Roman traditions are to be found in excavation reports rather than in physical remains above ground.

Within 200 years and after the Civil Wars of the fifth and sixth centuries, the Anglo-Saxons were the dominant cultural force in the area that later became England. Saxon villages abounded, their art flourished and blossomed into a colourful and precious flowering in the seventh century. They formed kingdoms, which by the early seventh century were taking on the shape they were to have for much of the Anglo-Saxon period.

At the point when the kingdoms were emerging, Rome sent St Augustine in 597 to rekindle the Christian flame in the province that had, apparently, lapsed into paganism. With some false starts, the new religion took hold and further ideas were adopted after contact with the civilized world. The adoption of Christianity in the seventh century marks the beginning of the *Middle Saxon Period*. Less is known about this archaeologically than about the Pagan Saxon period, because of the absence of grave furniture in Christian burials. During the Middle Saxon period the kingdoms unified into seven, the Heptarchy, and England was led by the most powerful – in succession Kent, East Anglia, Northumbria, Mercia and Wessex. The richly furnished royal ship burial at Sutton Hoo belongs to the transitional period between Pagan and Middle Saxon England. A number of churches or fragments of churches survive from the Middle Saxon period, the most important being the group centred on St Augustine's own foundation at Canterbury, though there are other early churches at Brixworth (Northants), Deerhurst (Glos) and Bradford-on-Avon (Wilts).

The Middle Saxon period came to an end with the arrival of the

Danes in England, and for a while the kings of Wessex, notably Alfred, were caught up in campaigns against them. The Danes were given lands in eastern England (the Danelaw) but conflict continued between the Vikings and the Anglo-Saxons into the tenth century. During this period Wessex had led England, and Aethelstan of Wessex became first King of All England around 927, a united England being ruled by the successors of Aethelstan until the time of Aethelred II (the 'Unready'), who ruled from 978 to 1016. Aethelred's reign is a saga of Scandinavian raids on England, and culminated in the conquest of England by the Danes. After a brief skirmish in which Aethelred's son Eadmund contested the throne, the Danish Cnut became King of All England in November 1016. He was succeeded briefly by Harthacnut, but in 1042 England returned to Anglo-Saxon rule under Edward the Confessor, whose death in 1066 led to the Norman Conquest.

The period when the Danes were active in England is known as the *Late Saxon Period*, and is characterized by the growth of towns and the expansion of trade. Apart from a few early towns, the first real town growth in England can be chronicled in the ninth century, Mercia probably taking the lead under her famous King Offa (d. 796), Wessex following with *burhs* established partly to counter the Danish threat. Many of these were laid out with grid-iron street plans. After a lull during the Danish raids, church building revived, and many good examples of Late Saxon churches, such as Earl's Barton (Northants) survive. Winchester was the capital of the newly unified England, and here the Winchester School of art (see p. 93) flourished. Anglo-Saxon coinage (which had been introduced in the seventh century) flourished in the Late Saxon period, and developed into one of the most sophisticated monetary systems in Europe. In this period, too, glazed, wheel-made pottery spread to many parts of England.

The Norman conquest of England did not bring about an abrupt end to the Anglo-Saxon way of life. Churches of Anglo-Saxon type continued to be built, and settlement patterns remained little altered to the end of the eleventh century and beyond. This period of Saxo-Norman overlap, however, lies outside the scope of this book.

Wales
The Welsh Dark Ages were almost devoid of Anglo-Saxon influence. It was not until Edward I's campaigns in the thirteenth century that the Welsh finally came under wider rule. The iron age

tribes had fought hard to maintain their independence from Rome in the first century AD, but by the late first century their fire was spent and Roman forts, conveniently spaced a day's march apart, kept the area subdued. Few villas and only two towns civilized this Roman military zone, and when the Romans were faced with problems on the northern frontier they did not hesitate to remove troops from Wales. The inhabitants had been relatively little affected by the rule of Rome in their everyday life. Many aspects remained unchanged from the iron age to the Dark Ages, in contrast with the situation in England. There was unrest in the third and fourth centuries when the Irish raided and subsequently settled in southern Wales and the Lleyn peninsula, and more when the usurper Magnus Maximus (Maxen Wledig) declared Britain a breakaway state from Rome. Around this time (c. 385) Roman administrative officials began to encourage the native Welsh to set up regional administrations under their general supervision, and the administrations thus formed grew during the fifth century into the first kingdoms of Wales, whose rulers traced their line back to men with Roman names and titles. Of the kingdoms that grew up the most important were Gwynedd in North Wales, with its capital at Aberffraw in Anglesey, Powys on the central Welsh Marches, Dyfed in Pembroke and Gwent in Monmouth. The names of these kingdoms have been revived in the counties that were created in 1974.

The remains of the Welsh Dark Ages are tantalizingly sparse. Historical sources are confusing, and archaeological remains limited. Apart from a few iron age hillforts re-used in the fifth and sixth centuries there are no excavated settlement sites of the Dark Ages in Wales, and few ecclesiastical structures that can be ascribed with any confidence to the period. Almost all the visible remains comprise inscribed and sculptured stones, which are abundant and span the whole period. Kings, princes, magistrates, a consul, a doctor and others are commemorated in stone. From the brief inscriptions summing up their lives we must piece together the real world in which they lived.

A few personalities illuminate early Welsh history: Maelgwn, the sixth-century king of Gwynedd who was made famous in later Welsh poetry, Cadfan, whose tombstone can be seen at Llangadwaladr on Anglesey and whose court was in contact with Continental culture, and his successors Cadwallon and Cadwaladr, of whom Cadwallon was an ally of the great Mercian king Penda in the seventh century. In the ninth century Rhodri Mawr (the Great) united most of Wales, and fought successfully against the Vikings. Rhodri's court had close links with the Continent. His grandson, Hywel Dda (the Good) completed the unification of Wales in the early tenth century and allied himself to England, effectively as a client king of Aethelstan.

Scotland

Scotland in the Dark Ages was a land of vigorous change and instability. The northern tribes had never been conquered by Rome – the most they had to suffer was Agricola's line of forts that lasted but a short while and which were established only as far north as Auchinhove in Banff. After the first century they fought fluctuating battles over the northern limits of the Empire, which Rome variously claimed as Hadrian's Wall or the Antonine Wall. The border tribes, while rarely giving lasting support to Rome, found after four centuries they had adopted many aspects of its civilization. The northern frontier was overrun by Picts, Scots and Attacotti in 367, and the Roman Empire, distraught from pressures elsewhere, finally left the north to its own devices around AD 400.

Three groups of people can be distinguished in Dark Age Scotland, with a fourth playing a later and lesser role in its development. The first of the three consisted of the Britons of the Scottish lowlands, who occupied the area between what had been the Antonine and Hadrian's Walls. Like the Welsh, to whom they were closely related, they started to form regional administrations under Roman guidance in the fourth century. Out of these emerged Dark Age kingdoms, of which the most notable were Rheged, centred on the Solway Firth, Gododdin, centred on the south-east, and Strathclyde, which evolved somewhat later on the Clyde valley. The peaceful development of the southern Scottish kingdoms was disrupted by the advance of the Anglo-Saxons of Bernicia (later part of Northumbria) into south-east Scotland from the end of the sixth century. By the middle of the seventh century Northumbrian influence had extended to south-west Scotland also, and the Anglo-Saxons were to remain a force to be reckoned with south of the Forth–Clyde line for much of the Dark Ages.

To the north of the Forth–Clyde line lay Picts and Scots. The Picts first make their appearance in history as one of the groups of northern barbarians menacing Hadrian's Wall – their name is a Roman one meaning 'painted people', though they called themselves

'Cruithne'. Their language is known only from a few personal names, place-names and brief inscriptions, which indicate that it was a mixture of Celtic and some older speech. It has been suggested that the Picts were descended from the prehistoric inhabitants of north-east Scotland who had migrated from Germany in the late bronze age.

Archaeologically the Picts are best known for their mysterious symbols, carved on stones and sometimes on small objects, and which may be found combined with crosses and other features of Christian iconography. They were distinguished metalsmiths, their work being known best from the hoard of silverwork found at St Ninian's Isle, Shetland, in 1958. Apart from their art, their culture was basically like that of the other Celtic peoples of the Dark Ages.

Throughout their history the Picts waged constant war with their neighbours the Scots, but were finally united with them under the Scottish king, Kenneth mac Alpin, around 842, at which point they disappear from history.

The Scots were Irish settlers who came over from Ulster in the fifth century to Argyll. Here, centred on their stronghold of Dunadd (see p 272), grew up the kingdom of Dalriada, which encroached on Pictish lands and extended its influence to some at least of the Western Isles. The Scots maintained links with their homeland, and St Columba came from Ireland to found his monastery on Iona in the sixth century, from whence a mission went out to the Picts.

The Norse began raiding Scotland at the end of the eighth century, one of the first targets of their attacks being Iona, which was sacked at the beginning of the ninth century. These early raids were soon followed by settlements. Orkney was settled by colonists from Norway around 800, and from there the Norse spread out, colonizing Shetland and the north Scottish mainland, particularly Caithness. The Isle of Man and Ireland were colonized partly as an extension of the settlements in the Western Isles, and somewhat later Galloway was raided and settled by Norse-Irish, who earned a reputation for their savagery.

Around 880 under Earl Sigurd the Mighty, Orkney became a Norse earldom which endured until the thirteenth century, taking under its sway the rest of the Northern Isles and Caithness, and sometimes even the Hebrides. The Norse were converted in Scotland to Christianity under Earl Thorfinn in the eleventh century.

Scotland was united under Duncan I in the early eleventh century. Under David I (1124–53) it became heavily Normanized.

Historical table

AD 367	'Barbarian Conspiracy' of Picts, Scots and Attacotti. Hadrian's Wall overrun.
383	*Magnus Maximus* (Maxen Wledig) takes troops from Wales and N. Britain to the Continent. Irish raids in Wales.
c. 396	Stilicho orders expedition against Picts, Scots and Saxons.
c. 400	Hadrian's Wall abandoned.
401	Withdrawal of Roman troops from Britain.
407	Usurper *Constantine III* takes troops from Britain to Continent in bid for the purple.
410	Emperor *Honorius* tells Britons to look to their own defence.
c. 428	Hengist and Horsa traditionally land, invited over by *Vortigern*.
c. 441	First Saxon revolt.
c. 446	'The Groans of the Britons' – appeal for military help to Aetius, consul in Italy.
c. 432–59	St Patrick active in Ireland.
c. 440–3	St Germanus combating the Pelagian heresy.
c. 460–75	Britons led by Ambrosius Aurelianus, forerunner of Arthur.
c. 475–515	Career of *King Arthur*.
c. 490	Battle of Mons Badonicus: Arthur's triumph over the Saxons.
c. 515	Battle of Camlann: Arthur killed.
c. 515–40	*Vortepor* king in Wales.
c. 520–51	*Maelgwn*, the 'Dragon of the Isles', king in Gwynedd.
c. 538	Gildas writing.
563–97	St Columba at Iona.
597	St Augustine begins conversion of pagan Saxons.
625	*King Edwin* of Northumbria baptized.
626–55	Rise of *King Penda* of Mercia.
664	Synod of Whitby. Northumbria decided to follow Roman rather than Celtic faith.
633–70	Golden Age of Northumbria, under *King Oswald* and *King Oswy*.
c. 681–735	Venerable Bede at Jarrow.
664–87	St Cuthbert active in Northumbria.
c. 740	Eclipse of Northumbria by Mercia.

757–96	*Offa king of Mercia*. Offa's Dyke built. Mercian supremacy in England.
789	First Scandinavian raid on England.
793	Sack of Lindisfarne by Vikings.
825	Eclipse of Mercia by Wessex, following Mercian defeat at Ellendun. Wessex supreme under *Egberht* (802–39).
844–77	*Rhodri Mawr king in Wales*.
c. 849	Picts and Scots united under *King Kenneth mac Alpin*.
871–99	*Alfred king of Wessex*. Wars against the Danes.
878	Agreement between Alfred and Guthrum of the Danes, establishing the latter in the area henceforward known as the Danelaw.
903	Winchester New Minster consecrated under *King Edward the Elder*.
c. 943–88	St Dunstan Abbot of Glastonbury and later Archbishop of Canterbury. Monastic reform, beginning of the Winchester Revival of the 'Winchester School' of art.
c. 946–84	St Aethelwold, monk at Glastonbury under Dunstan and later Bishop of Winchester, active in Winchester revival.
925–39	*Aethalstan* became *first King of All England*.
979–1013	*King Aethelred the Unready* dispossessed by Svein Forkbeard, king of Denmark: died in exile in Normandy 1016.
1016–35	*Cnut, king of Denmark* in 1014, became first Danish king of England.
1042–66	*Edward the Confessor* last English king. Westminster Abbey founded.
1124–53	*David I king of Scotland*. Settlement of Norman English in Scotland, and establishment of feudal system.

Some important churchmen

| Aidan | Monk sent from Iona to convert Northumbria. Founded Lindisfarne. Died *c*. 651. |
| Augustine | Sent by Pope Gregory to England in 597, where he converted Ethelbert, king of Kent, and thus began the conversion of the pagan Saxons. Founded church at Canterbury, and became its first archbishop. Died *c* 604. |

Bede	'England's first historian'. Born at Monkwearmouth, Co. Durham, *c.* 673, and spent most of his life as a monk at Jarrow, where he died *c.* 735. Author of a series of works, including the famous *Ecclesiastical History of the English Nation*.
Columba	Saint who went from Ireland to serve the Christian Scots of Dalriada, and who founded a monastery at Iona, in 563. From here he was active on the Scottish mainland, and went into Pictland. He died in 597.
Cuthbert	Northumbrian monk, abbot of Old Melrose, and later of Lindisfarne. He withdrew to Farne Island, and was an adherent of the Celtic form of religion. His coffin is still preserved in Durham Cathedral. He died *c.* 687.
David	Saint, active in the period *c.* 550–89, who founded a monastery at the place named after him in Pembroke. Although patron saint of Wales he was not the first Welsh saint – St Illtud had a famous school in the area at the end of the fifth century.
Dunstan	Abbot of Glastonbury and Archbishop of Canterbury. An active figure in ecclesiastical reform and a notable artist and craftsman, Dunstan had a chequered career – a brief period in the court of Aethelstan ended in his expulsion for supposed witchcraft. A key figure in the Winchester Revival. He lived 924–88.
Gildas	Western British monk, who wrote in Latin *c.* 538 an account of British history up to his time, the *De Excidio et Conquestu Britanniae*, in which he attacked important personalities of his day. Though unreliable, it is a key text for the period.
Nennius	A Welsh monk of the late eighth century, traditionally author of the *Historia Britonum*, a key compilation for early British history, but in reality the compiler of only part of it.
Ninian	Saint, who died *c.* 432. Founder bishop of Whithorn, Wigtown, and considered responsible for introducing Christianity to parts of Scotland.
Wilfrid	Saint, Bishop of York. 634–709. Upheld the Roman (as opposed to Celtic) form of Christianity at Synod of Whitby. In 681 went to the South Saxons to convert them, and taught them to fish.

Glossary

aisle Area of church separated by an arcade of columns or piers.

ambulatory Semicircular or polygonal aisle which encloses an apse, often provided so that worshippers can walk round an altar or shrine.

apse Semicircular or polygonal end of a chancel or a chapel.

arcade A row of arches on columns or piers; where attached to a wall instead of free-standing it is a *blind arcade*.

architrave The horizontal block between columns or piers that spans the area between them.

ashlar Carefully dressed masonry.

baluster A small column or pillar, often, but not necessarily, wider in the centre than at the extremities. Also called a *baluster shaft*.

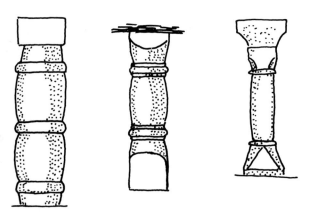

2 Examples of Saxon baluster shafts (a) Earl's Barton (b) Brixworth (c) Wing

barrow A burial mound.

basilica Term originally used to describe a Roman town hall, but later to describe a rectangular hall-like building, normally with a roof supported by two or more arcades (ie aisled).

beehive corbelling A technique of producing a dome-like vault by oversailing courses of masonry. Frequently used for Celtic monastic cells.

bellcote A turret, usually at the W end of a church, to carry bells.

boss A stone projection or knob, often used to ornament the intersection of ribs in a vault.

buttress A mass of brickwork built against a wall to carry the thrust and provide strength.

cable moulding Moulding imitating twisted cord.

capital The head of a column.

cell A small chamber or room, often used of the small detached buildings that are found in Celtic monasteries.

chamfer Surface produced by cutting across a square angle of a block at 45° to the other surfaces.

chancel The area at the E end of the church in which the altar is usually located. Normally used to describe the area E of the crossing that continues the line of the nave. Often narrower than the nave. Chancel arch is the arch dividing the nave from the chancel.

chevron Zig-zag pattern, normally on carved moulding.

clerestory Upper storey of the nave walls of the church, lit by windows.

corbel Block of stone projecting from a wall, usually to support a beam, or some other feature.

crypt Underground room, usually at E end of church.

curtain A connecting wall between towers.

cushion capital A capital cut from a square block with the lower angles rounded off to the column below. Also called a block capital.

Decorated Term used to describe a style of English Gothic architecture current *c*. 1300–50.

drystone Built without mortar.

dyke A bank, often used to describe a linear rampart.

Early English Term used to describe a style of English Gothic architecture, roughly covering the period 1200–1300.

gnomen The metal (or wood) finger on a sun dial.

graveslab A tombstone intended for laying flat on a grave.

Greek key Geometric pattern.

grubenhaüs Sunken-floor hut popular in Britain and on the Continent in the pagan Saxon period, but continuing in use later.

guilloche Geometric pattern.

herringbone Type of masonry in which the stones are set in a zig-zag pattern.

hogback Type of tombstone in the form of the hipped roof of a shrine or church, which bears a superficial resemblance to a hog's back (the shingles looking like bristles).

hood moulding Projecting moulding above an arch or lintel, normally intended to throw off water (sometimes called dripstone).

impost Bracket in a wall, often moulded, on which the end of an arch rests.

inhabited vinescroll Type of ornament popular in Northumbria, in which birds and beasts are disposed in a panel of stylized vine ornament, often pecking or biting the fruit.

in situ In its original position.

interlace A pattern made by intertwining a ribbon in and out of itself. Zoomorphic interlace is created when the ribbon takes the form of an animal's body.

jamb The straight side of a door, arch or window.

lacertine An animal with ribbon-like body used in zoomorphic interlace.

leacht An outdoor altar made from a pile of stones, normally square, which may mark a special grave.

light A window opening.

lintel A horizontal beam or stone bridging an opening.

longhouse A building with dwelling area and byre under the same roof-alignment, usually separated by a cross-passage. The commonest type of Viking house.

Manus Dei Literally 'the hand of God'. Visual symbol in the form of a hand emanating from a cloud representing God.

midwall shaft A shaft dividing a window of two lights, which is placed exactly centrally in the wall.

minster The church in a monastery; a church of major importance in the region.

monolithic Made of one stone.

narthex Enclosed vestibule or covered porch at the entrance to a church.

nave The main body of the church.

newel Central post in a circular staircase.

Norman Used in England as a synonym for 'Romanesque', it covers the style of architecture current between 1066–1200.

ogham A type of alphabet current in Ireland and in the Irish settlements in Britain in the Dark Ages, a variant of which was used by the Picts (see p. 44).

oratory A chapel without an altar.

parapet A low wall intended to protect a sudden drop, for example on a church or house top.

pelta A curvilinear shape, derived from that of a Roman shield.

Perpendicular A style of English Gothic architecture current
  between *c*. 1350–1530.

pier A mass of stonework or brickwork, usually of square section,
  which serves as a support instead of a column.

pilaster A shallow pier attached to a wall.

plinth The projecting base of a wall or column.

Pointed In English Gothic architecture, First Pointed is a style
  current in the Early English period (qv).

porticus A side chapel or chapels. In the early Anglo-Saxon church
  it was not permitted for burials to be made in the body of the
  church, but they were allowed in the flanking chapels or porticus.

quoin The corner of a building; also used of the individual stones
  (dressed) making up the corner.

rebate A recess cut in wood or stone to take the edge of another
  member that is to be secured in it.

relieving arch An arch constructed above a door or window to take
  the thrust of the masonry.

Renaissance The first period of classical revival, usually taken to
  begin *c*. 1453. Architecture influenced by it.

respond Half-pier bonded into a wall and carrying one end of an
  arch.

reveal The part of the jamb which lies between the door (or glass,
  in a window) and the outer wall surface.

revetment A facing of stone or timber in a rampart to stop it
  collapsing or eroding.

ring-chain A type of ornament popular in Anglo-Danish times.

ringwork A type of circular earthwork consisting of rampart and
  external ditch broken by an entrance. Constructed mainly by the
  Normans in Britain.

Romanesque In England called Norman, a style of architecture
  influenced by the Roman. Current in the eleventh to twelfth
  centuries. Some Anglo-Saxon architecture is called, misleadingly,
  pre-Conquest Romanesque.

rood Cross or Crucifix.

rune Alphabet of twig-like signs used by both the Anglo-Saxons and
  the Vikings. Variant forms exist.

scalloped capital Type of capital in which the semi-circular surface is
  carved into a series of truncated cones.

school A term used in art history to denote a group of artists
  working in a similar style or tradition.

screen A partition (of stone or wood). A rood screen was at the W end of the chancel, below a rood. A 'parclose screen' separated the rest of the church from a chapel.

scriptorium A place where manuscripts were copied.

shrine A structure of stone or metal in which a relic of a saint was placed.

splay A chamfer, usually on the jamb of a window.

spindle whorl A round weight, used to make the spindle revolve more readily and smoothly in spinning with a hand distaff.

squint A hole cut in a wall or pier to allow the main altar to be viewed from where it otherwise could not be seen.

string course A projecting band or moulding set horizontally in a wall.

transept Transverse portion of a cruciform church.

tread The flat part of a step.

tympanum The space between the lintel of a doorway and the arch above it. Often sculptured.

unicameral Single-roomed or -celled.

vallum A bank. Used to describe the enclosure bank of an early Christian church or monastery.

volute Spiral scroll.

voussoir Wedge-shaped stone used in an arch.

Types of field monument

Anglo-Saxon (England, parts of southern Scotland)

CHURCHES

Churches are by far the most common of Anglo-Saxon structural remains – over four hundred display Saxon or Saxon Norman features. They suffer from a double standard by which they can be judged. Compared to the more magnificent achievements of later centuries they are often dismissed summarily. Compared to the Celtic remains of the period, however, they are impressive; they display pleasing decoration and simple uncluttered lines particularly attractive to modern taste. Only a few survive more or less intact – many are represented by only a window or two in later buildings, the remainder having been swept away by successive rebuildings. The earliest are the oldest surviving buildings still capable of their original function, and the majority have remained in constant use since their erection. Those that have survived are merely those that were built in stone. The technique was a deliberate copy of that used by the Romans and sometimes, significantly, the Anglo-Saxon churches were built in Roman fort ruins, from old Roman tiles. The church plans were borrowed from civilized not pagan traditions. Every stone, every chancel arch and lintel is a statement of the desire of the Anglo-Saxons to establish their right to civilization. These are not pathetic remains unworthy of study, but the triumphs of men without the benefits of a long tradition of civilization, who could not be certain when the next barbarian or pagan raid would come.

Anglo-Saxon churches were first built after the arrival of St Augustine in 597, and were erected right up till the Norman conquest and in some areas even after 1066. Their characteristics thus tend to change over the centuries and indeed from region to

3 Examples of Saxon windows (a) Hardham (b) Tichborne, Hants (c) Thursley, Surrey (d) Swanscombe, Kent

region. By the time of the Norman Conquest many were showing marked Norman characteristics, and these have, by and large, been omitted from this book as belonging more to the traditions of the Middle Ages than the Dark Ages. The dating of churches is very difficult, and depends often on architectural interpretations in conjunction with historical evidence. Some are apparently earlier than others from structural evidence, but certain dating is often missing. In this book we have referred to 'Early' and 'Late' churches, to avoid giving an impression of very firm dating. Early in this context thus means roughly seventh or eighth century, and Late means after about 950.

Anglo-Saxon churches are usually simple in plan, with a *nave*, *chancel* and sometimes *porticus*. About a dozen are known to have been *basilican* (similar to a Roman basilica or public hall, with aisles). Some smaller churches were *unicameral* (ie consisting of one room). A number of features characterize Anglo-Saxon architecture, the most distinctive being the doors, windows and quoins. Arches are often constructed of through-stones (passing through the width of the wall), jambs laid in Escomb-fashion (through stones laid alternately upright and flat, as in the church at Escomb, p. 208, irregularly shaped voussoirs, strip-work round the opening (ie a rectangular-sectioned hood moulding). Windows can have single or double splays and can be round-headed, triangular-headed, square-headed. They can be simple slits or be of keyhole shape (in Lincolnshire and Norfolk especially). Belfry windows often have *baluster shafts*, turned on a lathe. These are central columns thicker in the centre than at top or bottom. The type of masonry is also distinctive, being of rubble or irregularly coursed, unlike the ashlar of Norman work. The quoining, too, is distinctive, the characteristic features being *random megalithic quoining* (the use of very large stones set at random), *long-and-short work* (tall, upright stones alternately set with short, flat stones), and *side-alternate work* (stones of similar size and shape placed so that they lie alternately along each side of the corner). (Fig. 4, p. 33.) These techniques are found in later walling, but with less differentiation between the quoins and the wall and usually with much more regularly shaped stones. Many churches are proved to be of Saxon date simply from the existence of quoins. *Walls* tend to be thinner than Norman work, often as little as 2 feet 6 inches (76 cm) thick. They are commonly set on *plinths*, which are flat in contrast to those of the Norman period which are splayed. *String courses* are found as decoration. Herringbone work is sometimes found. Other features can include stairs, belfries and crypts.

It is fairly certain that many Anglo-Saxon churches were built in timber, though only one still survives and that is heavily restored (Greensted).

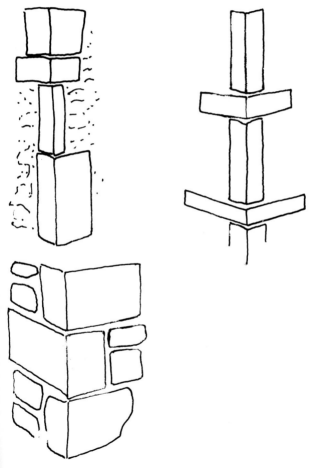

4 Quoining (a) random megalithic (b) long-and-short (c) side-alternate

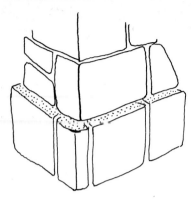
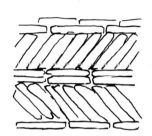

5 (a) Wall-plinths (b) Herringbone masonry

INSCRIPTIONS

Anglo-Saxon inscriptions are not common. They appear in a
number of scripts, and can be found on a variety of media, from
tombstones and architecture to coins and finger rings. The main
scripts are:

(i) *Insular Latin Majuscule*. Roman-type capitals. Used in
Northumbria, eg on the Whitby stones. A few Northumbrian
inscriptions are more 'Roman' in character, eg on the Ruthwell
Cross. Some miniscule letters may be combined with the majuscule.

(ii) *Hiberno-Saxon Half Uncial*. See p. 43.

(iii) *Runes*. Germanic alphabet, developed in the Roman iron age,
probably out of the Roman alphabet. Many variant forms of runes
occur, the Vikings having their own forms. Anglian runes belong to
the Anglo-Frisian futhorc, and appear on sculptures, such as the
Ruthwell and Bewcastle crosses, and on objects, such as rings.
Among the pagan Anglo-Saxons they had a magical significance and
in the Christian period were also used as charms.

SETTLEMENTS

The Anglo-Saxons built their homes of timber, and thus none
survive above ground. Saxon dwellings range from *grubenhaüser*,
small huts with sunken floors, through larger rectangular post-built
structures and halls to palaces, such as those found in excavation at
Cheddar (Somerset) and Yeavering (Northumberland). The Saxons

6 Scripts (a) Insular Latin Majuscule, from Whitby Abbey (b) Latin Majuscule, from Penmachno, Gwynedd

7 Runic alphabet

tended to live in *villages*, but all that is visible today, if anything, are a few hollows and bumps in the fields under which they lie.

Many Roman *towns* lingered on, and were occupied by Anglo-Saxon incomers, who built their huts adjacent to, and sometimes on, the Roman streets. A few towns may have survived with diminished occupation until revived in the Middle and Late Saxon period. Apart from a few mercantile centres engaged in the active overseas trade which grew up in the Middle Saxon period, such as *Hamwih* (the predecessor of Southampton), it was not until the time of Offa or Mercia that renewed contact with the Continent stimulated town growth in England. The Mercian towns were probably the first: the Danish threat in the time of Alfred the Great and his successors gave a new impetus to town building – defence. Late Saxon towns were laid out with grid-iron street plans and earthen ramparts, within which timber buildings and stone churches were erected. Late Saxon town defences are visible on a number of sites, such as at Lydford (Devon) and Wareham (Dorset), and have been investigated by excavation on others. Although extensively

excavated, nothing is now visible of the timber town houses at
Thetford (Norfolk). Towns were the focus of active trade, and each
had its own mint. Few traces of Saxon stone defences are now
visible, but portions of the stone rampart can be traced at South
Cadbury (Somerset), and what appears to be a very early Saxon
tower can be seen incorporated into the defences of York.

A few *ringworks* with circular earth ramparts can be seen which
predate the Norman conquest, and are the forerunners of Norman
fortification building in England.

BURIALS

Pagan Anglo-Saxon cemeteries consist of either *cremations* in urns,
which are found in the Anglian areas (ie north of the Thames), or
inhumations in unmarked cemeteries or under barrows, which are
found in the Saxon areas (ie south of the Thames), though there is
some overlap. *Ship barrows* are confined to East Anglia and are only
known from Sutton Hoo and Snape. In Christian times burials were
made in the churchyards attached to the churches, often in dug
graves, though stone coffins were sometimes used (as at Winchester).

EARTHWORKS

During the Anglo-Saxon period a number of earthworks were built,
most of which seem to have been territorial boundaries, the function
of which is now lost. Some were no more than estate boundaries,
but some were the result of more important political objectives. The
finest are Offa's Dyke and its predecessor Wat's Dyke, built the
length of the Welsh Marches to define the boundary between Mercia
and Wales. Earlier, but almost as fine, is Wansdyke, built in the
West Country, perhaps as a demarcation between Briton and Saxon.

SCULPTURE

Sculptures are among the commonest of visible Anglo-Saxon
remains. For the most part those surviving are fragmentary and late,
and all too often will consist of a few fragments of cross-shafts
decorated with poor interlace or debased vinescroll, or weathered
shafts in churchyards which will require the eye of faith to interpret.
The majority of sculptures are to be found in the north of England,
with a further concentration in the Midlands. South-east England is
almost without surviving examples of sculpture, and there are
relatively few in Wessex and the south-west. Virtually all the
sculptures recorded are *free-standing crosses*; in the late Saxon

period there are also a series of *hogback coffins and graves*, so-called because of their resemblance to a pig's back. They sometimes have bears holding either end (eg Brompton, Yorks), and are in fact representations of the coped roof of a church or church-shaped shrine. They were made popular by the Danes. *Architectural sculptures* are relatively rare, and usually consisted of friezes. The most famous are those from Breedon, Leics. *Roods* (representations of the Crucifixion) were sometimes built into churches in the Late Saxon period, notably in Wessex. The most famous is at Romsey, Hants. *Fonts* were on occasion decorated with sculpture, but these are rare. *Graveslabs* and *tombstones* were carved, as were the slabs used in *screens* and *shrines*. Some late Saxon churches had decorated *tympana* above the door.

In general terms, Anglo-Saxon sculptures fall into three main traditions: the *Northumbrian*, the *Mercian* and the *West Saxon*. The golden age of Northumbrian sculpture was the seventh to eighth centuries, that of the Mercian the ninth to tenth centuries and the West Saxon in the tenth to eleventh centuries. Northumbrian sculpture enjoyed a revival under Scandinavian influence in the tenth to eleventh centuries, while the West Saxon style was flourishing in the south.

Period I, AD 650–800. Sculpture appeared fully fledged in Northumbria with the free-standing crosses at Ruthwell (Dumfries) and Bewcastle (Cumbria). These display a naturalism new in Anglo-Saxon art, and combine figural ornament with inhabited vinescroll (characterized by panels of vines in which birds or sometimes other animals peck or bite), and (on the Bewcastle Cross) interlace and fret patterns. The subsequent works are less accomplished, and include the cross erected over the grave of Acca, Bishop of Hexham, in 740, and some early cross-fragments from southern Scotland, which at this period was under Northumbrian domination. Northumbrian sculpture became progressively barbaric until the end of the eighth century, when a certain softening of the style can be detected due to Continental influence. This can be seen on a cross-shaft from Brompton-in-Allerton (Yorks), and continued to manifest itself on a series of early ninth-century crosses, notably those from Otley (Yorks), Easby (North Yorks) and Rothbury (Northumberland). The figures have a greater naturalism and grace, and were more carefully modelled, but this skill rapidly degenerated – the Rothbury cross is crude compared with that from Easby.

Period II, 800–900. By 800 Northumbrian sculpture was beginning to be eclipsed by Mercian. The earliest Mercian works are architectural, and include the fragments of a frieze from Breedon (Leics) which combine both figural and abstract ornament in a diversity of styles. The rise in importance of Mercian sculpture is to be connected with the career of King Offa, who maintained contacts with the Carolingian Empire and under whose guidance Mercia developed a widespread trade. One early manifestation of Offa's trade links is the slab from Wirksworth (Derbyshire), decorated with figures copied from an imported ivory or manuscript.

Mercian influence soon extended to other regions. In Northumbria, the human figural work of the earlier crosses was ousted by designs composed of animals and interlace, typified by the slab from Melsonby (Yorks).

Politically, Mercia had given way to Wessex by 829, though her artistic influence lasted until the coming of the Vikings. From the beginning of the ninth century, however, some sculptures were produced in Wessex, one of the earliest being a fine cross-shaft from Codford St Peter (Wilts), with human figures which are stiff but dramatic, and which were influenced by new art styles introduced in manuscripts in Canterbury around the end of the eighth century. In west Wessex sculpture continued along its own lines in the later ninth century, rejecting Carolingian naturalism and drawing its inspiration from older, Celtic, models. This style is well exemplified by the sculptures at Colerne (Wilts).

Period III, 900–1066. In this period there are two conflicting traditions in Anglo-Saxon sculpture. In the south, focused on the New Minster at Winchester, a neo-classical style grew up. This drew heavily on Continental Carolingian models but developed into a distinct tradition which made 'Winchester school' art one of the most important in Europe. Outside Wessex, Scandinavian influence made itself felt, and gave rise to a tradition of Scandinavian-influenced Northumbrian sculpture.

The Wessex-based tradition of Winchester art is best seen in manuscripts and ivories, though a few sculptures are notable. Among these the finest are the angels from Bradford-on-Avon (Wilts), which share a delicacy of treatment with similar angels from contemporary manuscripts, and, somewhat later, the Crucifixion from Romsey Abbey (Hants).

On their arrival in Britain, the Scandinavians found a flourishing tradition of animal sculpture not too unlike their own, and in northern England an uninspired Anglo-Danish tradition grew up in the ninth century which combined some of the least interesting elements of both. The tradition was doomed to monotony, but was invigorated in the late tenth century by new Scandinavian elements. The most important of these was the 'Great Beast' – a creature developed out of an earlier Anglo-Saxon type of animal and the use of ribbon animals in irregular bands of interlace. Later still, from north Yorkshire, can be found an isolated dragon in a panel, well represented on a slab from Levisham.

Figural compositions from Norse mythology contribute to later Anglo-Danish sculpture. The culmination was the Gosforth Cross (Cumbria), erected around AD 1000, and showing Manx influence.

Celtic (Wales, Scotland, Northern Isles, Isle of Man, parts of England)

CHURCHES

Christianity probably reached the Celts in Roman times, and was revitalized in the fifth century by sea contact with the Mediterranean. Through the activities of early saints, such as Ninian and Columba in Scotland and David in Wales, Christianity rapidly spread in the fifth and sixth centuries, by which time it was the universal religion of the Celts. The most important remains are of inscribed and sculptured stones (see p. 43) but the remains of monasteries and chapels can also be seen. Until the seventh or eighth century churches and chapels (and presumably cells for monks) were all built of timber, and have been found only by excavation. The main types of ecclesiastical site are:

(i) *Monasteries*. Monasticism spread from the Mediterranean, where the first monasteries were regarded as the 'fortresses of God'. In keeping with fort plans, the early monasteries of the east Mediterranean were rectilinear in layout, and the first monasteries in Celtic Britain may have roughly followed this plan. Only Iona, however, can still be seen to lie within a rectilinear enclosure. Most Celtic monasteries are enclosed within a circular or oval *vallum*, an earth bank with outer quarry ditch which separated the sacred from the profane. The vallum is often the only visible feature on the site of a Dark Age monastery. Within the vallum the buildings were scattered at random – the *claustral* plan of medieval abbeys was not widespread until the Norman conquest. Typically a *church* or *oratory* would be surrounded by some rectangular or circular *cells* for the monks, and in the case of larger monasteries, artisans' huts, a 'schoolroom', or perhaps even a *scriptorium*, where manuscripts were copied. There would usually be a *cemetery*, and sometimes *shrines* or *special graves*.

The sites chosen for monasteries did not always require a complete encircling vallum. In some cases ruinous Roman forts were taken over, in others iron age forts may have been re-used. Some monasteries were sited on bends in rivers or on promontories, so that only the neck of land needed to be demarcated by a bank and ditch. Rock stacks were often favoured, as at Deerness (Orkney), or islands, as at Priestholm, off Anglesey. Here the sea served to isolate the monastic community.

(ii) *Hermitages* were very small monasteries, in very isolated situations, and usually consisted of a chapel, burial ground, and one or more cells within a vallum.

(iii) *Cemeteries* fall into two main categories, *undeveloped* and *developed*. An *undeveloped* cemetery, as the name suggests, consists of a series of burials dug in the ground or bedrock (*dug graves*) or in stone-lined cists (*cist graves*) or in stone cists with capping stones (*lintel graves*). The burial ground may be open, or enclosed by a circular or oval vallum, similar to that around monasteries. Occasionally these cemeteries may have memorial stones, cross-slabs or special graves. A *developed* cemetery has, in addition to the above, a church, oratory and perhaps living cells.

(iv) *Churches*. Celtic churches in Britain rarely survive above foundation level, and have few architectural features of note. They tend to be small (sometimes no more than 12 feet [3·66 metres] long), built in the ratio 3:2, with a door in the long side. They do not normally have a chancel – those that do were usually built after AD 1000. Churches of the Norse period and later tend towards the double square plan. *Chapels* are small churches with an altar, often stone-built. *Oratories* are similar, but lack the altar. *Beehive corbelling*, whereby a false vault is produced by oversailing courses of stones, is used for some monastic *cells* and possibly other buildings such as wells or baptistries. It can be seen at Eileach an Naoimh in Scotland and Llangybi in Wales.

(v) *Round towers*. Free-standing round towers were built in Ireland from the Viking period onwards, and served as places of refuge, treasuries and possibly bell towers. For protection, the door was set several feet above ground level, and inside were wooden floors accessible by ladders. The two examples in mainland Britain, Abernethy and Brechin, and the attached round tower in the Norse church at Egilsay, Orkney, were probably due to Irish influence.

(vi) *Special graves*. Cemeteries may contain special graves, often within their own enclosure. The best example of this is Eithne's Grave on Eileach an Naoimh, which has a circular stone surround, within which are two pairs of grave markers. Fragments of *shrines* are often found but cannot usually be seen *in situ*. The most common are *corner-post* or *corner-block* shrines, which have slabs slotted into end posts or blocks and which had hipped roofs, to resemble stone chapels.

(vii) *Leachta*. A *leacht* is a square pile of stones, like an open-air altar, sometimes surmounted by a cross-slab. The Mediterranean prototypes covered special graves, but in Britain it has not been determined whether burials lie under them. They have been found in Scotland, and there is one possible example at Tintagel, Cornwall.

(viii) *Caves* were sometimes occupied by Celtic hermits. Some may have engravings on the walls, as at St Ninian's Cave, Wigtown.

SETTLEMENTS

With the possible exception of nuclear forts, no single type of Celtic settlement in Britain is peculiar to the Dark Ages. Therefore the history of each site must be determined from excavation or documentary evidence, rather than its outward appearance. Because fortified sites are readily visible, more is known about these than open settlements (farms, farmsteads, villages) which do not leave any trace above ground, and thus can only be assumed to have existed – particularly after the late sixth century when many hillforts were abandoned. The existence of open settlements among the sand-dunes at places like Luce Bay (Wigtown), Culbin Sands (Moray) and Castlemartin Burrows (Pembroke) has been inferred from stray finds. Apart from occupation in a few caves and rock shelters, such as Lesser Garth Cave (Glamorgan), the main types of settlement which have produced evidence for Dark Age occupation are:

(i) *Nuclear forts* were usually built on rocky hills and made use of the natural defences: lengths of rock outcrop were joined with stretches of walling. A *citadel* usually commands the highest ground, surrounded by a series of interconnected 'courtyards'. The outer enclosures may have been for stock, and the citadels tend to be small (about 30 metres in diameter). They are confined to Scotland, but there are a few related sites such as Dinas Emrys (Gwynedd) where an earlier iron age fort has been modified in the Dark Ages. Dunadd, the citadel of the kings of Dalriada, in Argyll, is a classic example (p. 272).

(ii) *Citadel forts* are sometimes called 'defensive enclosure forts'. They have a small 'citadel' built within outlying defences, but not necessarily integral with them. The outworks frequently are of iron age date. Moncrieffe Hill (Perth) is a good example. They are mainly found in Scotland, but Garn Boduan (Gwynedd) is a related type of site in Wales.

(iii) *Refurbished forts.* The majority of hillforts occupied in the Dark Ages are iron age forts which have been refurbished. In some cases these renovations were extensive, and involved the construction of new ramparts and gateways (as at South Cadbury, Somerset).

(iv) *Primary forts.* There is very little evidence for hilltops being defended for the first time in the Dark Ages, but a few like Burghead (Moray) appear not to have been fortified before the fourth century, and some, such as the Mote of Mark (Kircudbright), not before the fifth. Future excavation will almost certainly bring many more to light.

(v) *Duns* are stone-walled Scottish forts which were developed in the iron age. The most distinctive are *galleried duns*, whose massive walls are often as much as 16 feet (4·90 metres) thick, and which enclose a courtyard 50 feet (15 metres) or more in diameter. They have a single entrance, checked for a door, and often have passages or chambers inside the walls and stairs, inside the wall or in the courtyard, leading to a wall walk. They contained insubstantial huts. Those built on rock stacks are known as *stack forts*. They are particularly common in the Western Isles and Argyll, but also occur in Galloway, Perthshire and Sutherland. Several were reoccupied in the Dark Ages, with or without alteration, while others appear to be entirely Dark Age in construction.

(vi) *Crannogs* are artificial islands on platforms in lakes on which houses were built. They were built from the bronze age to the Dark Ages in Ireland and Scotland, but none are worth visiting.

(vii) *Stone hut groups.* Groups of huts, enclosed by a wall (probably farm buildings) are found in Wales and northern Britain, where their construction may have been encouraged by the Romans. Additions were made to one at least (Pant-y-Saer, Anglesey) in the fifth or sixth century. So far there is no direct evidence for Dark Age occupation of hut groups in North Britain.

(viii) *Post-broch huts*. Brochs were iron-age tower-like constructions which fell into decay in the second century AD. From this time on, till the coming of the Vikings, new huts were built up round the ruins. Some rectilinear huts were distinctive and were perhaps built by the Picts.

(ix) *Wheelhouses* developed in Atlantic Scotland, probably in Shetland, in the second or third century AD. As the name suggests, they are stone circular huts with radial piers, in plan like a wheel, the hearth being the 'hub'. A few were reoccupied in the Dark Ages.

(x) *Souterrains* are underground passages, occasionally connected to huts. There are many different groups in Scotland, mostly of the early iron age. There is reason to believe, however, that the Fife and Angus souterrains were occupied by people whose descendants were known as the Picts.

INSCRIBED AND SCULPTURED STONES

The most common of all Dark Age Celtic remains are inscribed stones. Many of these are funerary monuments, but some were set up to commemorate events, possible as boundary markers or possibly even as preaching crosses. It is through them that Celtic Dark Age art can be most readily studied, and they shed a great deal of light on the life of the Dark Age Celts with their representations of human figures and inscriptions.

Inscriptions are found in different alphabets, which are readily recognizable even by non-experts:

(i) *Latin Majuscule*. This is the most easily read as it fairly closely resembles modern English capitals. It was an alphabet which evolved in the late Roman Empire, and inscriptions in this alphabet in Britain belong to the period AD 400–50 to 550 or even slightly later. Inscriptions in this are usually in horizontal lines, and may include some letters showing Greek influence, and some half-uncial letters, particularly in later inscriptions (fig. 6).

(ii) *Hiberno-Saxon Half Uncial*. Often thought of as Irish, this script represents a development in Britain and Ireland out of earlier scripts. Uncial lettering developed in the east Mediterranean in the Roman period, out of Latin majuscule, and first appeared in Africa in the third century. Out of this a book-hand (Roman half uncial) developed in Italy and Gaul in the fifth or early sixth century, employing a mixture of rounded letters. Some of these were adapted in Dark Age Britain, in Latin inscriptions, and by the seventh century inscriptions were mainly in half uncial letters. From the seventh century onwards Latin majuscule letters virtually disappear until the Norman Conquest (fig. 6).

(iii) *Ogham* script was developed in Ireland, probably in response to the Latin alphabet, during the fourth century. The ogham alphabet consisted of twenty letters, with additional symbols, arranged along a guide line, usually the edge of the stone. It was probably developed out of using a tally stick to count stock, or from a finger language. *Ogham bilingual inscriptions* are found in the areas settled by the Irish in Wales and Cornwall, and have the same memorial formula expressed in Latin majuscule and ogham. The Picts adapted the ogham alphabet from the Irish, but Pictish ogham, which appears meaningless when deciphered, differs from the Irish in that lines rather than notches are used for vowels. Pictish ogham inscriptions are late, dating from the eighth century. Oghams are usually set vertically (fig. 8).

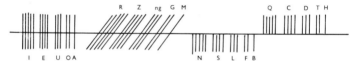

8 Ogham alphabet

Memorial formulae found on the tombstones of the fifth and sixth centuries are usually stereotyped, and derived from formulae used in the Mediterranean world. The most common are:

HIC IACIT 'Here lies', a corruption of the classical Latin HIC IACET. On the Continent this is found in Italy and Gaul from the fourth century.

FILIUS 'Son'. Usually in the form 'A filius B', the second name being in the genitive and thus ending in 'i'. Thus MELI MEDICI FILI MARTINI I(a)CIT, on a stone from Llangian, Gwynedd. Melus is rendered MELI because it is also a genitive, the words 'The stone of' being understood. In ogham FILIUS is rendered as MAQI, the Irish equivalent.

AVI 'Grandson' or 'descendant'.

INIGENIA 'Daughter'.

MEMORIA 'The memorial' or 'the tombstone'. This is found in Italy, but probably came to Britain from north Africa, where it is more common.

HIC IN TUMULO IACIT 'Here lies in this grave'. TUMULO originally
  meant 'in a burial mound' but in Dark Age inscriptions is not so
  specific. This is found in Italy and Gaul.
DM 'Dis Manibus', 'to the Shades of the Dead'. This is commonly
  found in pagan Roman inscriptions, and is here a survival of
  tradition.
NOMINE, NOMENA 'The special grave' or 'shrine'. This is also an
  African formula.

Inscribed stones fall into a number of different categories. The
main ones are:
  (i) *Inscribed memorial stones.* These usually are rough pillars or
boulders with Latin majuscule, ogham or ogham bilingual
inscriptions. From the sixth century onwards they also sometimes
have crosses.
  (ii) *Grave markers.* These are smaller uninscribed stones, many of
which were buried with the dead or laid on the ground to mark a
grave. Seventh to eleventh centuries.
  (iii) *Cross slabs.* These are flat slabs decorated on one or both
faces with some form of cross, often wheel-headed, in relief.
Recumbent cross slabs were laid flat on graves, but most cross slabs
stood upright. The cross is often in relief, and can be richly
decorated with interlace or other ornament. There can be figures,
ornament or inscriptions in the field not occupied by the cross. They
date from the eighth century onwards.
  (iv) *Free-standing* or *high crosses.* These appear to be stone
versions of wooden prototypes. They usually have a tapering shaft
and either a round *disc head* (which is solid, or projecting arms,
sometimes with a nimbus forming a *wheel head.* They would
normally have stood on a stone base. They are usually decorated
with figural ornament, interlace and other abstract patterns, and
belong to the ninth to eleventh centuries.
  Occasionally fragments of *shrines*, *altars* or other church fittings
are decorated with inscribed or sculptured ornament.
  The sculptured monuments of *Pictland* were classified in the
nineteenth century into three main groups, and the terms 'Class I',
'Class II' and 'Class III' monuments are still used.
  Class I. Rough undressed boulders or stones engraved with
distinctive Pictish symbols. No satisfactory explanation has ever
been advanced to explain the symbols, which are universal
throughout Pictland, and appear in various combinations of pairs or

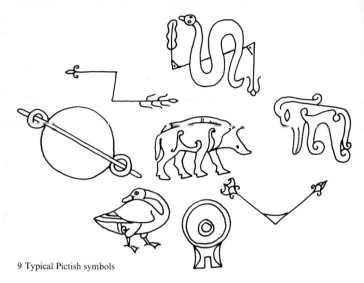

9 Typical Pictish symbols

larger multiples. There are two main series: animals done with great economy of line and in a distinctive style, and abstract symbols known by various descriptive names such as 'Z-rod', 'triple-disc', 'crescent and V-rod' or 'mirror and comb-case'. They probably date from before the eighth century, but how early they occur is problematic. The stones may be boundary markers.

Class II are dressed slabs of varying sizes with relief sculpture. This consists of a relief cross and Pictish symbols, often combined with other human, animal and abstract designs. They date from the later eighth to the tenth centuries.

Class III. These monuments in many ways resemble those of Class II but lack the Pictish symbols. They date probably from the time after the kingdom of Pictland disappeared, from the ninth and tenth centuries.

The study of the *ornament* on Celtic sculpture is complex, because of its eclecticism. Motifs and ornamental styles peculiar to one region can turn up in another, while one monument can display features of several regions. Nevertheless, it is possible to point to a number of 'schools' which seem to be focussed on distinct areas, and in some cases centres, at particular periods. The main schools are as follows:

(i) *The Whithorn School*. This was centred on the monastery of Whithorn in Galloway, and grew up in the tenth century when Galloway was extensively influenced by the Norse. Norse styles of interlace are characteristic of the school, the most distinctive products of which were crosses with dumpy shafts made out of a single slab of stone, and surmounted by a disc head, the arms of the cross being indicated in some cases by round holes. The head of the cross was usually plain, but with a central boss. Ring-chain ornament, common in the Isle of Man, was popular.

(ii) *The Govan School*. Centred on Govan in Lanarkshire, this was a very eclectic school which borrowed widely from the Picts and also from the Whithorn school. It flourished from the tenth to early twelfth centuries, and outliers of the style can be seen at Barochan (Renfrew) and elsewhere.

(iii) *The Iona School*. The Iona school is not so much a school as a long tradition, which was to persist into the full Middle Ages. A group of crosses on Iona (St John's, St Martin's, and St Matthew's), together with a number of outlying monuments such as the Kildalton Cross on Islay can however be regarded as a particular group of the ninth–tenth centuries. They are distinguished by the absence of a nimbus or ring, and waisted arms which expand into square ends, as do some Northumbrian crosses or that from Bealin in Ireland (which, however, has a wheel). They are decorated in a restrained manner with panels of ornament, and the head has a central boss, with further bosses on the arms.

(iv) *The 'Boss' School*. This is not so much a school as a style, found in Pictland in the ninth century. All the stones of this school carry bosses decorated with interlace. The Aberlemno Roadside Cross is a good example of the style.

(v) *The Carew School*. This is a convenient term to describe a small group of stones from Wales, of which the best example comes from Carew, Pembroke, dating from the tenth or eleventh century. These are wheel-headed crosses with tall splayed shafts, the head connected to the shaft with a tenon joint.

(vi) *The Margam Style*. This term may be coined to describe a distinct group of southern Welsh crosses, with plain round solid disc heads and wide shafts. Six examples of the eleven known come from Glamorgan. The finest is the Margam (Glamorgan) 'Great Cross'.

(vii) *Crux Xri Slabs*. These are found only in Glamorganshire, and have a lightly carved interlacing wheel-cross with the inscription *Crux Xri* ('The Cross of Christ') or a cross-symbol used to express the same idea. Tenth century.

(viii) *Monogram Slabs.* These are found in Pembroke, mainly at St David's, and have an outline cross in the angles of which are the abbreviations for IISOUS CHRISTOS, alpha and omega. They date from the ninth to the twelfth centuries.

Viking (North of Scotland and Isle of Man)

The visible remains of the Vikings in Britain are relatively few and are confined for the most part to the north of Scotland and the Isle of Man.

SETTLEMENTS AND FORTIFICATIONS

The only known Scandinavian settlements in England have been discovered through excavation and field survey in Yorkshire, and, because there are only slight visible remains, are not described in this book. More substantial remains of Norse settlements are to be seen in the Northern Isles of Scotland, where the most characteristic structures are the footings of *long houses*, which at their most typical have a dwelling area and a byre separated by a cross-passage, the byre being furnished with a central drain and the dwelling area having stone benches running along the long sides and a central hearth. In the Northern Isles turf was combined with stone in their construction. The best examples are to be found at Jarlshof in Shetland and Birsay in Orkney. These continued to be built until the twelfth century or even later. A few similar structures can be seen elsewhere in Scotland, notably at Little Dunagoil, on Bute, and in the Isle of Man, where good examples can be seen at the Braaid and in the Promontory fort at Cass ny Hawin.

This last is an example of a Norse house built within an earlier iron age fort, a phenomenon of the Isle of Man. In England a few earthworks are believed to be Danish, but without excavation this is usually difficult to prove. Three types have been distinguished:

(i) *D-shaped earthworks:* one side butting on to water, or situated on a small island in marsh or fenland.

(ii) *Harbour sites:* with one or more rectangular harbours, usually with substantial adjacent fortifications.

(iii) *Ringworks:* either with rampart(s) and ditch(es) or hollowed, on hill-slopes.

CHURCHES

Due to the relatively late conversion of the Vikings, most

Scandinavian churches in Britain are later than the main period of the book, ie after the mid-eleventh century. Some of the small stone unicameral churches of the Northern Isles and the Isle of Man were probably built under Norse rule; in Orkney there are a number of more substantial buildings including the ecclesiastical complex at Birsay, which shares features with that at Gardar, Greenland. The church at Birsay also shares features in common with Anglo-Saxon architecture. In the twelfth century the Norse built a number of unusual churches, including the church with round-tower, perhaps modelled on Irish prototypes, at Egilsay, Rousay (Orkney) and the round church, perhaps modelled on that of the Holy Sepulchre at Jerusalem, built at Orphir on the Orkney Mainland. Such buildings were put up following the participation of the Norse earls of Orkney in the Crusades.

BURIALS

Two types of Viking burial site leave some above-ground traces. *Ship burials* were made under long mounds, sometimes demarcated, as at Balladoole in the Isle of Man, with a ship-shaped setting of boundary stones. *Barrows* are round mounds, similar to those of prehistoric date, but on the whole larger. Examples can be seen in Orkney and the Isle of Man.

SCULPTURES

While a great diversity of Scandinavian-influenced sculpture survives in Britain, very little is purely Scandinavian in style and is instead the outcome of Viking influence on native Celtic or Anglo-Saxon work. Viking art styles are described under 'Objects in Museums' (p. 50). The finest Viking sculptures were undoubtedly those from the Isle of Man, which owe relatively little to Celtic antecedents, and depict scenes from Norse mythology and carry Norse runic inscriptions. The starting point for the series is Gaut's Cross, which bears the inscription, 'Gaut Carved this and all in Man', and which uses a type of ring-chain ornament usually associated with his name but which he may not have devised. Manx influence is apparent in the sculpture of Northern England, Wales, and to some extent Southern Scotland. Surprisingly, no Viking sculpture has been found in the Northern Isles.

INSCRIPTIONS

The Vikings used an alphabet of *runes* akin to the Anglo-Saxon runic alphabet, both stemming from the same North European origins. Runic inscriptions appear on sculptures and objects, and occasionally as graffiti on monuments in Orkney – they appear for instance in the prehistoric chambered tomb of Maes Howe and on the stones of the Ring of Brodgar.

10 Typical Kentish square-headed brooch, from Gilton

Objects in museums

Anglo-Saxon
From the **Pagan** period most objects on display in museums come from burials. Finds from Pagan period settlements are few, and consist for the most part of *pottery*, clay *loom weights*, *spindle*

whorls, bone *combs*, *beads* and perhaps the occasional metal object of types better known from burials. Virtually all that is known about the life of the pagan Anglo-Saxons comes from finds from graves. Although objects are sometimes found in cremation burials, they are few in number and usually damaged by fire. For this reason the finest collections of objects of Pagan date are to be found in museums south of the Thames, though a few northern museums (notably Liverpool) house objects from southern inhumation cemeteries. Certain types of object were selected for burial with the dead, and for this reason virtually nothing is known about many of the everyday objects which the pagan Anglo-Saxons must have possessed. The most common grave finds are of treasured personal possessions: *belt buckles*, *brooches* and other *items of jewellery*. These are usually found in women's graves. In men's graves are found weapons: usually a *sword*, one or more *spearheads*, and the boss and other imperishable fittings of a *shield*. After personal adornment and weapons the most frequent finds are containers: *pottery vessels*, *glass beakers and bowls*, *bronze-bound wooden buckets* and mounted *drinking horns*. Food sometimes accompanied burials, and on occasions women, horses or dogs were slaughtered to accompany their master to the after-life. Although the pagan Anglo-Saxons did not have a coinage of their own, *Roman*, *Byzantine* or *Merovingian coins* are sometimes found in graves, as well as other *heirlooms* or *exotic finds* such as bronze bowls imported from Coptic Egypt. *Hanging bowls*, or the enamelled escutcheons from them, are also sometimes found in graves – these are Celtic rather than Germanic in style.

11 Typical early Kentish Saucer brooch

12 Pagan period work-box, probably 7th century, from Kingston, Kent

From the archaeologist's standpoint the most useful objects are items of jewellery, pottery and glass vessels, as they can often be dated more readily than other artefacts. Art styles, which can be seen in the decoration of brooches, buckles and some other objects, provide one of the yardsticks for dating. Another is provided by Continental finds of similar type.

Two main art styles are recognizable on Pagan Saxon metalwork:

Style I is found mainly on brooches of the period AD 450–600, and consists of semi-naturalistic animal and sometimes human ornament, broken down into component elements.

Style II is current from *c.* 600 (or a little earlier) until the end of the Pagan period, and is characterized by intertwining ribbon-like animals (*lacertines*). It is for this reason sometimes called the *Ribbon Style*.

By the seventh century *polychrome jewellery* was being produced. This employed inlays of garnet, glass or other substances set in cells or *cloisons* on a metal ground. It is sometimes called *cloisonné* work. Not infrequently the ground was gold. Fine gold wire (*filigree*) and beads of gold (*granular work*) were also used to ornament the finest

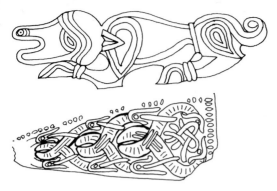

13 Styles I and II, Anglo-Saxon art

pieces. These were mostly produced in Kent and East Anglia in the seventh century.

Of the many types of brooch current in Pagan Anglo-Saxon England the following types are the most important:

Saucer brooches. Circular brooches, usually gilt bronze, with slight dish shape. Current from the fifth century, and among the earliest brooches found in England.

Square-headed brooches. There are many different types, all with a flat head, bow and flat plate foot.

Equal-armed brooches. Another early type, with expanded arms and narrow, bowed 'waist'.

Composite disc brooches. Found in Kent in the seventh century, and richly decorated in polychrome work. The most famous is the Kingston Brooch in Liverpool City Museum.

The pottery found in inhumation cemeteries normally consists of plain *accessory vessels.* The pots used for cremation containers, however, were often specially made and richly decorated with stamped ornament. The most distinctive are *buckelurnen*, which have pushed-out bosses on the sides decorated with stamped ornament.

Much less is known about the material possessions of the **Christian** Anglo-Saxons, as the settlement sites are no richer in finds than those of the Pagan period, and there are no burials with an array of furnishings. The Christian Saxons however made *wheel-*

14 Typical Anglo-Saxon pots

turned pottery (though some hand-made pottery continued), and in the Late Saxon period the most distinctive products are *Thetford Ware* (unglazed, grey sandy ware), *Stamford Ware* (hard, light-coloured ware with light green or yellow glazes) and *St Neots Ware* (coarse and shell-gritted).

The Christian Saxons also produced a fine coinage. The first Anglo-Saxon coins were small gold pieces struck in the seventh century; these were gradually debased to silver pieces of similar size known as *sceattas*. The silver penny was introduced by Offa (though a few had been struck in Kent before he annexed it), probably around AD 784. A few gold coins were struck, but the silver penny remained the main denomination until the Norman Conquest and later. It was very thin, slightly larger than our new penny.

Many Pagan Saxon traditions continued into the Christian period, including a taste for animal ornament. A new style developed, the *Trewhiddle Style*, named after a hoard found in Cornwall. This used niello (a black paste) on a silver ground, with animal and foliage patterns in irregular, sub-geometric shapes. The influence of Carolingian ornament made foliage popular. The successors to the Kentish composite disc brooches were large, silver *disc brooches* with bosses, current around the Norman Conquest, while Viking influence is apparent in some decoration. From the period survive some very fine *sword pommels*, usually with lobed crests, including one of silver from Fetter Lane, London. *Finger rings*, *coin brooches* (disc brooches with a coin or imitation coin in the centre) and a variety of *book clasps*, *strap ends* and *mounts* belong to this period. Naturalistic *ivories* in the Winchester style (see

15 Anglo-Saxon coins (a) St Edmund memorial penny, issued in the Danelaw
   (b) Hammer Cross penny of Edward the Confessor

p. 38) have also survived, as well as *manuscripts* decorated in the
same tradition.

Celtic
No pagan burials of the Dark Age Celts are known, and the
Christian graves are devoid of objects. Archaeologists depend
mainly on finds from settlement sites for information about the
Celtic way of life. The most important finds for dating purposes are
jewellery and *pottery*. The Celts made very little pottery of their
own, and what they did make is usually very crude and cannot be
closely dated. Imports from the Continent, however, can be dated in
their homelands and are therefore used to date Celtic Dark Age sites
in Britain. *Imported pottery* is surprisingly common on Celtic sites,
and seems to have been traded through the Irish Sea from the

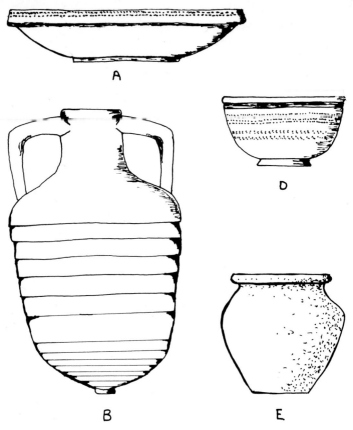

16 Imported Mediterranean pottery (restored)

Mediterranean. These are the main types (the other classes are very rare):

Class A: Bowls and dishes in red ware with a red or red-brown slip. Imported from the East Mediterranean, and dated to *c.* 400–600.

Class B: Amphorae or storage jars with handles. Red, pink or creamy buff in colour, sometimes with grooves on the body. Datable to the fifth and sixth centuries.

Class D: Mortaria (bowls for mashing fruit and vegetables) in soft grey ware with a blue-black wash. Imported from France, in the fifth and sixth centuries.

Class E: Cooking pots, bowls, jars and beakers in hard-fired gritty ware, usually dirty white but ranging from red and ochre to dark grey. Imported probably from the Bordeaux region from *c.* 550–700.

Of the types of jewellery, the most important are *penannular brooches* which are descended from iron age and Roman antecedents. As the name suggests, they consist of an open hoop with a swivelling pin. They have different types of terminal, and on the classification of these the dating has been worked out. By the seventh and eighth centuries some were very elaborate and richly decorated, such as the *Hunterston Brooch* from Ayrshire. Other types of jewellery include different types of *dress pins*, including *hand pins* which are so-called because of their superficial similarity to a partly clenched hand. Other personal items include different types of *beads*, *composite bone combs* made up out of plates of bone riveted together, and *jet bracelets*.

Metalworking finds are common, suggesting that this was done on most settlements. Particularly common are *clay moulds* for castings, *triangular crucibles* and *ingot moulds*. Sometimes *trial pieces* are found – pieces of stone or bone with designs scratched on them. *Iron* objects include *knives*, *spearheads* and a variety of small *tools*. *Bone* was used to make *pins*, *spindle whorls* and *handles*. In the Atlantic area of Scotland many of the earlier iron age types of bone objects continued into the Dark Ages. *Stone* was used for *whetstones*, *pot lids* and *spindle whorls*. *Glass* was imported from the Germanic world, though there is no evidence the Celts made glass vessels themselves.

Celtic ornament decorated metalwork and sometimes other materials. It differs from Anglo-Saxon in that abstract patterns are preferred to animal ornament, though in later Dark Age Celtic art, birds' heads and other semi-naturalistic creatures sometimes appear. Simple ornament, partly derived from Romano-British art and partly perhaps from older iron age Celtic traditions, is found in most of the Celtic areas of Britain in the fifth and sixth centuries. The finest products are *hanging bowl escutcheons*, which usually have a triskele as the main motif, though peltas, trumpet patterns, spirals and voids were also popular motifs. By the seventh century most ornamental work appears to have been done in Ireland and Scotland, and *Pictish metalwork* is particularly important, reaching its peak in the *St Ninian's Isle Treasure*. *Champlevé enamelling*, produced by melting enamel in hollows cut in the metal ground, was very popular, at first in red, later in other colours also. *Filigree* and *granular* work was copied from the Anglo-Saxons.

The material assemblage of the Dark Age Celts shows a mixture of iron age and Roman survivals, as well as new elements from the Germanic world.

Viking

There are very few excavated Viking settlements in Britain, and most information comes from the site of Jarlshof in Shetland, amplified by stray finds and burials, and now artefacts which at the time of writing are coming to light in York.

The Vikings did not make pottery in their homelands and in Britain they used *steatite bowls* (ie made of soapstone) similar to those they had used in Scandinavia. Later, however, in Scotland, they learned how to make very crude hand-made pots of jamjar shape, and in the Danelaw the Danes used Saxo-Norman pottery in the Thetford ware tradition, the most notable being *York Ware*. *Wooden bowls* were used in York, and no doubt elsewhere.

The most common finds on Norse sites are stone *loom weights*, *net* or *line sinkers*, *pot lids*, *bowls*, *lamps*, *pounders* and *whetstones*. *Bracelets* of canal coal or jet are sometimes found. *Bone needles* and *pins* are quite common finds, the dress pins sometimes having elaborate heads in cross, axe or animal shape. Bone was also fashioned in distinctive types of *combs*, the most characteristic being one-sided and hump-backed. *Glass* was used for *beads* and for *'linen smoothers'* which are often found in graves.

Bronze pins often have polyhedral heads, though many other types are known. Particularly common are *loose-ringed pins* which were adopted from the Irish. Bronze was also used for a variety of small objects, including *mounts* and *buckles*.

The Vikings introduced the *stirrup* to Britain, and examples of these and of *bits* have been found in York and London.

Norse women's graves frequently contained a pair of *tortoise brooches*, richly decorated and shaped roughly like a small tortoise shell. *Celtic* (ie penannular) brooches, brooches made out of Celtic mounts and *trefoil brooches* are sometimes found in graves. Burials were frequently accompanied by a *sickle* of iron, *comb and comb-case* of bone, *shears*, a *necklace*, *axes*, *whetstones*, *knives*, *pins* and *buckles,* in various combinations. A *beam balance,* sometimes with accompanying *weights,* is a common grave find. Male burials were accompanied by weapons, notably an *iron sword, spearheads, shield boss* and perhaps an *axe.*

Treasure hoards of the Viking period usually comprise *hack silver* – pieces of silver including ingots intended for melting down – along with *rings* and *armlets,* sometimes carrying limited decoration. Characteristically Viking *thistle brooches* (penannular brooches with thistle-like terminals) and *penannular silver brooches* with bosses on the end plates are also found in hoards. *Arab coins* and *Anglo-Saxon pennies* turn up (often in large numbers) in such hoards, of which the most famous is the Cuerdale hoard from Lancashire and the Skaill hoard from Orkney.

The Vikings did not have a native *coinage,* but took up the idea of coins from the Anglo-Saxons, striking coins at York and in the Danelaw.

Many objects are decorated in Scandinavian ornamental styles. The main styles found in Britain are:

(i) *Jellinge,* named after the royal seat at Jellinge in Jutland. The style began in the late ninth century and continued until *c.* 1000. It uses animals with sinuous, double outlines and with pigtails and lip-lappets. It is found in the earliest phase of the Viking settlement of England, and a version of it was taken up by the Irish. It is found on both metalwork and sculpture.

(ii) *Ringerike.* This developed out of preceding styles and was current in the early eleventh century. It takes its name from a group

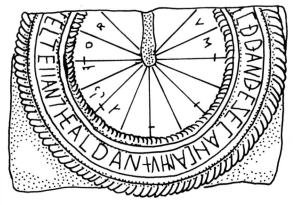

17 Anglo-Saxon sundial from Orpington, Kent

of sculptures from Ringerike in Norway. It continued to use animal ornament, but from the animals tendrils of acanthus leaf foliage sprout to dominate the pattern. A distinctive version developed in England, which blended with the Winchester style under the Danish kings of England in the eleventh century. It is found in both metalwork and sculpture.

(iii) *Urnes*. This style developed around the mid-eleventh century, and is named after the stave church at Urnes, Norway, which has this style of carving on it. It continued until the mid-twelfth century. The tendrils are very elongated and the foliage less apparent. It is a feature of both metalwork and sculpture.

South-West England

South-west England offers a richer diversity of Dark Age and early medieval remains than any other part of Britain. After their rapid expansion over south-east England the Anglo-Saxons were slower to colonize the West. A dual expansion up the Thames valley and down from Middle Anglia brought some Germanic incomers into Wessex in the fifth century, but until the end of the century there was no Anglo-Saxon settlement in Somerset, Dorset or Hampshire.

The Saxon advance continued, however, from the mid-sixth century, with the campaigns of Ceawlin of Wessex, which culminated in the defeat of the British in the battle of Deorham, fought in Gloucestershire in 577. In this year Ceawlin captured Gloucester, Cirencester and Bath. In the early seventh century a frontier was established for Wessex with the construction of Wansdyke, a remarkable linear earthwork which is one of the most notable remains of Dark Age Britain (see p. 77). Although by this date the Saxons held the best lands in Somerset, the British seem to have maintained their identity in the marshy lowlands of the Somerset Levels. In 614 the Anglo-Saxons penetrated Devon, and by 682 Devon was effectively under Saxon control. Cornwall, however, remained staunchly Celtic until the ninth century, and retained much of its Celtic character even after the Norman Conquest.

Wessex and the south-west, then, offer both Celtic and Anglo-

Saxon remains for the traveller. Several of the sites in this region
have the added attraction of figuring in lore about King Arthur, and
indeed, for the Arthurian enthusiast, there are many other places
without any Dark Age remains round which later ages have woven
stories about the semi-legendary hero. In Cornwall, for instance, at
Dozmary Pool, a mile (1·6 km) south of Bolventor on Bodmin
Moor, local tradition will inform you that an arm came out of the
waters to give Arthur his trusty sword, Excalibur. But the region
also boasts some of the finest Dark Age remains in Britain: the early
monastic Celtic complex at Tintagel, the reoccupied hillfort at South
Cadbury, believed by some to be Camelot, and the picturesque
Anglo-Saxon church at Bradford-on-Avon, to name but three.
Apart from some Anglo-Saxon churches and sculptures, there is a
diversity of Celtic memorial stones, settlements and ecclesiastical
remains.

The most spectacular Dark Age site in Cornwall is also one of the
most interesting in Britain. **Tintagel** (SX 0489) [AM;S] is intimately
associated in medieval legend with King Arthur, and holds an
honoured place as one of the key sites in Celtic Christian
archaeology.

The medieval castle and Dark Age monastic remains straddle a
fallen land bridge, and are approached from the village of Tintagel
on the B3263, about 4m (6·4 km) SW of Boscastle. A path leads
from the central car park (adjacent to a bookshop and café), across
a small bridged stream running between plunging cliffs. Thence the
zig-zag path leads up to the well-preserved walls of the castle. This
stronghold with its almost fairy-tale charm was built in the mid-
twelfth century by Reginald, Earl of Cornwall.

For some years the inner ward (and Dark Age remains) were
inaccessible except by the intrepid, but in Easter 1976 the
Department of the Environment opened a magnificent bridge to the
'island' reached by steep stone steps on each side. The site was
excavated in 1933–4 by Dr C A R Radford, and interpreted as a
fifth–sixth century monastery. Some aspects of this interpretation
have recently been modified in the light of later thought.

The Dark Age remains appear as low drystone walls in clusters on
the exposed headland, and are referred to by letters. A path from
the medieval castle leads to *Site F* – perched on a rock platform.
The largest building was porched and has one large room containing
a stone base with slots for what must have been a wooden structure.
The excavator suggested that these might have been the remains of a

scriptorium or library. The smaller building may have been a school. The path leads on to a further cluster of rectangular buildings grouped round a courtyard (*Site B*). These were possibly simple living cells, and one may have had two storeys. Lower down the slope are some isolated buildings, all small, one possibly a sauna. Further along the path, the terrace above three buildings (known as *Site C*) may have been cultivated.

A somewhat hazardous scramble up the slopes from Site C takes the visitor to *Site D*. Situated on the open plateau at the summit of the island, this can also be approached more gently from the castle. Three buildings are grouped round a courtyard, open on the fourth side. One was subdivided by stone slabs forming stalls for cattle. Another produced the foundations of a corn-drying kiln.

In the centre of the plateau the rectangular walls of a medieval garden partly overlie the fragmentary Dark Age foundations of *Site E*, which can be seen running out under the garden walls at the N angle, but were badly disturbed by cultivation.

Little can be seen of *Site G*, which lies between the garden and the main complex. Site A, however, on the edge of the plateau, should

18 Tintagel, site B

not be missed. Here the remains of a twelfth-century chapel overlie a long range of Dark Age buildings facing on to a court. The small square room with a projecting stump of walling at the S end may have been a gatehouse. A square block of masonry in the courtyard was interpreted as a *leacht*, a type of open-air shrine commonly found in Ireland, which may have been built above graves. Due S of the medieval chapel, between it and the *leacht*, are the remains of what may have been a small Dark Age oratory.

The settlement was defended by a rampart and ditch, which is now crowned by the thirteenth-century curtain wall of the castle. The bank itself was heightened in the twelfth century, but the lower portion (some 30 feet [9·14 metres] across and 8 feet [2·44 metres] high) belongs to the Dark Ages. This can be seen underlying the curtain wall on the N side of the inner ward.

Tintagel is unique in Dark Age Britain. Pottery was imported to the site from the Mediterranean in the fifth and sixth centuries – red bowls (Tintagel Class A ware) and amphorae (wine storage jars) in reds and buffs (Tintagel B ware). Study of the Tintagel pottery fragments has led to the closer dating of other Dark Age sites with similar wares.

In Arthurian legend Tintagel was the King's birthplace, and was made famous in the twelfth century by Geoffrey of Monmouth in his *History of the Kings of Britain*. The castle was traditionally that of Gorlois. Uther Pendragon became enamoured of Ygerne,

19 Entrance to Chun Castle, Cornwall

Gorlois's wife, and laid seige to Tintagel after defeating and killing Gorlois. Ygerne was captured and forced to marry Uther. She gave their son Arthur over to the care of Merlin. Traditionally Merlin's Cave is the first on the left-hand side if, instead of crossing the stream up to the castle, you follow the right-hand path along to the beach below the castle.

After Tintagel the most imposing Dark Age site in Cornwall is **Chun Castle** (SW 405339), though most of the visible remains belong to the iron age. A lane, approximately 1m (1·6 km) SW of Morvah, off the minor road from Penzance to Morvah, is signposted to Chun Castle. At Trehyllys Farm a path leads behind the farmhouse to the hilltop. From the summit there is a superb view across the fields to the sea.

Two concentric drystone walled ramparts built in the iron age (c. 200 BC) are broken by a single staggered entrance on the W. The whitish-grey stones are very tumbled and overgrown with grass and gorse, but the footings of Dark Age structures built against the inner rampart can be discerned. A Dark Age well on the N side is partly infilled with fallen stones but still runs with clear water. Secondary walling at the entrance, which makes the approach more difficult, was possibly erected in the Dark Ages. Tintagel B pottery has been found there.

Castle Dore (SX 103548) stands on a ridge 3m (4·8 km) N of Fowey, on the line of an ancient trackway running from Bodmin to Pridmouth, now the B3269 to the N of the road. As at Chun, building began in the third century BC when two banks, each now about 8 feet (2·44 metres) high, with an outer ditch, were thrown up. The inner enclosure is off-centre, and the outer courtyard or barbican thus formed gave added defence.

The site was abandoned in the Roman period but occupied again in the fifth or sixth century. A large enclosure with insubstantial bank which lies below the main enclosure may be a Dark Age cattle compound but is undatable. N of the gate a stone revetment was added to the original bank half way down its inner slope, and a new cobbled path laid down (not visible). During excavations inside the fort Dr C A R Radford found the postholes of various buildings, two of which were interpreted as long halls. The largest was possibly 90 feet (27·43 metres) long.

Five miles S of Castle Dore, opposite the lodge gates of Menabilly, stands the re-erected tombstone of the chieftain who owned Castle Dore in the sixth century. It is to the S of the A3082 to Fowey, and is known as **Tristan's Stone** (SX 0954). It is a 7 feet (2·13 metres) high monolith, with an inscription on one face reading

DRVSTANVS HIC IACIT FILIVS CUNOMORI
(*Tristan lies here, son of Cynvawr*)

The name Tristan (Drustan) is Pictish, which is unusual for so far south, and there is little doubt that this is the same character who figures in medieval romance in the story of Tristan and Iseult. Cynvawr is also known to history as a sixth-century king of Dumnonia, and may be the same Cynvawr who, in Breton folklore, was a wicked opponent of the saints.

In West Penwith, the Land's End peninsula, the **Men Scryfa** (SW 4235) – the name means 'written stone' – stands in a field on the N side of a track leading off the unclassified Penzance–Morvah road, opposite the lane to Chun (p. 67). It is probably in its original position, and dates from the late fifth or sixth century. It is inscribed

RIALOBRANI CVNOVALI FILI
(*Rialobran, son of Cunoval*)

The **Selus Stone** (SW 3732) stands inside at the W end of St Just Church, reached by the A3071 from Penzance. One side has a chi-rho – the first two letters of Christ's name in Greek in the form of a monogram – and the other an inscription recording that it marked the burial of Selus. It may be as early as the fifth century.

King Doniert's Stone (SX 2468) [AM; A] stands 3m (4·8 km) NW of Liskeard. On leaving St Cleer take the minor road to Commonmoor, and turn W towards Redgate. The stone is to the S of the road. It is part of a cross-shaft of the late ninth century, inscribed

DONIERT ROGAVIT PRO ANIMA
(*Doniert has prayed for his soul*)

It probably relates to King Durngarth, known to have reigned in Cornwall at this period. Part of another cross shaft is adjacent.

Of the free-standing crosses in Cornwall, few can be ascribed with any certainty to the pre-Norman period. Of those that can be dated to the Dark Ages, three are in West Penwith. The first is the **Penzance Cross** (SW 4730), which now stands outside Penlees Museum, off the W side of Morrab Road, Penzance. It has a wheel head and ornamented panel. On the base is an inscription,

REGIS RICATI CRUX
(*The Cross of King Ricatus*)

It dates from the tenth century.

In the churchyard of the small village of **Sancreed** (SW 4229), 3m (4·8 km) W of Penzance, approached by minor roads to the N off the A30, there are five crosses, two of which are at least partly of Dark Age date. One, 9 feet (2·74 metres) high, stands by the path and may in its present form belong to the twelfth century. On the shaft, however, is a virtually illegible inscription probably of the sixth century. The second cross, near the S porch, dates from the mid-tenth century and boasts a head with a Crucifixion and some fine ornament. An inscription RUNHO may refer to the sculptor.

The finest of all the Cornish Dark Age crosses is at **Cardinham** (SX 1268), 3m (4·8 km) NE of Bodmin, approached by minor roads from the S off the A30 or N off the A38. The circular-headed cross with its tapering shaft stands outside the S porch of the village church. It is carved with interlace, running spirals and ring-chain of the type used by Gaut on the Isle of Man (p. 49). It is the only example of ring-chain in S England, and dates probably from the tenth century.

Devon is not rich in Dark Age remains. The only notable sculpture is the cross-shaft at **Colyton** (SY 2493), discovered after a fire in 1933 had destroyed considerable portions of the church of St Andrew. The shaft, which is dated to the tenth century, is decorated with inhabited acanthus scrolls, with a bird and a lion on the front. The sides have interlace. Colyton is reached by taking the A3052 to the W out of Lyme Regis and turning N on the B3161 a mile past its junction with the A358 to Axminster.

Lydford (SX 5184) in W Devon lies on a wedge-shaped promontory and figures in the Burghal Hidage, a Late Saxon list of *burhs* and their men. On the S and W it is isolated by the gorge of the Lyd and on the NW by a steep valley of a tributary. To get there, take the A386 N from Tavistock – the village lies on it about 9m (14·5 km) from Tavistock. The modern road passes through the bank of the *burh* near its centre, adjacent to where the original Anglo-Saxon E gate must have been. This point is reached 300 yards (274 metres) from where the road crosses the gorge, and here the bank cuts off the promontory, running for 650 feet (198 metres). Excavation has shown it to turn along the NW scarp, and that underneath the Norman capping it was about 40 feet (12·2 metres)

20 Sancreed 10th century churchyard cross

21 The Cardinham Cross

wide, with a steep slope rising to a height (now) of 6 feet (1·82 metres).

Nor is Dorset rich in Dark Age remains. At **Winterbourne**

Steepleton (SY 6289) 4m (6·4 km) W of Dorchester on the B3159, the nave of St Michael's and All Angels' church is of Anglo-Saxon origin. The aisleless church was probably erected between 950 and 1100, of small stones and rubble with large dressed blocks of side-alternate work at the quoins.

The 7 feet (2·13 metres) high round-headed N and S doorways have semi-circular solid stone tympana and hood moulds, and are themselves evidence of a pre-Conquest date of construction, as are the huge side-alternate quoins of the nave, and the 32-inch (0·81 metre) thick walls.

Not to be missed on a visit to Winterbourne Steepleton, however, is the famous angel, carved in stone and similar to those at Bradford (see p. 74). Now built into the external S wall, this winged being awkwardly trails its feet upwards. It dates from the tenth century: undoubtedly it was carved before the church was put up.

The name Steepleton comes from the fact that it had one of the three spires in medieval Dorset.

At **Melbury Osmond** (ST 5707), reached by a side road about ½m (0·8 km) W of the A37, 7m (11·3 km) S of Yeovil, the church of St Osmund has in the N chancel a portion of cross shaft with a strange creature entwined in interlacing. It could represent the Ram Caught in a Thicket.

At **Stinsford** (SY 7191) the Church of St Michael offers outside the W tower a weathered carving of St Michael with his wings spread, of late Saxon date. Stinsford lies on the A35, about 1½m (2·4 km) E of Dorchester.

At **Melbury Bubb** (ST 5906), reached by side roads about 1m (1·6 km) E off the A37, 7½m (12 km) S of Yeovil, can be seen a font which was once part of a round-shaft. It is in the church of St Mary, a picturesque building in a leafy setting. The font is cylindrical and tapering, with shaft and base in one. The column has been turned upside down, and is decorated with interlace and with animals, including a fine stag.

A curious seated figure adorns a slate relief inside the church of the Holy Rood at **Buckland Newton** (ST 6904) on the B3143, about 10m (16 km) N of Dorchester. The figure, which dates perhaps from the early eleventh century, is a strange composition, its arms outstretched in the early Christian attitude of prayer. Various suggestions have been made about its date and affinities. Its closest parallels are in Germany.

Wareham (SY 9287) is one of the most interesting Anglo-Saxon

22 10th century cross inverted, used as a font at Melbury Bubb

burhs. The site lies at the point where the rivers Frome and Piddle
are closest together, before emptying into Poole harbour, and here
there were iron age and Romano-British settlements. Wareham lies
on the junction of the A352 from Dorchester with the A351, about
6m (9·75 km) N of Swanage. The site was certainly occupied between
the sixth and ninth century, for no fewer than five inscriptions have
been found of this period, indicating a church of some importance,
established by the Britons before the arrival of the Saxons in the late
seventh century. It can be presumed that the Romano-British
community survived until the coming of the Saxons, and their
flourishing church was taken over by the incomers, who built a new
one around 700, later dedicated to Lady St Mary. Some of the
memorial stones were incorporated into the fabric of this church,
and remained until it was demolished in the nineteenth century. All
but the latest of the stones bear British names, and the discovery of

so many on one site is without parallel in Britain, though matched by major cemeteries in France and Germany. This church was the only surviving example of a minster in the south-west. The extant inscribed stones are now to be found in the present St Mary's church.

However another Anglo-Saxon church does survive, dedicated to St Martin. It stands astride the Late Saxon defences of the *burh*.

The church has been much modified by later changes, which have left only parts of the N, W and S walls of the nave and most of the chancel intact from the tenth or eleventh century. Evidence for this dating: the quoins, the double plinth, the N wall window in the chancel, about 8 feet (2·44 metres) above ground, and, in the N aisle, remains of a N door and above its level vestiges of a small window. The chancel arch is the most outstanding feature, but the proportions are Norman.

The Saxon *burh* was founded probably in the early tenth century – it is mentioned in the Burghal Hidage. The first phase was an earth bank, which has survived to a height of 9 feet (2·74 metres) above ground level, perhaps with a front revetment of timber. This was enlarged by heightening the rearward slope, which was then capped with mortar and provided with a wall walk. A massive ditch was dug in front of it in the Norman period. Three stretches of the bank still survive, two crossing the area between the two rivers and one facing the Piddle – no rampart faced the Frome. The area enclosed was between 80 and 90 acres (32–36 hectares). The street plan of Wareham preserves the grid-iron layout of the original Saxon *burh*.

On the border between Hampshire and Dorset lies **Bokerley Dyke** (SU 0319). This is essentially a late Roman linear earthwork that continued in use in the Dark Ages. The best section can be seen by taking the A354 just beyond Martin for about 1¼m (2 km), just S of the Hants–Dorset border, where the bank can be seen running for 100 yards (91 metres) covered with bushes at the S of the road. It is a multi-period rampart, originally designed to protect the NE Dorset downs from northern raiders. It was begun AD 325–30 and, later in the century it was extended across the Roman road. By the end of the century the road was reopened, and a new earthwork was subsequently constructed. This can be seen to the W of the road.

Moving northwards into Wiltshire, there is a considerable diversity of remains to be visited. The most notable is without doubt at **Bradford-on-Avon** (ST 8261), where the town centre boasts a gem of Anglo-Saxon architecture in the form of the chapel of St

Lawrence. Take the A36 out of Bath for 3½m (5·6 km), then turn E on the B3108 for a further mile (1·6 km).

The church stands complete (nave, chancel and N porch), except for the S porch. In 1125, William of Malmesbury recorded it as having been founded by St Anselm in the early eighth century. The lower half of the walls may be this original construction, but the pilaster work that is so prominent and the higher areas were probably erected during the late tenth or eleventh centuries.

In 1856 the chapel was a school and the chancel a cottage – there are still very obvious traces of these habitations inside the now reconsecrated ancient monument. The chapel is tall and narrow, typically Anglo-Saxon. The height of the walls actually exceeds the length of the nave (25 feet 2 inches [7·67 metres] by 1 inch [2·5 cm]). The most immediately recognisable feature from the outside is the stone pilaster stripwork that decorates the corners and the middle of each wall. Below the eaves a frieze of two squared string courses is connected by an arcade of round arches on short pilasters. Reeded pilasters run up to the east gable of the nave.

Inside, visitors should notice first the tall (9 feet 9 inches [2·97 metres]) narrow (3 feet 6 inches [1·07 metres]) chancel arch, the three double-splayed windows in the chancel, nave and porch and the most famous remains – the Bradford Angels. These are now built into the east wall of the nave above the chancel arch but originally were probably lower down, above the arms of a now destroyed Crucifixion. Notice, too, that the doorways and chancel arch are cut straight through the walls in typically Anglo-Saxon fashion and are ornamented with stripwork.

In complete contrast to this architectural monument is **Oldbury Camp** (SU 0469) which lies on the Cherhill Downs and can be approached by a footpath leading southwards from the A4 about 3m (4·8 km) east of Calne on the way to Marlborough, just opposite the N turning to Yatesbury. This interesting iron age hillfort is close to a White Horse and within 5m (8 km) of one of the most famous prehistoric complexes in the country – Avebury, West Kennet and Silbury Hill. The remains are mostly of the prehistoric period – a double rampart and ditch which was later divided by a low internal bank. Excavations produced a coin of Valentinian I, late Roman pottery, a post-Roman class G brooch, and significantly a bone comb decorated with ring and dot ornament. This indicated that the fort was reoccupied and used either in the very late Roman period or in the Dark Ages. It is thus worth visiting as a site of Dark Age

23 Bradford-on-Avon Anglo-Saxon church

occupation but there is nothing actually visible from the period.

A similar lack of definitive features distinguishes **Liddington Castle** (SU 2081) nearby, though this oval iron age fort was associated in tradition with Mons Badonicus, the scene of King Arthur's great victory over the Anglo-Saxons. Excavations in 1976 showed that its single rampart and ditch was given extra height in the later or post-Roman period, giving credence to the folk memory. It is to be reached by a steep uphill climb from the Ridgeway in Liddington, a village that lies on the A419 some 4m (6·4 km) S of Swindon and at junction 15 of the M4. The hillfort lies to the S of the village.

Iron age hillforts were occasionally the sites chosen for *burhs* in Late Saxon England, with some additions and refurbishing. The predecessor of medieval Salisbury was one such settlement and can be seen as the hillfort of **Old Sarum** (SU 1332). It is approachable about 2m (3·2 km) N of Salisbury to the W of the A345 to Amesbury. The sharp contours to banks and ditches are very impressive and although recut at later times they originated in the iron age. There may have been a Roman site here, though evidence suggests that this was not, as once believed, the Roman town of Sorviodunum. The area was reoccupied in the ninth century when the Late Saxon town was founded, and this continued to be inhabited into the Norman period. The Saxon *burh* was known as *Searisbyring*, and the fortifications were repaired by Alfred. In 960 King Edgar held court here. From the reign of Aethelred II until the time of Henry II a mint was situated at Old Sarum, but surprisingly almost nothing was found of the Saxon settlement during excavations. By the fourteenth century the site was effectively abandoned and the chief surviving remains are of the medieval cathedral and castle. The inner earthwork and the two transverse banks and ditches are entirely Norman.

Wansdyke (SU 0566) is a major linear earthwork which runs for nearly 50m (80·5 km) in Wessex, though it probably comprises two separate works connected by a stretch of old Roman road. Its length can be walked. It begins at Dundry Hill, SE of Bristol, and crests the hills S of the valley of the Bristol Avon between Bristol and Bath. There it stops, and the Roman road takes up its line until it appears again as a second earthwork which runs from Morgan's Hill near Devizes along the summit of the Marlborough Downs until it ends W of Savernake. This second section is more impressive than the first. The date of Wansdyke is disputed, though it certainly belongs to the Dark Ages. The W section may have been put up as a defence against the expansion of Mercia under Penda, around 628, or, less probably, by the Britons defending their frontier against the expansion of Ceawlin of Wessex after the battle of Deorham in 577. The eastern work was probably to define the limits of Wessex against the Angles of the Midlands after the battle of Fethanleag, 584. An alternative, but less probable, explanation for Wansdyke is that it was put up by Ambrosius as a defence against the expanding Anglo-Saxons around 470. It consists of a single bank and ditch, with the ditch on the N side. The best section is the 10m (16km) stretch along the S edge of the Marlborough Downs. The most impressive points to see it are where it crosses the A361, 3m (4·8 km) NE of Devizes, where it can be seen on each side of the road, and where it crosses the A345, about 1½m (2·4 km) SW of Marlborough, where it can be seen best to the W of the main road. It can also be reached by two side roads S of the A4.

Very close to this section of Wansdyke is the church of St Mary the Virgin, **Alton Barnes** (SU 1096), where the four megalithic quoins and four pilasters prove the nave to be Anglo-Saxon in date. It is in an attractive setting, close to the church of Alton Priors, and is reached by several minor roads to the E off the A361 from Devizes to Beckhampton; it is about 6m (9·4 km) E of Devizes.

Wiltshire is not rich in Anglo-Saxon sculpture, but what does exist is of considerable interest. Perhaps the finest is at **Codford St Peter** (ST 9640), on the A36 to Warminster about 15m (24 km) NW of Salisbury. The sculpture in question is a section of cross-shaft in St Peter's church, dated to the ninth century, but without any real parallel. The shaft depicts a man with a mallet, his head craned upwards, raising a branch. The angle of his head recalls some figures in Ottonian and Winchester manuscripts, but the drapery seems too stiff for mainstream Winchester art. On the sides are foliage scrolls. The interpretation of the figure has baffled commentators.

At **Ramsbury** (SU 2771), about 1m (1·6 km) W of the A419 to Swindon, 4m (6·4 km) NW of Hungerford, the church of the Holy Cross contains a number of interesting sculptures. The most notable are the fragments of one, or possibly two, ninth-century crosses, decorated on the lowest register with a dragon biting its own tail, with inhabited vinescroll above. There is interlace on the sides. The dragon is in Ringerike style, and shows the permeation of Danish influence into the heart of Wessex. In addition, there are two coped tomb-stones of the ninth century, with rounded ends and interlace and foliage scrolls.

24 Carving from Codford St Peter

A piece related to the Ramsbury cross, perhaps even by the same sculptor, can be seen in the church of St John the Baptist at **Colerne** (ST 8171), approached by a minor road NW off the A4 and about 6m (9·4 km) SW of Chippenham. The church crowns a hill, in a picturesque village. The sculpture is a ninth-century cross shaft, now in two pieces, decorated with intertwined animals in Jellinge style.

'Tosti', the brother of Harold, was staying at **Britford** (SU 1528) with Edward the Confessor when news was brought of a rebellion in Northumberland, of which Tosti was Earl. This connection with royalty accounts for the fairly elaborate church of St Peter in which, despite many Decorated additions, the nave is undoubtedly that which these illustrious personages would have seen. In fact, it was probably built in the ninth or early tenth century: notice the stripwork and very elaborate plinths. Foundations were found in excavation to the N, proving that the N arch in the W of the nave wall originally opened to a side chapel. A similar arch opposite presumably led to another chapel. The northern arch is richly decorated with vinescrolls and interlace. The church was restored in 1875.

Sculptures can be seen on the jambs of a door which originally led into a porticus, and which now forms the N door of the church. The reveals have two uprights bridged by square connecting slabs, giving a ladder-like effect. The slabs are ornamented with vinescroll and other decoration, including interlace, assignable to the ninth century. The S entrance has a similar arrangement of slabs, except for some interlace on one of the bridging slabs.

Two farm grounds enclose the church of St John the Baptist at **Inglesham** (SU 2098), where there is an interesting eleventh-century sculpture of the Virgin and Child surmounted by a *Manus Dei*. The village lies just off the A361, about 1m (1·6 km) S of Lechlade. Although weathered, it is a good example of the Winchester style (see p. 38). The church itself has a pre-Conquest nave, as defined by the slight evidence of the SW quoin, the S doorway which has been erected in the S aisle, and the height and thickness of the walls.

At **Cricklade** (SU 0993) the Anglo-Saxon *burh* was rectangular, and covered about 80 acres (32·3 hectares). Most of the line of the defences is still visible, though in places it is marked by a modern hedge or little more than a rise in the ground. They are best preserved on the E side of the town, where the now-denuded bank has been spread out between 50 (15·24 metres) and 60 feet (18·29 metres) wide and about 3 feet (0·91 metres) high. Excavation

between 1948 and 1964 showed the rampart to have been made of
piled clay subsoil, revetted with turf. In front of the rampart was a
mortared wall 4 feet (1·22 metres) thick, added later, perhaps shortly
before the Norman conquest. Ninth-century pottery was found in
the bank. It lies 7m (11·3 km) SE of Cirencester on the A419.

Somerset is King Arthur country. The hillfort of **South Cadbury**
(ST 6325) made news during the years 1966–70 due to the
excavations of Professor Leslie Alcock. The site has been claimed to
be Camelot, and was so identified by the antiquary John Leland as
early as the sixteenth century. Follow the A303 from Wincanton
and turn S. The village of South Cadbury lies about 7m (11·3 km)
NE of Yeovil, and is reached by several minor roads from the A359
or A303. The fort dominates the village, and is reached by a path
(Castle Lane) from the village centre up through the tree-clad slopes
and plunging ramparts, through the NE gate. These impressive
earthworks, built in the iron age, enclose an area of some 18 acres
(7·3 hectares), now an open field from which very fine views can be
obtained on a clear day across to the islands of the Bristol Channel,
the hills of Glamorgan and the whole of the Somerset basin. The
conical hill of Glastonbury Tor (itself occupied in the Dark Ages)
thrusts up against the skyline 11m (17·6 km) to the NW.

In the Dark Ages the site was reoccupied and a rampart of
drystone construction, tied together with a framework of timbering,
put up, following the line of the iron age rampart and broken at two
points (in the SW and NE corners), where there had been iron age
entrances. The excavators found that the SW gate was similar to the
type found in Roman forts, which suggests deliberate copying of
Roman defensive ideas. Inside the fort a Dark Age timber hall was
excavated. South Cadbury was probably abandoned at the time of
the Anglo-Saxon advance into Somerset (after 577), but was
reoccupied and refortified between 1010 and 1017, when Aethelred
II (the 'Unready') occupied it in the face of Danish attack. A mint
was founded on the site (which was known as *Cadanbyrig*). A
mortared stone wall was put up with a rubble core and a new
gateway constructed on top of its Arthurian predecessor in the SW
entrance. The foundation trenches for a cruciform church of this
period were also found in excavation.

It is now difficult to distinguish between the Dark Age additions
to the iron age innermost rampart and the original rampart itself,
though the top of the bank is certainly made up of Dark Age
additions. Sections of the stone wall of the Aethelredan fort (*burh*)

and gateway are visible in places where they have been exposed.

The site of **Glastonbury** (ST 5039) is also famous for its Arthurian associations – Arthur's grave is marked with a plate in Glastonbury Abbey. Remains of the Anglo-Saxon monastery were found in excavation on the Abbey site, but nothing of these are now visible. A few carved stones and some small finds of Anglo-Saxon date attesting its importance in Anglo-Saxon times can be seen in the site museum. The Anglo-Saxon monastery was preceded by a Celtic one, but again traces of this found in excavation are not now visible. Glastonbury lies on the A39, about 5m (8 km) SW of Wells. Adjacent to the town, and dominating the surrounding countryside, Glastonbury Tor was found on excavation to have been occupied in the fifth or sixth century, though later activity on the site made the interpretation of the remains very difficult. The Tor itself is very prominent and is approachable from the A361 to the E. The earthwork known as Ponter's Ball (ST 5337) which is cut by the A361 between Glastonbury and West Pennard has been claimed as Dark Age, but recent research suggests otherwise.

Cadbury Congresbury (ST 4465) can be reached by taking the A370 SW out of Bristol for about 10m (16 km) to Congresbury, then following a path which runs just W of Rhodyate Hill at ST 446651. The hilltop is much overgrown, but the site is one of major importance in Dark Age studies as it was reoccupied in the late Roman period and continued in occupation into the fifth century. It has produced much imported pottery. The existing remains consist of the univallate defences with a rock-cut quarry ditch – this rampart, which belongs to the fourth and fifth centuries AD, had a timber or turf façade. It may have been refurbished with D-shaped bastions or annexes in the fifth century, which flank the entrance on the E. A second rampart can be seen on the NE, where the ground is less steep.

Somerset is not rich in Anglo-Saxon sculptures. The finest is that in **Bristol Cathedral** (ST 5872). It is a depiction of the Harrowing of Hell, and probably dates from *c.* 1050, being an outstanding example of the late Winchester style. It stands on a pair of Norman colonettes, in the S transept.

At **Rowberry** (ST 4558), just E of the A38, about 14m (22·4 km) SW of Bristol, an interesting sculpture can be seen in St Michael's church. It is from a cross, and has rich interlace, reminiscent of that on the stone at Colerne, Wilts.

South-East England

The south-east has some very distinguished Dark Age remains, though in general visible monuments are few in number in this region because the massive redevelopments at various periods in the past have swept away earlier remains. What examples do survive must represent merely a minute part of what must have once existed. Fortunately, the remains that have escaped are on the whole well preserved.

The area was probably the first to receive extensive Saxon settlement in the fifth century, and certainly became Anglo-Saxon in character very early. Kent was the key area: here St Augustine arrived in 597 to begin the conversion of the pagan Anglo-Saxons, and here in the seventh century one of the richest of the Anglo-Saxon cultures flourished, nurtured by close overseas contact. The pagan cemeteries of Kent are famous for their rich burials filled with gold and garnet jewellery, exotic imports from Coptic Egypt, France and even India, and Kent was the first of the Anglo-Saxon kingdoms to be pre-eminent, before it was eclipsed by Northumbria and later still by Mercia.

Among the Christian Saxon remains are the earliest in Britain – the foundations of Augustine's church at Canterbury – and later Christian activity is well exemplified by the churches at Worth and Sompting in Sussex. Some Celtic remains in the form of iron age hillforts reused after the Romans had left (before the Anglo-Saxon settlements had taken hold) can also be found, and though the area is not distinguished for sculpture there are a few fine pieces, notably in the church at Sompting.

25 Worth, window in N wall of nave

A very fine church though heavily restored in 1871, when the present NE tower was built by Anthony Salvin, is that of St Nicholas at **Worth** (TQ 3036). It is reached by the B2036 and lies some 2m (3·2 km) E of Crawley. It is a cruciform building constructed some time in the early eleventh century or before. Some features that look to be Saxon, such as the pilasters on the apse, may not be original features, but part of the imaginative rebuilding. Nevertheless, there are long-and-short quoins, a plinth and pilasters topped by a string course to look out for, and three double windows in the nave (two in the N, two in the S), with bulging midwall shafts. The three arches to the chancel and transepts are superb, and of the two narrow doors into the nave, one has been blocked and one cut into by a fourteenth-century door. The chancel arch is blocked and extremely impressive, with hood moulding. These are the only features that are certainly pre-Conquest – the cruciform shape of the church is a pre-Norman plan.

One of the most remarkable church towers in the south-east is attached to the church of St Mary the Virgin at **Sompting** (TQ 1605). Worthing has expanded almost into the village which lies just S of the A27 to Brighton. The village name is Saxon and means 'the marsh dwellers'. It is only a mile or so (about 1·6 km) from the English Channel. The church was rebuilt in the early twelfth century by the Knights' Templar.

The tower is decorated with pilasters and each face is different. Tradition records that the tower was lowered 25 feet (7·6 metres) in 1762, but it is now considered that the tower is intact and that the Rhenish-type spire was lowered. The chief features to look out for on the outside are the double belfry windows on the N and S, the single belfry windows in the W and E, and the two round-headed windows in the N face about 35 feet (10·5 metres) above ground level along with the two triangular-headed windows some 10 feet (3 metres) lower. There is a small round-headed window in the N face lighting the ground floor. A triangular-headed window lights the S face about 25 feet (7·6 metres) above the ground. Inside, the splendidly decorated tower arch is worth seeing, with its capitals adorned with volutes, scrolls and bunches of grapes. Since it is slightly off-centre it suggests that an altar was placed N of it. A large number of eleventh-century carvings can be seen in this church.

Both the nave and chancel of the church of St James at **Selham** (SU 9320) date from the late Saxon period. The village lies between Petworth and Midhurst, 1m (1·6 km) S of the A272. Unfortunately no windows have survived from the original structure, but the N door is intact and the chancel arch is particularly attractive. It has a different decoration on each side and good capitals and imposts. The capitals are interesting since they are square at the top and round at the bottom and have been decorated not with a volute, which would be the classical answer to this mason's problem, but with animals or monsters with interlacing bodies. The N impost seems to have been a Roman architrave which was reused by the Saxon mason – the classical mouldings on the soffit face are still clearly visible. The only other features of interest are the side-alternate quoins and the herringbone work which is abundant. The W wall of the nave has been rebuilt. The village name means an 'estate by a sallow copse', and is Anglo-Saxon.

At **Bosham** (SU 8003) the church of the Holy Trinity is worth looking at, for the main body of the building – W tower, nave, chancel arch and the western portions of the chancel – date to the late Saxon period. The A27, and then a minor road S, only 4m (6·4 km) W of Chichester, will take you to this attractive harbour-side. It was here that Wilfred preached to the South Saxons (from

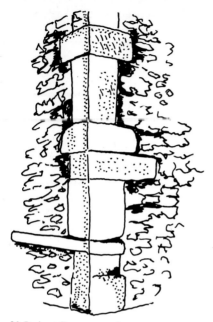

26 Bosham, Saxon NW quoin

whom Sussex takes its name) in AD 681. Here, too, was a seventh-century monastery where a monk called Dicul lived with half a dozen brothers. The Bayeux tapestry has a stylised illustration of the church since it was from here, too, that Harold sailed to Normandy. The village and church are thus unusually well recorded historically and of especial interest. As befits a place with such historical associations, Bosham has a legend concerning the tenor bell of the church. This is supposed to have been stolen by the Danes in the tenth century. When the pirates were on their way across the waters the church bells were rung to proclaim that all was now safe. The tenor bell joined in, tipping up the boat and drowning its abductors in what is now known as Bell Hole.

The Saxon remains are very fine. The tower rises sheer – 55 feet (16·7 metres) of Saxon work with two string-courses breaking its height. At first sight the tower windows may look Saxon but only one in the S face (which is blocked), one in the west and one double-belfry window are pre-Norman. A window on the second floor in the N face has the original Saxon frame around a modern opening. Notice too the quoins of the Saxon nave, the rest of which is now demolished, which appear near the tower in the N and S of the W nave wall.

Inside, the most important feature to note is the chancel arch, which is wide and tall with jambs set on plinths. A recess or blocked door can be seen above it, with another to the N. There are remains, too, in the N wall of the chancel of a round-headed window. The arcading in the nave is post-Conquest but almost certainly cut through the original Saxon walling, since three circular windows remain as evidence in the N wall above the roof of the later aisle.

Turning now to the W wall and the tower inside, the tower arch and the triangular-headed door above it preserve a pattern common in churches of this date and are authentic Saxon work. So, too, is the round-headed doorway high in this wall. The chancel preserves one more piece of evidence of its Saxon construction which can be seen outside – the blocked door in the S wall near the nave.

The memory of an otherwise unknown Saxon called Eadric is preserved at **Bishopstone** ('Bishop's Farm' in Anglo-Saxon), where the church of St Andrew (TQ 4701) dates possibly as early as the seventh century.

It is reached only by taking a minor road for less than a mile to the N off the A259 mid-way between Seaford and Newhaven. Few definitive features have remained to prove the date of the building, but it seems clear that the present nave and south porch are all that remain of a more complicated church, of which the porch was a chapel and which had a square chancel. The long-and-short quoining of the nave and its thin walls are immediate clues to its date, and the fact that structural evidence shows the Norman tower and porch door to be later than the nave and porch respectively clinches the argument. It is the Anglo-Saxon sundial in the porch gable above the N door that has the name Eadric inscribed on it. The only other features of interest are the two blocked windows (only visible inside the tower) in the original W wall of the nave.

Stoughton (SU 8011), some 6m (9·7 km) NW of Chichester, picturesquely means 'enclosure by the dairy farm' in Anglo-Saxon. Take the B2178 out of Chichester till it meets the B2146 and follow this for 2m (3·2 km). Then turn NE to Stoughton on a minor road. Here the church of St Mary is enclosed in a circular churchyard. The main fabric of this building belongs to the very latest Saxon period and Stoughton was a wealthy manor noted in the Domesday

Book. It was held by Earl Godwin in the time of Edward the Confessor. The church shows many Norman features, although it was built before the Conquest. Of the nave, transepts and chancel, the visitor should note the fine side-alternate quoining and the thin walls (only 30 inches [0·76 metres] thick and 30 feet [9·1 metres] high). Outlines of the original N and S doors can be seen and the transepts have large Saxon windows. The arch of the chancel has unusual mouldings.

Apart from the fine sculpture in Sompting church only one carving is of note in Sussex. This is a graveslab at **Bexhill** (TQ 7407), in the church of St Peter, Old Bexhill (Church St). It is a coped slab, in curiously Celtic style, showing Danish influence. It dates from the eleventh century, and has Maltese crosses, fine interlace, animals and fret and plant patterns. Some of the designs are reminiscent of Northumbrian work of the Golden Age, and it is without parallel in England. Bexhill is reached by the A259 about 5m (8 km) W of Hastings.

Cissbury (TQ 1408) is a remarkable fort, justly famous. It can be reached by a path from the village of Findon, from where it is signposted. To get to Findon, take the A24 N out of the centre of Worthing for about 4m (6·4 km). There is parking space near the fort. The earliest features are the hollows of a neolithic flint mine: the impressive hillfort belongs to the iron age, and was abandoned early in the first century AD, after which the interior was ploughed during the Roman occupation. At the end of the fourth century or early in the fifth it was reoccupied, and a turf wall was built on top of the old ramparts. The ditch was also widened at the entrances.

About 9m (14·5 km) S of Salisbury on the A338 is **Breamore**, Hants (SU 1518), a village whose name means in Anglo-Saxon the 'broom-covered moor'.

Unusual features of its church of St Mary are the inscription over the S chapel door and a Late Saxon rood. Of the structure itself the nave, central tower and one transept still remain from about the year 1000, though a second transept or chapel is visible only as a roofline in the N wall and the jambs of the door connecting it to the nave. On the outside there are quoins to indicate Saxon date and a blocked window in the S face near the later porch. Most of the surviving windows are in the tower, in which three out of the original four can still be seen. A window in the E wall of the S transept is echoed by a partly removed one in the S wall. In the N face of the nave are two double-splayed windows, high up. The

27 Breamore, inscribed arch

pilaster work is interesting, but it is the interior of this church that has the inscribed door. The precise form of the lettering (which could mean 'Here the covenant is manifested to thee') is such that the church could not have been built after the second decade of the eleventh century. The other interior doors or windows have long since been removed. However in the porch, over the S door of the nave, is the Rood, which narrowly escaped destruction during the Reformation. The mourners can still be seen on each side of the Cross, with the hand of God coming down from a cloud.

Hampshire has a famous Saxon church of no known dedication at **Corhampton** (SU 6120). It is fairly complete, with an eleventh-century nave and chancel, though the E end of the latter collapsed and was extended in 1855. The village is reached 11m (17·6 km) SE of Winchester, either almost directly from minor roads off the A33, or by the A333 out of Winchester for 10m (16 km), then NE along the B3035 for a further 4–5m (6–8 km).

There are pilasters, long-and-short quoins and a plinth: where the pilasters meet the plinth decoration is afforded by three upright leaves. Originally the side walls were higher – there is a string course on the W wall of the nave which crosses it about a third of the way up, and presumably the gable was higher, with the string course at its base. Only the stripwork of the N door survives, and the window above the string course was probably a bell-cote since there are grooves cut in the jambs as if by bells. A circular sundial in the S face of the nave is 2 feet by 18 inches (0·61 × 0·45 metres), and the chancel arch has Escomb-fashion jambs, but otherwise there is little of note from the Dark Ages inside the church. The village name means 'corn farm'.

Within a mile of the M27, 2m (3·2 km) NE of Fareham and reached by minor roads to the N off the A27, lies the church of St Nicholas, **Boarhunt** (SU 6008). The nave and chancel were built in the tenth or eleventh century and there are side-alternate quoins, a string course and vertical pilasters to be seen. The string course runs along the W face of the nave wall, over the chancel arch which is itself outlined in stripwork. In both the N and S nave walls faint remains of round-headed doors can be seen. On the outside only the remains of this S door and one double-splayed window in the N wall remain.

A notable Rood can be seen at **Headbourne Worthy** in the church of St Swithun (SU 4832). The village is approached by minor roads to the S off the A34, and lies 1½m (2·4 km) N of Winchester. Various modifications have taken place to the nave and chancel, culminating in very extensive restoration in the nineteenth century, but there are still a number of original features to note. The NE angle of the nave preserves the long-and-short work built in the eleventh century and a horizontal string course still adorns the W external gable of the unrestored W wall. Also in the W, but inside, is a door with Escomb-fashion jambs. There are vestiges of the original stepped bases under the pilasters, of which one is to be seen in the S wall of the chancel and three run up the N wall of the nave. The Rood was cut back almost to the face of the wall, possibly in the sixteenth century, but the hand of God is still clearly to be seen issuing from a cloud above the head of Christ.

Hampshire does not, in general, have much sculpture to offer, but what it does have is of good quality. Amongst the earliest remains is a cross-shaft at **Steventon**, which lies between the B3400 and the A30 about 5m (8 km) E of Whitchurch. It is in the church of St Nicholas (SU 5447) and can be assigned to the ninth century. On one panel intertwined dragons can be seen and on another there is interlace.

At **Whitchurch** (SU 4648), on the B3400 about 6m (9·7 km) NE of Andover, a very unusual gravestone is housed in All Hallows

church. It is shaped like a Roman tombstone, with an arched top
and recess in which is a representation of Christ, half-length. Along
the top is an inscription in Roman letters reading

HIC CORPUS FRITHBURGAE REQUIESCIT IN PACEM SEPULTUM
(*Here the body of Frithburga lies buried in peace*)

The reverse carries a plant scroll.

Two crucifixion slabs of Late Saxon date are to be seen at **Romsey**
(SU 3521), 10m (16 km) SW of Winchester on the A31. Romsey
Abbey was founded in 907 by Edward the Elder for his daughter
Elflaeda, but the existing building was mostly rebuilt in the
twelfth century. The larger of the two slabs can be seen on the
outside of the W wall of the S transept. It is over 6½ feet (1·98
metres) high and now somewhat weathered, with a hand of God
above, perhaps a recut. It dates from the early eleventh century. The
second panel is in the S chancel aisle of the church and is set into a
piece of screen used as the reredos of the SE apse. It shows the
Crucifixion flanked by the Virgin and St John, with Stephaton and
Longinus below. On the arms of the Cross are two angels. It dates
from the tenth to eleventh centuries, and is one of the most notable
examples of Winchester style sculpture surviving. Some dispute has
surrounded the dating of the larger piece, which has been claimed as
post-Conquest.

28 Winchester, late 9th century fragmentary Anglo-Saxon wall painting

Winchester (SU 4829) has nothing visible of its once important
Anglo-Saxon town and cathedrals, though large-scale excavations
during the 1960s and 1970s have done much to unravel the early

history of this former capital of England and base of King Alfred. But you should not miss the museum in the Square (10–4, 5 or 6 according to season, Sun. 2–4.30), for it houses an important collection of objects not just from Winchester but from the region. The placename comes from the Anglo-Saxon, and means 'Roman fort called Venta'.

In Berkshire there are only two sites of note. St Swithun's church in **Wickham** (SU 3971) has a W tower under a nineteenth-century belfry, dating to after 950, but there are still good long-and-short quoins despite restorations in the nineteenth century which swept away any further Saxon remains of the church itself. It is reached from turn-off 14 on the M4 via the B4000, some 5m (8 km) NW of Newbury. The name means 'homestead with a dairy farm'. St Swithun, who was buried in Winchester (where he was bishop 852–62), was to have been re-interred on 15 July 971, but it was too wet, so the burial was postponed – hence the superstition that if it rains on St Swithun's day it will rain for forty days.

Note the remains of a blocked round-headed door about 8 feet (2·4 metres) above ground level in the S: some have suggested it was in this odd position for defence. Above this the chamber has only one small round-headed window. The second floor has double belfry windows in the N and S and a single one in the W.

The aisle roof is decorated with papier mâché elephants that were featured in the 1862 Paris exhibition.

The *burh* at **Wallingford** (SU 6089), about 20m (32·2 km) NW of Reading and reached by a variety of main roads (the A329 from Reading or the A4130 from Didcot), was situated on the W bank of the Thames, controlling a river crossing. The fortification is rectangular, with massive bank and ditch enclosing about 100 acres (40·5 hectares). It is mentioned in the Burghal Hidage. The defences are very clear on the E side of the town, above the flood plain of the river, and a depression under the E bank in the NE corner of the *burh* may represent a Norman dock connected with the castle, for many of the earthworks may date from the late eleventh century in their present form. Excavations within the castle, however, have shown a two-phase Saxon rampart, similar to that at Wareham (see p. 72). The grid-iron street plan is probably Saxon.

Godalming (SU 9643) originally had a Saxon two-cell church, but the later additions to SS Peter and Paul have all but obliterated it. Nevertheless, within the present nave and tower slight remains can be detected. The chancel arch even managed to survive until 1879.

Two circular double splayed windows still exist in the area above the bellringers' chamber in the tower. Godalming is reached on the A3100, about 5m (8 km) SW of Guildford.

Guildford, though in the heart of Saxon country, preserves only the tower of St Mary's church from after 950. It can be found in Quarry St, S of the High St (TQ 0049) and the lower part of the tower is entirely surrounded by later additions. There are merely pilasters to note and, from the inside only, a double splayed window in the N and S faces of the tower. Outside no remains are definitely Saxon. Guildford lies 13m (20·9 km) SW of Leatherhead on the A246, and the church can be most readily located by looking for the castle. The place-name comes from the Anglo-Saxon and means, picturesquely, a 'marsh-marigold ford'.

At **Taplow** (SU 9082), 1½m (2·4 km) NW of Maidenhead, can be seen the remains of a famous Saxon barrow (burial mound). Take the A4 out of Maidenhead until it meets the B476 to the N: Taplow is ½m (0·8 km) from this junction. The barrow stands on high ground above the Thames, at Taplow Court, in the old churchyard. When it was opened in 1883 it produced a rich array of finds, now in the British Museum, including a Coptic bowl (from Egypt), drinking horn mounts, four glass beakers, thirty bone counters, a gold buckle and an embroidered garment. Taplow means 'Taeppa's tumulus'.

London is extraordinarily lacking in Dark Age remains, though recent excavations are proving that it was occupied from pagan times onwards and probably was never deserted. The church of St Andrew, **Kingsbury** (TQ 2086), within a mile of the Edgware Rd, shows four quoins of long-and-short work on a plinth that indicate a date around the time of the Norman Conquest for the nave. No other early features make it worth visiting, however.

All Hallows by the Tower (TQ 3380) is included here not for its fine Saxon features so much as its uniqueness in the capital: it is the only London church with standing fabric dating to around the eighth century. It is to be seen in Great Tower St, and was discovered to be ancient only after an attack by fire bombs in 1940, when a Saxon arch was exposed in the S wall. A series of fragments of eleventh-century cross-shaft, decorated with interlace, vinescroll, figures and an inscription, were also discovered. The arch is similar to those at Brixworth, and this fact causes it to be dated to around the time when it is known that the Abbey at Barking was founded for Ethelburga by her brother Earconwald, bishop of London, who died about 694.

What London lacks in Anglo-Saxon sites, it more than makes up for in museum exhibits. The finest collection of Dark Age objects in Britain can be seen in the new medieval gallery in the **British Museum** [10–5, Sun. 2.30–6] in Great Russell St. Of the many objects on display, particular note should be taken of those from the Sutton Hoo ship burial (see p. 160) and from Taplow (p. 95). There is a fine collection of Kentish goldwork with garnet inlays, and this can be compared with the adjacent collection of Migration Period continental pieces. Do not miss the gallery devoted to objects from a pagan cemetery excavated at Dover, and notice too the case of Late Saxon metalwork, notably the fine Fuller Brooch and other examples of the Trewhiddle style. A few sculptures are represented, but no pottery, for typical examples of this can be seen in the separate pottery gallery at the end of the medieval gallery. The Celts are not unrepresented either, and among the exhibits notice the Pictish bull-carving from Burghead (see p. 268) and the magnificent Breadalbane Brooch from Scotland, one of the masterpieces of Celtic metalwork in Britain.

Further Anglo-Saxon and Viking antiquities can be seen in the **Museum of London** [Tue.–Sat. 10–6, Sun. 2–6], London Wall. This houses finds made in the city and its environs, and includes some fine pieces very attractively displayed. Neither must you miss the **Victoria and Albert Museum** in South Kensington [10–6, closed Friday; Sunday, 2.30–6], which has some masterpieces of Anglo-Saxon art, including ivories of the Winchester school.

Kent is famous for its profusion of rich pagan Saxon cemeteries, and also for being the starting point for the conversion of the Saxons. Here are to be found the greatest number of remains of very early churches.

The church of All Saints at **Lydd** (TR 0421) is interesting: in a very fine ecclesiastical building, approached by the B2075 S out of New Romney, 4m (6·4 km) NW of Dungeness, are the W and N walls of a formerly aisled Saxon nave with a clerestory. The 30 feet (9·1 metres) of N wall and 14 feet (4·27 metres) of adjoining W wall are datable by the three round-headed arches, now blocked, with one clerestory window above. The NW quoin of the original structure is still visible. A modern tradition holds that the font at this church used to be locked up so gypsies could not steal the Holy water to give to Mother Shipton, the famous sixteenth-century prophetess.

The white cliffs of Dover provide the setting for another Saxon church, this one remarkable for its proximity to the only standing Roman lighthouse in Britain. It lies picturesquely within the castle grounds at **Dover** (TR 3241), between the keep and the sea; it is reached by the A258 from Dover to Deal, and is a short distance to the E of the road.

Heavy restoration has left the church as much a product of the nineteenth century as the tenth or eleventh century, when it was first built. However (with the exception of the gable), as far as can be ascertained the more recent restorers kept to the model of the ruins as they appeared in 1860–2. Its history had been somewhat chequered since the building was roofless for a short period in the eighteenth century and was used as a military coal store for some time until restoration. Visitors should notice the original plinth and six original windows in the nave. The lighthouse was built in the second century AD and is an ancient monument [A;S]. The top 19 feet (5·8 metres) are medieval but the rest is original. Of the windows and doors, the entrance to the S is the original Roman work, and a Saxon door gave access from above the W doorway of the church. There are two openings to the belfry in each face and seven circular windows below. Inside, two arches support the tower. Taking into consideration the exceptionally fine Norman castle at Dover, this site provides a veritable feast of architectural features.

Dating back to the earliest period of Saxon ecclesiastical development is the church of St Mary and St Sexburga at **Minster**, Isle of Thanet (TQ 9573). This small area was an island until the sixteenth century, but is now easily accessible by the A249 from Maidstone. Minster itself is reached by turning to the W when this road forms a T-junction with the A250 on Thanet itself, and continuing for about 3m (4·8 km). In 1027 the buildings were rebuilt from earlier beginnings, but have the unique claim of being the oldest inhabited edifices in England, since parts are still used to house some nuns of the Benedictine order. Only the N and S walls of the nave of the church can still claim to date from the time when Queen Sexburga founded a religious house for over seventy nuns, after the death of King Erconbert of Kent in 664. The Queen became the first abbess six years later. St Mildred was abbess later and died in 725. Part of her tomb was found during excavations in 1929 when the original apse was uncovered. Nowadays, visitors should notice the fragments of four early windows – two in the S wall and two visible externally in the N wall. The string course on the N wall and the NE quoin, too, are original features.

Also in Kent is one of the most outstanding churches in Britain, though sadly little remains standing – **Reculver**'s church of St Mary (TR 2269). Apart from the twin Norman towers which stand prominently over the ruins and are useful to shipping, the entire building with its unusual triple chancel arch was deliberately demolished in 1805. The site is of exceptional interest since its history is known for nearly two thousand years – from long before the church was built around 669, when King Egbert of Kent gave the land to a priest called Bassa.

The site was chosen because it contained the ruins of the Roman fort of Regulbium. As was the custom, tiles and other Roman building material were used in the erection of the new church. The sea has now encroached extensively on the Roman fort, though walls are still visible in the characteristic rectangular layout, to about 8 feet (2·44 metres) high in one part. Excavation has discovered the complete plan of the early church: the nave, apsidal chapel and flanking porticus which presumably were built by Bassa, and a later porticus which enclosed the nave and formed the W porch. It is thus well worth taking the A299 for about 3m (4·8 km) E out of Herne Bay and then turning N for another 1½m (2·4 km) to reach the seaside settlement of Reculver. The plan shows the remains to be complex but similar to other Kentish churches – it is partly this which proves the stones are indeed those put up by Bassa. Of the chancel arch demolished in 1805 little remains, but two columns from it are now in the crypt of Canterbury Cathedral. The excavations in 1927 found some of the original flooring which was a ten-inch thick layer of mortar and rough flints. It was covered with a red burnished surface of cement and pulverized brick, which in itself belies the unfounded tradition that the Saxons endured insalubrious conditions in their buildings. Notice the remains of sills and splayed jambs of two windows faced with brick which remain in the N wall of the N porticus. In the N wall of the later porticus are three windows with a fourth below.

Leland, the antiquary, described in the sixteenth century a Great Cross in front of the triple arcade, but this is now in fragments and the remaining pieces can be seen in Canterbury Cathedral.

Canterbury itself offers unusual remains from the Dark Ages, for here there are the foundations at least of four churches, three with important historical associations.

This ecclesiastical building began with the foundation of the Abbey by St Augustine in the late sixth century, followed by the

29 Reculver (a) from an old print, (b) from the air

building of the Abbey church by the newly converted King Ethelbert of Kent. Several alterations were followed by a rebuilding in the eleventh century. Excavation has found three seventh-century churches on a common axis – the main church dedicated to SS Peter and Paul (later rededicated to include St Augustine as well), the chapel of St Mary nearby which was incorporated into the main church in the eleventh century by the building of a Rotunda, and a third church dedicated to St Pancras. A fourth is that of St Mildred in Stour Street where the only evidence of pre-Conquest date is the megalithic nature of the quoining in the S wall.

The visible remains of the Abbey Church are not very impressive compared to many Saxon standing buildings, though the original plan has been discovered under the later Norman rebuilding – in some places all that is left of the plan are markers on the ground to indicate the results of excavation. The church was rectangular with two chapels each side, a narthex in the W and probably an apsidal E end. The NE chapel is the most interesting because it is known that many archbishops were buried here until the chapel became full. Augustine himself was first interred outside the church, but at its

30. St Augustine's, Canterbury

dedication was brought into the side chapel. The N chapel was enlarged but not used for interment until the Rotunda was built by Wulfric. The Rotunda's building operations demanded the disturbance of the E wall of the Abbey church and the W wall of the chapel of St Mary. In the process the mortal remains of St Mildred (which had already been removed once from their resting place in Minster in Sheppey) were taken into the new chapel dedicated to St Gregory. Of the Rotunda itself only the lower part of the lowest storey is original under Norman work, though it is unique in Britain. It was never completed by Wulfric, whose death was thought at the time to be due to St Mary's displeasure at the demolition of the W end of her chapel. The original work is slightly below ground level and was approached by steps in the W wall. The building was round inside, octagonal outside and its function was to amalgamate the two churches. St Mary's chapel is now destroyed by late Norman work except for the W wall. It had a simple plan with side chapels and an apsidal E end.

The church of St Pancras on the same axis survives rather more fully, one wall of the W porch is almost intact and most of the building is visible, at least as foundations. The monastic remains of St Augustine's Abbey are not now above ground, and the only wall which has been claimed as early is that of the boundary which runs

31 Brooch from Kingston, Kent

some 130 feet (39·6 metres) E of the NW angle of the Cemetery
Gate – though if it is original it certainly has many later additions.

Canterbury, the county town of Kent, has long been a centre of
pilgrimage, and inspired the *Canterbury Tales* of Chaucer. Its
Archbishop is Primate of All England, who crowns the monarchs.

Central England

Central England offers the traveller a wide range of landscapes and a varied selection of Dark Age remains. In landscapes ranging from the Derbyshire Peaks and the Shropshire heights to the gentle Cotswolds and the soft countryside of Northamptonshire with its distinctive stonework can be seen some of the finest sculptures and

churches in England. This was territory dominated by Mercia, the leading kingdom of England in the later eighth and ninth centuries, and on it the Mercian tradition of sculpture was focused, classic examples of which can be seen at Breedon-on-the-Hill, Leics. The remains are varied. They range from the impressive Wat's and Offa's Dykes which run partly through counties now in Wales along the western march of Mercia to some of the finest Anglo-Saxon churches in England. Several cluster together in Northamptonshire, and within a day's travelling it is possible to take in Brixworth, Earl's Barton and Barnack, while also in central England lie the two remarkable churches of Deerhurst and Odda's Chapel in the Cotswolds and the similarly important Wing in Buckinghamshire.

Deerhurst, with its outstanding church of St Mary (SO 8729), lies 3m (4·8 km) SW of Tewkesbury. To get there, take the A38 until it meets the B4213 to the W, follow this for 1m (1·6 km) then turn N along a side road. The church is extremely complex architecturally, and has been the focus of many a learned dispute. The dating of the various phases is still not certain, and excavations are being carried out at present to try to resolve some of the problems.

The building looks simple enough from the outside, with its magnificent 70 feet (21·3 metres) Anglo-Saxon tower, but a series of demolitions and alterations have drastically transformed its appearance over the last millennium.

Originally the building was a small rectangular church, with an apsidal chancel, that began life in the seventh or eighth centuries. During the same period a W porch was added and two-storeyed side chapels transformed its appearance. Later still in the same general date bracket the W porch was raised to three storeys and the side chapels were extended W to flank the nave. Possibly about 1000 the chancel was replaced by a now ruined apsidal chapel (the modern chancel merely uses part of the main body of the church). The W porch was further extended to produce the present prominent tower. Still later modifications have included the medieval tower stair, perpendicular windows and other features which have obscured many earlier features and made interpretations difficult.

Historically, it is known that a monastery existed at Deerhurst (which derives from the Anglo-Saxon place-name meaning a wood frequented by deer) in 804, when Aethelric, son of Aethelmund, is recorded as having bequeathed lands to the foundation. It is possible that the latest Saxon features were added after the tenth-century Danish raids which may have made restoration necessary –

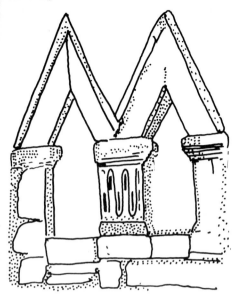

32 Deerhurst, Saxon window

the Danes were particularly prone to ravaging monastic settlements.
The confusion about what are late or early features does not help.

A visit is however well rewarded, and should begin with the
scrutiny of the tower – notice the remains of an original W door,
partly obscured by a Pointed door. There is a weathered Saxon
sculpture of the head of some beast above it, and higher still a
square-headed window of uncertain date. Above these features,
some 25 feet (6·62 metres) above ground level, a round-headed door
can be seen, with a square hood mould and a very crude beast's
head above.

Inside the tower can be seen by climbing the medieval stair to the
second floor chamber where a large stone is probably all that
remains of a door. Square-headed windows on the side walls can be
seen, too, though they are obscured from view from outside. One
has a flat head and hides behind the stair. Close inspection of the W
door will reveal that it was once rebated for a door to be hung. The
third floor of the tower contains a notable E doorway. The E wall of
the tower can be seen from the nave and is broken by a blocked

door, a window with a triangular head and a unique double triangular-headed window above. The siting of the blocked door has led to suggestions that it was the entrance to a second floor chapel. Under this hypothesis the altar would have been placed in a central position under the window: access would have been gained to the church by means of a platform or gallery in the nave. Two corbels just below the level of the door seem to bear out this theory. The double window is outlined with stripwork and the north opening was modified at some stage when its base was cut back to form a door.

   The aisles of the nave contain string courses along the N and S walls and small triangular windows prove that the walls predate the early English arcades cut through them. The most important Saxon feature is the magnificent blocked archway that led originally to the chancel, which dominates the E and focal point of the church. The ends have two large beast heads as decoration and traces of original colouring have been detected on them – a reminder that architectural details and sculptures were not always as they are today. Other remains are the faint traces of blocked triangular-headed windows flanking the perpendicular E window and two corbels in the same wall that indicate a possible gallery. Blocked narrow doorways to the N and S are all that are extant of the original openings to the side chapels.

   One of the few Saxon fonts in the country has had a chequered career in Deerhurst and the nearby church at Longdon. This, an oolite bowl, was used for an unspecified period until 1844 as a washtub on a village farm. However, the Dean of Westminster saw it and bought it for Longdon church where it was used for baptism for a generation; then the discovery in a garden of what was thought to be the font stem resulted in the returning of the bowl. It is now considered that the stem and font do not belong together, but the bowl is very delightfully decorated with double spirals, vinescroll and rosettes.

   Only a few hundred yards from Deerhurst church is **Odda's Chapel** (SO 8629), which was not recognized as Saxon until 1885 because it had been incorporated into a house. The church is still attached to the medieval half-timbered farmhouse and the exterior of the chancel is totally obscured by the farm walls. It is a simply planned building with nave, chancel and chancel arch, although three centuries of domestic use have taken their toll: the nave was used as a kitchen and the chancel had an upper bedroom in it. The dedication is known to have been to the Holy Trinity from an inscription discovered in the building material. The two double-splayed windows, one in the N and one in the S nave wall, the long-and-short work of those quoins that survive and the mutilated north door and chancel arch are the most definite Saxon features still visible. Why the church should have been used for secular purposes is a mystery. It is presumably the building referred to in an inscription found in 1675 and now in the Ashmolean Museum, Oxford – this was a church built by Earl Odda and dedicated on 12 April 1056, a rare instance of an exact dating for a Saxon building.

The church of the Holy Cross at **Daglingworth** (SO 9805) is 3m (4·8 km) NW of Cirencester, reached by minor roads to the W of the A417. The nave with its ornamented S doorway and the chancel belong to the Late Saxon period. Drastic rebuilding of the chancel in 1845–50 made use of ancient materials and has thus obscured much of the dating evidence. An Anglo-Saxon door was reused in the S porch, too, at some point, so that although the porch looks pre-Conquest, it is almost certainly medieval. It is certainly later than the Saxon nave, since its erection left a Saxon sundial useless. The sundial is 10 inches (25·4 cm) square and has a circular dial with a raised roll moulding. Notice the gnomen hole. Outside the church the long-and-short work of the original quoins of the nave are intact, except for that at the NW. Those to the chancel look original but are rebuilt. The sculptural decoration in this church is its outstanding feature. The S door has an attractive wheat-ear ornamentation and placed in a lofty position above the E gable is a rough stone Crucifixion with a plain Cross and Christ wearing a knee-length tunic. The face is moustached and possibly bearded. Inside the church are three further sculptures, in the nave and the north aisle walls. These were originally part of the chancel arch jambs, but were removed in 1845. One piece is badly mutilated and appears to show a seated Christ in Majesty. Another is a bearded and moustached Christ in a girdled tunic of some transparent material (the body shows through). A soldier carries a cup and bag and another bears a spear. The third sculpture is of an apparently clean-shaven St Peter who carries a large key in his right hand and a book in his left. All three are almost certainly contemporary with the church – about the eleventh century. Before restoration the E end of the chancel was lit by an original window of which the outer face was made from a single slab with a Roman inscription on it: it is still visible. This placename refers to the original Saxon 'homestead of Daeccel's people'.

Langford has a Late Saxon axial church tower of unknown dedication (SP 2402). It lies 3m (4·8 km) NE of Lechlade, reached by minor roads to the E of the A361. The Saxon origins of the tower are indicated by the quoins, the string courses and the pilasters with their stepped bases and capitals. The masonry is authentic Saxon work right up to the Norman corbel table, and each side of the belfry has a pair of unique windows with sculptured imposts. In the south of the middle stage the double-splayed windows have keyhole-shaped apertures. Also in this wall the observant will notice two kilted figures who are carrying a sundial above their heads: they decorate a panel in the central pilaster. The lower part of the tower is visible only inside the church and has two fine arches, of which the E is the more elaborate. Above these, square-headed doors can be seen, that to the chancel being blocked. The line of the original roof is to be seen on the upper wall in the E. Finally, the medieval porch incorporates two Roods. That in the E wall shows one of the very few English examples of Christ dressed in a long clerical garment with sleeves. The second has been incorrectly put together, for St Mary and St John should be looking towards the Crucified Christ, not away. The dates of these sculptures are subject to some controversy: they have been claimed both as Saxon or from as late as the twelfth century.

33 Langford, impost on s belfry window

Fragments of another Rood can be seen by taking the A431 from Bath to Bristol as far as the village of **Bitton** (ST 6869), where the church of St Mary has a Late Saxon nave. Originally there were side chapels to N and S, and the most important feature for dating the structure is the one remaining chapel arch now blocked in the N wall of the nave. Other original remains are more fragmentary, since the chancel arch was replaced in 1843 and only a few lengths of stripwork and one intact and one mutilated capital remain. The S wall has been rebuilt on the existing Saxon plinth. There is some evidence that the church was much higher when built: firstly, there is the string course that has survived above the chancel arch, which suggests a much higher roof originally, and secondly there are the sculptured fragments of a massive Rood. The natural place for this to have been placed would have been above the string course, to dominate the congregation in the nave. This would necessitate a much higher church. Of the remains of the Rood there is only the stone carved with huge feet with a serpent emerging from waves beneath that definitely came from the carving. Other fragments were discovered in a blocked-up squint, of which one seems to be the hand of Christ belonging to the Rood. The head that was discovered may not belong.

34 Serpent on the Bitton Rood

Seven miles (11·3 km) NE of Cirencester on the A433 lies the village of **Bibury** (SP 1106) and the church of St Mary. Many later additions have all but obscured the Late Saxon nave and chancel, but close scrutiny will reveal a short piece of the S wall that is not hidden by the aisle, where a string course 27 feet (8·23 metres) above the ground delimits the original work. A double-splayed window in this wall and a fragment of long-and-short work in the NE quoin still exist. On the chancel, the short pieces of pilaster work with stepped bases and the plinth at the western ends of the walls show that the walling at this point is a thousand years old. Inside, the original exterior of the nave can be seen from the N aisle where three pilasters remain, of which the most northerly has Saxon carvings on it. A blocked window is visible only from the aisle. The chancel arch has been drastically remoulded in the Middle Ages, but the jambs and the finely carved imposts are still Saxon. The Saxon village name means the 'fort of Beage'.

The British Museum now houses a fine eleventh-century gravestone from Bibury, which shows some modifications of English taste in response to Scandinavian influence with its foliate figure-of-eight scroll and interlacing branches.

Only 6 miles (9·7 km) NE of Cirencester, reached by minor roads E of the A429 is **Coln Rogers** (SP 0809), where the nave and chancel of the church of St Andrew belong to the Late Saxon period. It is almost intact, except that the E of the chancel has been rebuilt. Of the features determining its date, only one window (in the north of the chancel) remains. Visitors should notice the long-and-short quoining on all but the NE corner of the nave, and the Saxon plinth and four pilaster strips. The chancel arch is constructed in Escomb-fashion and the blocked thirteenth-century door in the N wall of the nave must originally have been Saxon.

Somerford Keynes (SU 0195) lies about 4m (6·4 km) S of Cirencester, reached either directly by minor roads or by minor roads E of the A429 or W of the A419 out of Cirencester travelling S. The church of All Saints contains only a fragment of the early Dark Ages: the blocked N door of the nave which may date from the foundation of Bishop Anselm (later Saint) who was granted land here in AD 685. It has been included in the main guide merely for its antiquity in an area otherwise rich only in Late Saxon remains. The door has pleasing decoration and Escomb-fashion jambs. Two monsters play with a ball in a carved recess inside the arch. The village name is an interesting mixture of Anglo-Saxon and French origins, meaning 'Keynes's manor of land at the ford only available in summer'.

One of the very few sculptures of Anglo-Saxon date in Gloucestershire can be seen in the chapter house of **Gloucester** Cathedral (SO 8318). This dates from the mid-tenth century, and depicts Christ as Pantokrator (ruler over all) in a roundel, with a border ornamented with a running dog motif. It shows strong Continental influence in the Carolingian artistic tradition.

To reach **Newent** (SO 7225) follow the B4215 for about 8m NW of Gloucester to its intersection with the B4216. Two interesting sculptures can be seen in the church of St Mary. The first is an eleventh-century memorial slab, a mere 8 inches by $6\frac{1}{2}$ inches (20·3 × 16·5 cm), imitating an ivory or metal prototype, with an inscription to someone called Edred. The second is a fine cross-shaft set up in the porch, and probably dating to the ninth century. It is somewhat dumpy with Adam and Eve on the front. One edge has a panel with a creature known as the 'Carolingian lion with worried brow'. The edge is bounded by a symmetrical wiry scroll. It is Mercian, rather than West Saxon, in its overall style.

At **Beverstone** (ST 8593), $1\frac{1}{2}$m (2·4 km) W of Tetbury on the A4135, there is a relief of Christ holding a stemmed cross, built into the S wall of the church tower. It stands about 5 feet high, and dates from the first half of the eleventh century. It is similar to the sculpture in Bristol Cathedral (p. 82).

Oxfordshire is not rich in Dark Age remains. **Oxford** (SP 5106) is worth a visit not only as a famous University and County town, but also for the W tower of the church of St Michael which is a fine sturdy example of Saxon work. It stands in Cornmarket St, and the long-and-short quoins, blocked W door and double-splayed window in the N prove its age. Other Saxon windows light the first floor in the N and W (the latter has been enlarged to form a door). The door 30 feet (9·14 metres) above ground is original, as are the belfry windows above. Similar windows can be seen above this under the modern parapet (except that the E window is modern).

Also in Oxford and a must in any tour of the town is the Ashmolean Museum [10–4, Sat. 10–5, Sun. 2–4], which has a notable collection of Anglo-Saxon antiquities as well as a few Celtic. Its most famous Saxon treasure is the Alfred Jewel, probably owned by Alfred the Great. It was probably part of a reading pointer. On the front under a piece of crystal is an enamelled personification of Sight. It is made of gold and the edge is inscribed with the words 'Alfred had me made' in Anglo-Saxon. It was found in 1693 near Athelney, Somerset. The museum also boasts the important Minster Lovell jewel.

The famous Roman villa at **North Leigh** (Anglo-Saxon 'northern wood') lies not far from the church of Saxon origin in the village (SP 3812), 3m (4·8 km) NE of Witney, slightly N off the A4095 to Bicester. The tower, now at the W, was probably built in the tenth century and is topped by a medieval parapet. Notice that there are gable lines on the E and W, that there is a W arch and that the quoins under the level of the nave roof are not well dressed. All

35 North Leigh, Saxon tower

these features indicate that the tower was originally axial, flanked by buildings that no longer exist. Keen observers will see a blocked door outlined in the W face of the tower high up, and original round-headed windows in the N and S. Four belfry windows are unmistakably Late Saxon. Inside, the only Saxon features are parts of a round-headed window above a pointed arch in the S wall.

Moving into the West Midlands, slightly W off the A34, 6m (9·7 km) NW of Shakespeare's birthplace, Stratford-on-Avon, lies the church of St Peter at **Wootton Wawen** (SP 1563) in an idyllic setting. The central tower under the perpendicular belfry belongs to the half-century or so before the Conquest. Its main interest lies in the four fine arches that prove it to have been cruciform with flanking buildings when it was first built. Three are still in use, all show Escomb-fashion construction and there are long-and-short quoins and a string course to be seen. The place-name is Anglo-Danish and means 'Vagn's manor of woodland farm'.

Tredington ('The farm of Tyrdda's people') (SP 2543) has the church of St Gregory. The village is approached from the A34, 8m (12·9 km) SSE of Stratford, just S of its crossing with the A429. The side walls of the nave above the arcades are all that remain from the Saxon period. However, they are of more interest than usual, since eight windows and two doors have been preserved. The windows are visible from each side of the nave walls, the doors only from in the aisles.

The attractive Marches countryside boasts several Anglo-Saxon churches. That at **Stanton Lacy** (SO 4979) has been much modified but the N and W walls of the nave and the walls of the N transept date from the late tenth or eleventh century. It is reached by taking the A49 northwards out of the picturesque town of Ludlow for about 2m (3·2 km) and then turning N on the B4365. Stanton Lacy lies just off the main road to the E. The nave walls display side alternate quoining and there are five pilaster strips in the W wall, nine in the N wall and one in each of the transept walls, all standing on corbels. Only two original doors remain – a fragmentary opening in the N wall of the transept and a fine though blocked door in the N wall of the nave. This has a cross in relief above it and a window to the E of it is of uncertain date.

Those who follow the B4365 N out of Ludlow without turning off to Stanton Lacy could turn NE along the B4368 some 4m (6·4 km) further on, to reach the village of **Diddlebury** ('Dudda's fort') in the Shropshire Heights. The church of St Peter (SO 5185) still retains its

Saxon N nave wall and what used to be the annexe, but is now the tower. The date for its erection is very close to the Norman conquest. A Saxon plinth runs along the N wall of the nave and part of what is now the tower. About 2 feet (0·61 metres) W of the transept the nave plinth turns S, proving that this was the E quoin of the original nave. The north nave wall displays a double-splayed window and a blocked round-headed door which is decorated with stripwork. Herringbone work is very prominent in this church, and is important since such work used to be considered wholly Norman in date. The evidence at Diddlebury, however, changed this view, since here it has been proved to be Saxon. The chancel is Norman, even though there are tendencies for the quoins to look Saxon.

Wroxeter (the name means 'Roman fort of Viroconium') (SJ 5608) is more famous for the Roman fortress and town of that name than for the church of St Andrew. Take the B4380 to the S off the A5 some 5m (8 km) E of Shrewsbury and then continue past the Roman ruins which are signposted, to reach the church. Although much of the Roman town was robbed to build the church and the gateposts of the churchyard started life as classical columns hewn by a legionary, only the eastern 40 feet (12·19 metres) of the N wall of the nave are Saxon. The seventh or eighth century building was shorter than the present church, since its quoins are readily visible incorporated into the N wall. The S wall contains a piece of Saxon cross-shaft with vinescroll and an animal of indeterminate parentage. A band of birds continuously eat worms in a carving over the S jamb of the chancel arch.

Open to the elements on Wenlock Edge is the church of St Giles, **Barrow** (SJ 6600), some 3m (4·8 km) E of Much Wenlock on the B4376 to Ironbridge. The church, with its eleventh-century chancel stands almost within a farmyard. The tower and nave seem to be Saxo-Norman and the E wall of the chancel was rebuilt in 1844, 1848 and 1895. The plinth is similar to that at Diddlebury and there are remains of a pilaster strip in the N wall of the chancel. A double-splayed window high in the E of the N wall of the chancel is Saxon, as is the impressive chancel arch of which the imposts were chamfered in 1851 to make them look neat! The change in masonry in the E wall indicates the existence of a former narrower nave with a steeply pitched roof.

Next to the Mytten pub in **Atcham** (SJ 5409) is the church of St Eata which has a few Saxon features of the seventh or eighth centuries. The side walls of the nave are all that remain, however,

36 Barrow, details of Saxon church

and visitors should note the large stones in the lower parts of these walls, the side-alternate W quoins and the plinth under the N wall. A small window in the nave has been the subject of discussion, but it is probably original despite the chamfering on the round-headed exterior. It is triangular-headed inside. Atcham lies on the A5, some 5m SE of Shrewsbury.

Moving north from Shropshire, Cheshire generally lacks Dark Age remains. **Eddisbury** (SJ 5669) can be reached by the B5152, and a side road W, from Delamere. The site is approached from the nearby farmyard, where permission must be sought before a visit. It is a multi-period iron age fort, which was reoccupied in the post-Roman period. Huts of presumed fifth-century date were discovered in the partly silted-up ditches. Queen Aethelflaeda of Mercia refortified the *burh*, and built a new rampart and gateway similar to that at South Cadbury, Somerset.

Of the numerous fragments of Cheshire sculptures that survive, few are of any outstanding note. By far the finest are those which stand in the market square at **Sandbach** (SJ 7661) [AM:A], which lies on the junction of the A533 and A534, 5m (8 km) SE of Middlewich, and is easily reached from turn-off 17 on the M6. There are two crosses, datable to *c.* 850. They are richly ornamented in a manner which reflects West Saxon taste modified in a Northumbrian style. Cheshire however lay within Mercia, so it is not surprising that some Mercian influence is apparent in the animal at the bottom of the W face of the larger cross. Both crosses stand on a plinth, and were probably erected at the same time – twin crosses of later date are not unknown in Mercia. On the large cross the figural ornament is rich, derived from New Testament iconography. On the smaller cross the E face has a series of unique scenes, perhaps representing the introduction of Christianity to Mercia by Penda.

In **Chester** (SJ 4166) nothing of the Late Saxon occupation is now visible, except for a number of cross fragments of the Scandinavian period in St John's church, just to the E of Newgate. Nine fragments survive, though others have been lost. All date from the tenth to eleventh centuries. The finest is a complete ring-headed cross in two pieces, arms decorated with a triquetra pattern and the shaft ornamented with 'scales'. The Grosvenor Museum in Grosvenor St [10–5, Sun. 2–5] displays a number of interesting finds, of which the most notable in this context is a stone from Overchurch, with a lengthy runic inscription, the only one known from Cheshire. Reused by the Normans from an Anglo-Saxon church, it is a memorial to one Aethelmund. Chester is more famous for Roman and Medieval remains.

Sometimes in England, sometimes in Wales, **Offa's** and **Wat's Dykes** run the length of the Marches, and their total length can be considered together here. These mighty ramparts were constructed by King Offa of Mercia and his predecessor down the length of the frontier between Mercia and Wales and are two of the most outstanding archaeological remains in Britain. They can be compared with the Roman frontier works of Hadrian's Wall and the Antonine Wall, though they lack the forts associated with the Roman lines. In terms of length, however, they put even Hadrian's Wall in the shade – it is a mere 73m (117·5 km) in length compared with the 120m (193 km) of Offa's rampart, which runs through some of the most breathtaking scenery in England. Offa's Dyke runs from near Treuddyn down to a point near Chepstow on the Severn, with a number of gaps where dense forest probably made the dyke unnecessary. Wat's Dyke, somewhat shorter, runs from near Holywell to the middle Severn.

The authority for believing **Offa's Dyke** to have been the work of Offa of Mercia (757–96) is provided by Asser, King Alfred's biographer, who reported that Offa built his frontier from 'sea to sea'. As it would appear at present, this is not strictly accurate, but recent research suggests that Offa incorporated part of Wat's Dyke into his scheme at its northern extremity.

37 Offa's Dyke

Excavations have shown that Offa's engineers first marked out the line of the dyke with a small ditch and bank, perhaps crowned with a wall, and at least at some points along its length the rampart was constructed with turf and not merely earth from the quarry ditch.

Offa's Dyke can first be observed at **Treuddyn** (SJ 2558). To find it follow the A5104 S of Chester in the direction of Treuddyn, then turn S on the B5101. The road follows its line from Coed Talwrn to Llanfynydd and Ffrith. Thereafter it leaves the road and heads due S to Brymbo Hill, which it crests (but where it is obscured by modern development). Just before Brymbo it can be seen crossing the B5102 at SJ 2854. From SJ 291525 a stretch of over a mile can be followed from modern lanes. A particularly good section is visible between SJ 297493 and SJ 298487. This can be reached by side roads from the A483 or B5426 at Bersham – at one point it crosses the B5426. The next fine stretch can be reached from just W of Ruabon – the Dyke has followed the line of the A483 approximately, but here it crosses the A539 and A483, and is well preserved from SJ 297448. The next section of the Dyke worth visiting lies just beyond Froncysyllte. To find it, take the first minor road running south from the A5 just E of Froncysyllte to Fron Isaf. The Dyke is to the E of the road, and carries on down intermittently until it reaches the B4500 near Chirk Castle. It carries on to cross the B4579 at Craignant, then further south crosses the B4580 about 2m (3·2 km) W of Oswestry. The best points at which to view it are at SJ 281406, SJ 271391, and at SJ 263374. Just beyond the B4579 a good section can be observed at SJ 252349.

South of the B4579 the Dyke runs due S towards the A495. It can be reached by side roads from these and from the A483. It crosses the A495 about 1m (1·6 km) W of Llynclys, then it curves round to meet the A483, which it follows for a short distance before it swings slightly E then stops short before the Severn is reached. It starts up again just S of Buttington, on the A458 about 2m (3·2 km) NE of Welshpool, then follows the B4388, running to its E. Where the B road swings W the Dyke carries on to Pentre, but meets the B4388 again at Kingswood, crossing the A490 about 4m (6·4 km) S of Welshpool. About 1m (1·6 km) E of Montgomery the Dyke crosses the B4386, and again meets the main road where the A489 and B4385 intersect. It can be reached by side roads from the A488, and crosses the B4368 at Lower Spoad. Thereafter it runs slightly E towards Knighton, and can be reached by side roads from the A488. The best points at which to view the Dyke from roads are at

SO 249077, SO 243026 and SO 238020. A particularly fine section is visible at SO 235975 and SO 245947.

The section immediately to the N of Knighton is particularly suited to exploration on foot – virtually the whole length of the Dyke is traversed by footpath, and walkers will find this, and Wansdyke in Wessex, an enjoyable exploration. It is in many ways the finest section, and was probably completed first. At SO 283720 a fine length can be observed at the golf course, and it can be followed to the B4355 where it can be seen continuing over Hawthorn Hill at SO 282688, about 2m (3·2 km) S of Knighton. It runs roughly parallel with the B4355, and can be observed where it crosses lanes to the E of the B road at SJ 272651 and SJ 269639. From Eywood, a section of the Dyke runs W to Radnor Hill, which is National Trust property. This is the last appreciable section of the Dyke (though short sections can be seen) until it takes up again for its last, almost continuous, run to the sea from Highbury, Glos. It can be easily observed from the A466, starting about 3m (4·8 km) S of Monmouth, where it follows the line of the river Wye (and the road) for about 2m (3·2 km). Where the road crosses the Wye it swings out E but continues to follow both road and Wye down to Chepstow. To see the end of the Dyke, take the A48 out of Chepstow and turn E down side roads to Sedbury. From the park gates the Dyke runs to the Severn cliffs.

Wat's Dyke is generally less impressive than Offa's; it averages about 4 feet (1·22 metres) high and 50 feet (15·24 metres) in width (Offa's Dyke is several feet higher and wider). It was built probably in the period immediately preceding Offa, perhaps by Aethelbald (716–757), and extends from Basingwerk, Flints, to the river Morda between Oswestry and Maesbury in Shropshire. The first good section is visible from SJ 233697, where it runs across the A55 to SJ 239674. It crosses the A55 about ¾m (1·2 km) W of Northop. The next good section can be viewed at Buckley, at SJ 258646, where it crosses the A549 and continues to cross the A5188 E of Padeswood. A good section can be seen at SJ 308591. This section can be viewed by taking the A550 into Hope, Flints, then following Stryt Isa – the Dyke runs parallel to the road on the E side, and is cut by a side road which runs E from Stryt Isa. The next good section is not visible until a point beyond Wrexham, but short sections can be seen at SJ 333525 and SJ 326494, between the A541 and B5425 just N of Wrexham, and S of Wrexham, to the E of the A483, reached by side roads. The best section however can be seen starting at SJ 323476, where it can be followed on foot for about 3m (4·8 km), crossing the B5426 about 1m (1·6 km) E of Johnstown. It carries on to cross the A539, but fades out in Wynnstay Park. There is a break in the Dyke until it starts up again between Chirk and Gobowen, but this section runs virtually unbroken to its end. The start of it can be reached by following the A5 to the junction with the B5068 about 1m (1·6 km) S of Chirk. This should be followed E towards St Martin's Moor, just before which the Dyke can be seen on the S of the road. The best place to view it next is at Old Oswestry, the fine multivallate iron age hillfort just N of Oswestry, and signposted on a side road (the site is in state care). The fort lies astride the Dyke, and this section is exceptionally fine (at SJ 2930). The last 2m (3·2 km) of its length can be followed by taking side roads running S from Oswestry.

Leaving the Marcher lands, and moving eastwards, the modern county of Worcestershire boasts one fine monument, the **Cropthorne Cross** (SO 9944), which can be seen in the church of St Michael. Only the head survives, dating from around the mid-ninth century, but it is richly decorated with beasts and birds, with Greek key patterns on the sides. Cropthorne can be reached by taking a side road N of the A44, between Pershore and Evesham, about 3m (4·8 km) W of Evesham.

The north Midlands is a key area for the study of Mercian sculpture. In Derbyshire the cross at **Bakewell** (SK 2168) is one of the finest, and can be seen in the yard of All Saints church, reached by following the A6 NW out of Matlock, to its junction with the A6020. Nothing survives of the Saxon church except its general plan. The cross is in exceptionally good condition but is incomplete, and is decorated with vinescroll, animals and figural work of the early ninth century. It would appear that Bakewell was the centre of a Mercian school. Other Anglo-Saxon fragments can be seen in the S porch and N aisle.

The very fine cross at **Eyam** (SK 2278) lies about 6m (9·7 km) N of Bakewell. Take the A623 for about 11m (17·6 km) E from Chapel-en-le-Frith, then turn N on the B652 for a mile (1·6 km) or so. It stands in the churchyard of St Lawrence's and is restored with its Northumbrian-style head set on the lower part of the shaft. The shaft has vinescroll ornament, the head figural work in early ninth-century style.

The Wirksworth slab can be seen in the church of St Mary at **Wirksworth** (SK 2854), 4m (6·4 km) S of Matlock, on the intersection of the B5023 and B5035. This fine recumbent tombstone is one of the earliest examples of Mercian sculpture, and is related in style to the Bakewell cross. The decoration consists entirely of human figures, set out in two registers, representing events connected with the life of Christ. Some of the scenes have their closest parallels in the Byzantine world, or slightly nearer home, in France. One scene is the Crucifixion, with the Cross surrounded by evangelist figures, and a slain lamb upon it. It dates from around 800. In spite of the stiff, tubular draperies, the figures have a certain vitality, and show that a vigorous tradition was emerging in Mercia around the time of Offa's supremacy.

Pride of place amongst the Dark Age remains of Derbyshire must be taken by the church of St Wystan in **Repton** (SK 3026). The church spans the period from the seventh to the eleventh centuries as well as having many later additions, and is now close to the twelfth century Augustinian Priory that has been incorporated into Repton School. Hrewpandum (Repton) was the capital of Mercia under King Penda and lies 6m (9·7 km) SW of Derby. Take the A38 southwards for about 5m (8 km) till it forms a junction with the

38 Repton (a) exterior of crypt

A5132, follow this for about a mile eastwards and then turn southwards along the B5008 to Repton.

Repton is well documented in history, having belonged to an abbey of mixed sex that was founded in *c.* 660. An eighth-century life of St Guthlac records how the saint renounced the world at the age of twenty-four and came to Repton. The earliest work in the church (the lowest courses of the crypt wall below the chancel and visible in a trench at the E end) are probably those which St Guthlac would have seen in 698. King Ethelbald was buried here, according to the Anglo-Saxon Chronicle, which mentions too that the Danes wintered here in 873 and 874. The monastic buildings were indeed destroyed by the Danes in 875, and a new church was built and dedicated to St Wystan a century later. The later Saxon work in the church thus presumably dates from this rebuilding.

Only the chancel, crypt and parts of the original central crossing and transepts remain from the Saxon period, but from the outside, almost all the chancel is original. It is of three separate builds, including the earliest parts of the crypt beneath. In the side walls and the E wall, the rectangular recesses that are clearly visible may have been used for shrines or tombs before those in the N and E were adapted to give access to the crypt stairs. The change in walling above this work is very evident – high up, the latest phase of building is clearly shown by the pilasters and a string course which decorate it. This is probably eleventh-century work. That below it dates somewhere between the seventh and eleventh centuries. The external walls are of interest, too, since part of the original transept remains as the E wall of the N aisle and the lowest three courses of the E part of its N wall. The church originally had a central crossing and in both E walls of this (attached to the chancel walls) string courses are visible. The crypt itself can be entered from a passage and steps from the nave – originally there were two passages functioning. It was discovered accidentally in 1779 when a workman fell in from the chancel above. It is a cold dank place and the atmosphere was not improved in our view by a modern blue cross (when we visited it in 1977). The crypt is 16 feet (4·87 metres) square with 9 square bays vaulted from four monolithic columns. These are carved with spiral ornament, with rough bases and capitals which give a sombre, cumbersome air. Recesses in the middle of the side and S walls of the crypt now hold windows but, like those outside, they probably held tombs or shrines in the eighth century.

Inside the church, remains of the central crossing are extant: near

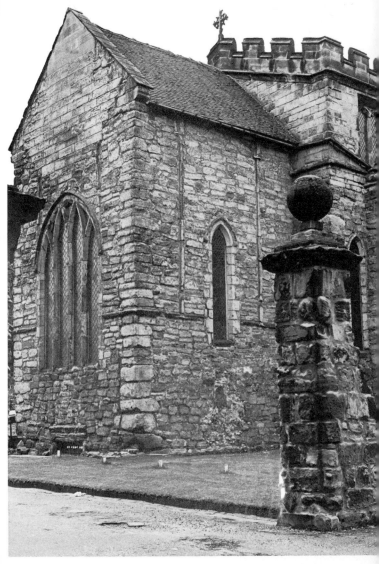

38 Repton (b) Saxon chancel

the ends of the passages to the crypt are sections of the Saxon flooring with the bases of the circular columns that took the arches of the transepts. These have now been replaced, but the walls above the later arches are proved to be original by the presence of a string course 23 feet (7 metres) above ground level. Over the medieval chancel arch is a square-headed door with a S jamb in Escomb-fashion technique.

Much further south, in **Leicester** (SK 5804) the church of St Nicholas has a nave built in the tenth or eleventh centuries and standing in the centre of this county town. This city was the Roman RATAE CORITANORUM (the capital town of the Coritani), and the famous Jewry Wall stands close by. The street in which the church stands is called Holy Bones. The Jewry Wall has been proved in excavation to have been part of a fifth-century occupied area and finds can be seen in the site museum [AM; 10.30–7, Saturday 9.30–7, Sunday 2–5]. The Saxon church had been much modified – Norman arches have been cut into the N wall of the nave, though two round-headed windows with two rows of tiles above them survive. Outside the only Saxon remains are in the W wall of the nave where the SW quoin in particular is of side-alternate work. The See was established here in 737.

Nottinghamshire and Leicestershire generally lack notable Saxon ecclesiastical remains but there are a few sculptures worthy of a visit. The best is a cross at **Stapleford** (SK 4837), conveniently reached from turn-off 25 on the M1, or by the A52 from Derby and then the B5010, since it lies 8m (12·9 km) due E of Derby. The cross stands in St Helen's churchyard, with a shaft 10 feet (3 metres) high on a base which, along with the top, was restored in 1820. The decoration is mainly interlace, but there is one figure at the top. It is a late work, probably dating from the eleventh century.

At **Shelford** (SK 6642), which lies about 5m (8 km) NE of the centre of Nottingham, approached by side roads S off the A612 or north off the A52, the church of St Peter, in picturesque river meadows by the Trent, offers the visitor a fine sculpture of the Virgin and Child. It is probably mid-eleventh century, and stands 2 feet 10 inches (0·86 metres) high with interlace on one edge and a scroll on the other. The opposite face has a bearded seraph. It is one of the finest examples of late Saxon sculpture in the Midlands.

The church of the Holy Trinity at **Rolleston** (SK 7452), which can be reached by a minor road running SW from the A617 at Averham, about 3m (4·8 km) W of Newark, has an attractive free-standing cross-shaft with interlace. An inscription on this eleventh-century work reads RADULFUS ME FE (cit).

The famous sculptures of **Breedon-on-the-Hill** (SK 4022) lie in the church just W of the A453 about 6m (9·7 km) N of Ashby-de-la-Zouch. The church is signposted from the village green, and is dedicated to St Mary. It can be seen from afar, since it has a very prominent position on the edge of a quarry. There are almost 30 fragments of sculpture at Breedon, in a distinctively Mercian style, and these rate amongst the best Anglo-Saxon sculptures to have survived. They are probably late eighth-century, and most seem to have come from friezes in the Saxon monastery of Brindum, mentioned by Bede and known to have been in existence as early as 731.

The monastery was destroyed by the Danes, and an Augustinian priory built on the site early in the twelfth century, though only the W tower of this survives, the remainder of the church belonging to a later period. The largest section of frieze can be seen behind the altar, and runs for about 18 feet (5·49 metres), depicting geometric ornament, Greek key patterns, peltas, interlace and vinescrolls. The total surviving length of frieze amounts to about 60 feet (18·29 metres); it is only about 7 to 9 inches wide (17·7 to 22·8 cm), and because of being set high on the wall is not easy to study. Human figures appear in the frieze, including some on horseback, some kneeling and some seated. There are a number of figures belonging to the friezes which are now isolated, as well as a number of other compositions which clearly do not come from friezes. The most notable of these is a figure of an angel, about 3 feet (0·91 metres) high, and a figure of Christ, on a panel about 2 feet (0·61 metres) high, Byzantine in style and also recalling the style of the figural work in the Mercian manuscript known as the Book of Cerne.

Also in Leicestershire, at **Sproxton** (SK 8524) there is a complete tenth-century cross in the churchyard of St Bartholomew's. It is very weathered, but has an animal and some interlace on it. It lies 7½m (12·1 km) NE of Melton Mowbray, N of the B6763.

Rothley (SK 5812) is on the B5328, reached by taking the A6 N out of Leicester for about 4m (6·4 km), then turning W. Here a cross-shaft in the churchyard dates from the ninth century and is decorated with interlace. There is an animal in one panel. The church is dedicated to St Mary and St John the Baptist.

Northamptonshire has some of the finest Anglo-Saxon churches

39 Earl's Barton (a) Saxon church tower

39 Earl's Barton (b) Saxon w door to tower

that survive anywhere. Of all these, the most outwardly impressive is
Earl's Barton (SP 8563). All Saints church lies high above the
junction of a minor road with the B573 in the centre of the village. It
can be reached by several minor roads to the south off the A45 some
6–7m (9–11 km) NE of Northampton. The late tenth-century tower
is a very famous architectural feature, remarkable chiefly for its
pilaster and stripwork decoration. The tower was probably
incorporated at some stage into the defences of the Norman castle,
of which vestigial remains are visible outside the churchyard. It has
been erroneously suggested that the upper belfry windows were used
in defence. These five windows with their triangular heads pierce the
fourth of the decreasing stages of the tower. The upper eight feet of
walling and battlements are perpendicular. Triangular-headed
windows can be seen on each face linked by pilasters of St Andrew's
crosses.

The second stage boasts a tall round-headed door, with its sill resting on a string course 22 feet (6·71 metres) above ground level. The tower was probably the main part of the original church, with other annexes, and remains of this earlier plan can be seen in the much modified door in the E face (second stage).

In the lowest stage a double window ornamented with small roll-moulding and carved with small crosses survives in the S face, and a very fine doorway pierces the W face. Note, too, the plinth and the long-and-short work in this most attractive and remarkable tower. The village name was originally Anglo-Saxon and means the 'grange of the earl'.

Brixworth (SP 7470) (the name is Anglo-Saxon, meaning 'Beorhtel's homestead') lies about 7m (11·3 km) N or Northampton on the A508 to Market Harborough, and can be reached almost directly by minor roads from Earl's Barton. Where Earl's Barton impresses by its ornamentation, Brixworth is almost overpowering in its complexity. It has been much altered and is a rare example of an originally aisled nave whose side arches have been blocked in an almost eerie fashion. The original church, probably dating to around 700 or later, had nave, aisles, porch and narthex (both destroyed) as well as a presbytery and apsidal chancel. In about 850 the semi-circular ambulatory was added. The tower was built up from the W porch, the W stair turret added and the apsidal chancel was rebuilt sometime after 950. The church is 160 feet (48·79 metres) long and offers much to be appreciated both inside and out. It belonged to a monastery which is known to have been founded by the Abbot of Peterborough after 675. The latest changes were probably after the Danish raids in the tenth century.

The most noticeable feature is probably the sunken 6 feet (1·82 metres) deep trench around the chancel, which is all that remains of the ambulatory. This was entered by doors to the main body of the church which are still visible and very prominent inside. The ambulatory was possibly added to allow viewing of relics in the recesses that remain, or possibly in an original crypt underneath.

It is relatively easy to distinguish the Saxon from the later work by the Saxon tufa used. The doors in the N and S of the present tower and the fragments of walls to the N and S of it are the main evidence for the existence of a now destroyed narthex.

A blocked round-headed door cuts through the N wall of the presbytery below a decorated window. Notice, too, the Roman bricks and tiles that edge the doors and windows with very little regard to careful alignment. On the inside, the nave and presbytery are now in one, though originally separated by a wall and a three-arch arcade, the outer parts of which support a fifteenth-century arch. The angle of the remains of the arches indicates that the original was triple. There is a blocked round-headed window in the S wall of the presbytery and the four blocked arches that led each side to the aisles are very prominent. Notice, too, the chancel arch and the two windows on each side of it.

Inside the tower the door (the original entrance) to the church still exists and a similar door above is now cut into by a triple-headed window of the tenth century. The original W door to the tower was blocked slightly in about the tenth century when a smaller door was fitted to give access to the stair.

The tenth-century staircase is of great interest and is unusual for its remarkable state of preservation. It is lit by a series of small windows and leads to a door which cut through the window of the original porch. The tower room looks into the church through the triple-window.

To the left of the door as you enter the church, notice the

40 Brixworth (a) Saxon church

40 Brixworth (b) Saxon chancel

sculpture behind the glass. It represents an eagle, and is a fine example of Mercian work, reminiscent of the eagle-evangelist symbols that appear in manuscripts.

After these two gems, the next two churches may seem almost a disappointment. Half a mile (0·8 km) to the S of the A5, some 6m (9·7 km) NW of Towcester is **Stowe** with its parish church dedicated to St Peter and St Paul (SP 6357). The W tower and adjoining parts of the nave walls date from the tenth or eleventh century. This church is datable by part of a cross-shaft built into the NW quoin of the tower, by the string course that divides the belfry from the lower stages, the pilasters on the E and W belfry stage and the blocked square-headed door in the W, with an original window high above it. Notice, too, the plinth at the NW angle of the tower and, inside, the small modified Saxon door that leads from nave to tower.

Green's Norton (SP 6649), about 1½m (2·4 km) NW of Towcester, reached by minor roads from the A5 or A43 has a tenth-century Saxon nave. The church of St Bartholomew looks almost completely medieval but keen observation will pick out the W quoins of the tower. Above the chancel arch a door has been blocked, and the existence of corbels under its jambs suggest that there was a gallery at this point in Saxon times. Three windows have been blocked and can be seen in their fragmentary condition above the N arcade. Those who go into the ambulatory will be able to see a plinth and the original E quoins of the nave. The long-and-short work on that in the north is easily identifiable.

Geddington (SP 8983), which lies about 3½m (5·6 km) N of Kettering on the A43 and within a short drive of another outstanding church at Brigstock, has two attractions. The first is the superb Eleanor Cross, which stands in Gothic splendour opposite the second – the church of St Mary Magdalene, which, though superficially unremarkable from the Dark Age viewpoint, displays some early and fascinating Saxon work inside. The chief interest in Geddington lies in the evidence it seems to give for the dating of Saxon features. The nave arcades are Norman, but close inspection of the N wall of the church, from the north arcade, will prove it to be of Saxon date. It shows a triangular-headed arcade and the remains of a round-headed window above the Norman arches. It will be seen that the arcade is contemporary with the NE quoin from the easy way the two meet, and that the window cut through the arcade. The Norman arches in turn cut through the window. Thus at Geddington at least two stages of building before the

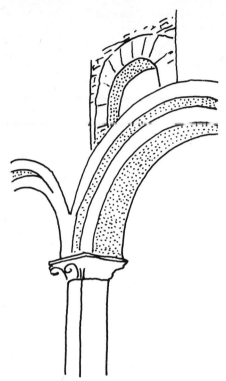

41 Saxon window cut through by later arcade in Geddington Church

Conquest are shown in what is merely a short section of walling. From this it is inferred that the church must date back to the ninth century at least. Saxon Geddington was the 'farm of Gaete's people'.

Brigstock (SP 9485) boasts the outstanding church of St Andrew on the A6116 some 7m (11·3 km) NW of Thrapston. It has been well camouflaged by its spire, its decorated windows and its early English chancel and chapel, but the Anglo-Saxon work is there to be seen too. The lower part of the W tower and nave walls were probably built before 850, and the upper part of the tower and the round W stair turret were added some time after this date.

Before entering the church look at the bold plinth on which it stands, the long-and-short quoins of the tower and the change in character of the masonry, which is evidence for its two stage construction. A double-splayed round-headed window in the first stage of the tower is intact and another has been hidden by the clock.

Inside the church, the tower arch is a splendid example with its stripwork outlining and from the evidence of the Saxon window that has at some time been blocked, in the N arcade, and the string-courses above it, it can be presumed that parts of the nave walls are the original build. The Saxon-looking Norman arch in the N wall of the tower might well trap the unsuspecting into thinking it an original feature. The round-headed windows in the tower are genuine Saxon work however as is the short section of plinth near the pulpit and the long-and-short quoin nearby which was the original SE corner of the nave.

42 Brigstock (a) Saxon tower arch

42 Brigstock (b) Saxon tower and stair turret

The turret deserves some consideration, since there are so few remaining from the period. Access is gained through a door with a triangular head. Originally the turret would have been furnished with wooden stairs. The square-headed door that is now blocked gave access from the nave to the upper room of the tower. The place name proclaims that the village grew up from the Saxon 'dairy farm by a bridge'.

Buckinghamshire has only a few examples of Anglo-Saxon architecture but one of them is of outstanding note. This is the church of All Saints at **Wing** (SP 8822) some 3m (4·8 km) SW of Leighton Buzzard on the A418. The nave of the original church has aisles, and that on the N side is unusual in that it still retains its external wall. It may have had a seven-sided chancel which underlies the seventh- or eighth-century crypt, but the nave and chancel were both the subject of alterations after 950, to judge from the architectural features. On first approaching the building it is the perpendicular west tower, clerestory and windows that are the dominant features, but the vertical pilasters connected by an arcade of round arches decorating the chancel immediately proclaim its Saxon date. Above the perpendicular windows in the N and S part of the polygonal chancel, sections of original windows can be seen with four intact examples above. On the lowest level, the crypt is lit by three Saxon windows: all have round heads in rubble and that on the S had been adapted to form a door. The crypt itself is octagonal with an ambulatory, and the barrel vaults of the central chamber are supported by four huge piers. The original entrances to the crypt are blocked. Outside it will be seen that the E end of the north wall contains a blocked door with a triangular head which is of uncertain function, though it does give a Saxon date to this wall. Inside, the impressive chancel arch could be of Saxon date, and the double window surmounting it that was discovered in 1892 is certainly Saxon. The arcades on each side are original and unusual for their completeness. In 1954 two doors with round heads were found, one in each of the nave walls at the W. It has been suggested that they indicate the presence of a gallery – perhaps for the lady of the manor, Aelfgifu, who may have been the widow of King Aedgar's brother in the early tenth century.

About 8m (12·9 km) SW of Bedford on the A428 to Northampton is the village of **Lavendon** (SP 9153), where the church of St Michael dominates a dangerous bend with only a narrow footpath to preserve pedestrians from the heavy traffic. The rather forbidding W tower is topped by a fifteenth-century belfry, but the lower 50 feet (15·24 metres), devoid of any relieving decoration, are late Saxon. Notice the uppermost windows on the N and S sides, and two others below: these, along with a carved stone in the S face (in the eastern quoin), are original. This church is notable for the herringbone work. Inside, the nave has been cut through by thirteenth-century arcades, though there is no reason to suppose that the walls themselves are not Saxon. The most impressive Dark Age remains inside are, however, the tower arch and the door which leads from nave to tower.

Not far from Peterborough is **Wittering**, a village about 4m (6·4 km) SE of Stamford (the Danish borough) off the A1. Here the church of All Saints (TF 0502) has a nave and chancel that were first put up in the late tenth or eleventh century. Six long-and-short quoins remain and a well-defined plinth on the S face. The chancel arch is grandiose and very remarkable with three-rolled moulding.

Also approachable by the A1 and then a series of minor roads, or from Stamford by the B1443, is **Barnack** (TF 0705). This very charming village is fortunate in having the church of St John the Baptist for its focal point. The two lower stages of the tower and the W angles of the nave date back to the late tenth or early eleventh century. The tower is immediately recognizable as Saxon from the pilaster work, and closer inspection will reveal a round-headed S doorway, N and S windows (with a sundial over the S window), triangular-headed W window and similarly shaped belfry lights. Barnack stone, subtly coloured and pleasingly weathered, has been used since Roman times in the area, and in this church it has been intricately carved. There is the head of a beast over the W window and decorated slabs enhance the wall above the first cornice with acanthus leaves and birds. The midwall slabs of the N and S belfry windows have fine openwork.

Inside, the tower arch is impressively simple – 20 feet (6·1 metres) high and 13 feet (3·96 metres) wide. The only decoration is the stripwork and hood moulding. A triangular-headed recess in the W wall of the tower has been claimed to be the seat of the president at local legal proceedings (which were carried out in churches in Saxon times) or of a member of the clergy. There are also aumbries in the N and S walls, and the original S doorway of the tower is now partially blocked by the thirteenth century stair turret.

There is, too, the bottom of a door that originally led from tower to nave which has been cut in half by the roof and which is partly visible outside. In the N wall of the nave six stones that might have belonged to a pre-Conquest arch can be seen, and a carving of Christ in Majesty is built into the outer wall of the N aisle, possibly datable to well after the Conquest but showing strong Saxon features.

Eastern England

The eastern counties of England are very well off for Anglo-Saxon remains. Many finds have come to light by chance or excavation, while the visible remains, as in other areas, are those of the Christian Saxons. In this region in particular, many churches that survive were put up just before the Norman conquest. Some churches show signs of several periods of modification or rebuilding.

Generally Norfolk (which comes from the Saxon 'north people') has few sculptures, but is noteworthy for its round towers, often in idyllic settings. These are a feature of later periods, too, because of the lack of good stone for quoins and corners.

Suffolk ('south people') has few remains, but has the rare pagan Saxon tumuli or barrows at Sutton Hoo – these are interesting for the finds now on display in the British Museum, rather than for the visible remains on the site.

Essex ('east Saxons') has the unique wooden church at Greensted, and the very well-preserved church at Bradwell-on-Sea which dates from the early seventh century and is still standing.

Cambridgeshire, although well off for pagan Saxon finds, has only a few churches, but it does have the impressive linear earthwork known as the Devil's Ditch.

The traveller in the north of the region will find a further gem at Barton-on-Humber. The east was one of the first parts of England to be settled by the Anglo-Saxons, and although remains of other periods are relatively few, its best Dark Age remains are now among the finest in the entire country. Lincolnshire has very distinctive Anglo-Saxon towers, tall, plain and rather gaunt. Keyhole-shaped windows and round windows are common here and elsewhere.

Bedford makes a convenient place to begin a tour of the area. The town was fortified by the Saxons in 915, but despite these precautions, fell to the Danes in 1010.

The church of St Peter (TL 0550) stands in the NE angle of the main cross-roads of the A6 with the A428, and is notable for its axial tower (originally in the W) and its chancel which was the original Anglo-Saxon nave. The remains are therefore interesting to disentangle. Sculpture enthusiasts will enjoy the carved picture of two dragons who fight with protruding tongues and twisted tails, above the door over the chancel arch. Only the outer part of a window remains in the N wall of the chancel and the quoins of the W face of the tower can be seen by observers inside the church. The quoins of the chancel are visible – that in the SW is of long-and-short work and that in the NW can be seen only from in a vestry.

Outside there are parts of blocked windows on each side of the clock in the S face and an arched opening obviously once looked out from the belfry stage. Bedford is probably more famous for its associations with John Bunyan than for its Saxon remains.

Leaving Bedford on the A6 northwards, some 2m (3·2 km) out of the town is the village of **Clapham**, with its church dedicated to St Thomas Becket (TL 0352). The church was mostly rebuilt in 1861, but the tower escaped and remains impressively of Saxon build. For about 60 feet (18·29 metres) under the Norman belfry it rises sheer, broken only by round-headed windows; one in the E and two in each of the other sides. Inside, and partly hidden by the nave roof above the tower arch, an upper door leading to the first floor of the tower can be seen. The tower and chancel arches are original but unremarkable.

Moving into Lincolnshire, within a radius of about 10m (16 km) of Sleaford lie a number of churches with Saxon remains. The first worth a visit is **Hough on the Hill** (SK 9246), which has extensive remains in the church of All Saints. The village is approachable most easily by minor roads to the W off the A607, 7m (11·3 km) N of Grantham. It has a W tower, an exterior stair turret and nave walls above the later arcades, which were all probably erected in the late tenth century, though the tower was constructed after the nave. Outside, several quoins are visible, the tower plinth can be seen in the N, and string courses break up the height. Round-headed windows can be seen, one in the S and one in the N. Under the latter is a third window that is better preserved on the inside. Two further, original windows light the top of the W face. The stair turret is of great interest since the lowest forty-five steps are intact from the tenth century and are still in use. The stairway is formed with a central newel and separate treads, which are notched into it and built into the the external walls. The turret is lit by three windows on the W and four of different shapes on the S: one diamond, two circular and one pentagonal. The door giving access from tower to turret inside is square-headed and built in Escomb-fashion. A similar door opens to the first-floor room and the second-floor access is by means of a triangular-headed door.

Fatigued visitors can rest on an original stone bench in the tower at this church, having entered through a door that has been much altered since Saxon days. There are a number of Saxon features still to be seen within the nave, though none of great consequence. A section of plinth is to be seen in the SE respond and the line of a roof is clear on the W wall. The height of the Saxon walls is about 30 feet (9·14 metres) – keen observers will distinguish the two builds by the definite offset in the walling. The quoins in the W and the NE of the nave still exist outside.

At **South Kyme** (TF 1649) the church (which is part of an Augustinian priory) has some important pieces of sculpture. They are in the N wall at the E end, and were probably part of a screen. They have Celtic-looking trumpet-spirals and foliage scrolls, and date from the seventh or early eighth century. The church is on the B1395, about 7m (11·3 km) NE of Sleaford. South Kyme was a grand priory of Augustinian canons founded before 1169.

Lincoln (SK 9771) was a town of major importance in the Dark Ages, and current excavations are bringing to light much information about the town in Anglo-Saxon times. Visible evidence of its importance are three churches (see Appendix One for the third) within the city with Anglo-Saxon remains in them, and a further four within a radius of 8m.

St Mary Wigford, between the High St and main railway station in the lower part of the town, has a very Late Saxon tower and W wall of the nave. Its history is controversial. An inscription in Anglo-Saxon is built into the W face of the tower; it announces, 'Eirtig had me built and endowed to the glory of Christ and St Mary', but the Domesday Book records that a Saxon called Colswein had two churches in Lincoln, which has led to suggestions that this might be one of them. Whatever its origins, the church preserves varied remains from the Saxon period. Inside, visitors should first notice the doorway to the tower which has been cut through the wall above the very large tower arch. A carved stone has been incorporated into the E face of the S jamb and depicts an animal's head. Outside, the W wall of the original nave can be pinpointed by the remains of its quoins that exist each side of the tower. The tower itself was built with side-alternate quoins, a string-course and four double belfry windows. A door in the W face has been considerably modified over the centuries and the further indications of Saxon work can be seen in the W window and the round-headed window in the S.

Another example of a Saxon tower can be seen on the church of **St Peter-at-Gowts** in the E side of Lincoln High Street, though there are only few indications of its date to be seen. Inside there is a fine arch leading from nave to tower with a triangular-headed doorway above it. On the outside visitors can note the plinth, the string-course and the double-belfry windows to the tower. The W wall of the original nave still remains where it meets the tower – the long-and-short quoins can be distinguished from the side-alternate work of the tower corners. Saxon windows are sparse in this building – there is one in the S face and a similar opening in the W. Over the latter is a carved stone representing Christ in Majesty, though this has claimed to be Norman.

Leaving Lincoln southwards on the A15, the traveller after 2m (3·2 km) will arrive in the village of **Bracebridge**, and be able to see another very late Saxon tower in the church of All Saints (SK 9667). The nave predates the tower slightly and you should look out for the three long-and-short quoins outside and one in the chancel. In 1875 parts of a Saxon N door were rebuilt into the N aisle and are therefore not *in situ*, and not an indication of the date of the wall. Notice the string-course on the tower, the W doorway with window above, the four double-belfry windows and inside, the Saxon tower and chancel arches.

Only 4m (6·4 km) to the SE of Lincoln on the B1188 is **Branston** church, dedicated to All Saints (TF 0267), with its two-stage late-Saxon tower and demonstrably earlier W wall of the nave (proved by the fact that the plinth passes behind the tower). There is a string-course and four double belfry windows of which the heads of those in the S and E are probably nineteenth-century neo-Gothic reconstructions.

Eight miles (12·9 km) NW of Lincoln, and reached by taking the A57 out of the city and then turning N along the B1241 at Saxilby, is St Mary's, **Stow** (SK 8881). This is one of the most interesting and unusual Saxon churches in the country, and was traditionally the cathedral church of Lindsey, founded in 674 by King Egfrith of Northumbria. There is no proof of this, but it was certainly a major pre-Conquest church, for it is large, despite its simple cruciform plan. The Saxon work consists of a central crossing under the tower (noticeably wider than the width of the transepts), and transepts, though there have been extensive Norman additions. The Saxon quoins are distinguishable from the small ashlar Norman masonry by large side-alternate stones.

Outside, the visitor should note the original plinth around the transept, and the change in quoins in the crossing and transepts at a height of about 9 feet (2·74 metres): below this level they are red and fire-cracked, suggesting a rebuild at some stage following a fire. Other details include the windows – one is in the S transept, and

43 Interior of Stow Church, from 19th century engraving

parts of two others in the N transept. That in the S is decorated in pleasing palmetted ornament, and has dowel holes for shutters.

Inside, the 33 feet (10 metres) high walls of the transepts are impressive, though the interior is partly obscured by the perpendicular piers. Notice the four splendid Saxon arches that support the crossing – that on the W has a hood moulding with palmette ornament. In the transepts can be seen plinths, and the original door to the N transept through the W wall can be observed, with Escomb-fashion jambs. The head is so cut that it would be neat if the wall were plastered.

Three miles W of Stow, on the A156, 5m (8 km) S of Gainsborough is **Marton** (SK 8481), where the church of St Margaret is notable for a very late Saxon tower. Fragmentary evidence shows that the original church too was Saxon, but almost all details of this have been obliterated by later building. The name of the village itself is derived from the Anglo-Saxon 'lake farm'. First look at the tower outside, where you will see an original window in the W face and a gable-line in the E face above parts of an early doorway. This church has many features that are Norman and may be confusing to the visitor. The slight remains of the original nave W wall project sideways near the tower and otherwise the features of interest are inside. Notice the tower and chancel arches and the Crucifixion carving in the N wall of the chancel. Seven pieces of interlaced cross-shaft are now to be seen in the W wall of the aisle.

Corringham (SK 8791) lies on the A631, 3m (4·8 km) E of Gainsborough, and possesses the church of St Lawrence with its fine Late Saxon tower and nave walls. The original length of the nave is fixed by the quoins now some distance along it. The original SW quoin of the nave is to be seen outside. The tower is in two stages, with side-alternate quoining. Traces of a door can be made out in the W face. There are four double belfry windows and what might be the remains of a first floor window. There is a blocked door above the Saxon tower arch.

South of Corringham, reached by minor roads S from the A631 about ½m (0·8 km) further out of Gainsborough are Springthorpe and Heapham. **Springthorpe** boasts the church of St Lawrence and St George (SK 8789) which has a fine Late Saxon tower with side-alternate quoins (original up to the roof ridge), a chamfered plinth and a modern belfry with confusingly pseudo-Saxon windows. There is, too, a blocked W door and a small original window high in the S face. **Heapham** with its church of All Saints (SK 8788) is a mere mile away to the S and has a W tower of Late Saxon date with the N and S walls of the nave of the same period. The two stage tower has a string course, chamfered plinth and the remains of a W doorway with a tympanum, under a restored keyhole-shaped window. Double windows to the belfry, the S door to the nave and the tower arch are the remaining Saxon features.

About 10m (16 km) N of Lincoln on the B1398 is **Glentworth** (SK 9488), with its church of St Michael which has another late Saxon tower, with rather more doors and windows than those already described from this area. In Saxon times a bell rang out from the W window of the belfry to summon the faithful; evidence of this is the groove and hole still visible. Inside the church there is just the tower arch to see, with a blocked door at first floor level that can be seen only from in the tower. Outside however, the outline of the original W doorway can be discerned. Four keyhole-shaped windows give light to the tower – two in the lower stage and two much higher up. The belfry has the usual arrangement of four windows.

Alkborough (SE 8821) has fragments of Saxon work in the church of St John the Baptist, reached by the B1430 N out of Scunthorpe (Lincs) for 5m (8 km) and then by a minor road N out of the village of Burton. The village lies almost on the Humber. The lowest three stages of the W tower, and possibly the nave walls up to the offset, visible inside, are very Late Saxon. A W doorway, a keyhole-shaped window and the W and N belfry windows are extant. The semicircular tower arch is of reused stone, and a trapdoor under the foot of its N jamb reveals a carved Saxon stone. The gable line of the original nave roof is visible in the E.

Although there is a good deal of Anglo-Saxon sculpture in Lincolnshire, most of it is late and unexceptional. The most notable is at **Edenham** (TF 0621) where the church of St Michael has two fine pieces. It stands on the A151 to Colsterworth, 2m (3·2 km) W of Bourne. The first is a roundel, reused in the S aisle at the W end, and is over 2 feet in diameter. It is decorated with four scrolls. At the W end is part of a ninth-century cross-shaft with St John and a seated figure in a niche, perhaps the Virgin. The church itself is Saxon but only the S wall of the nave above the arcading remains from the ninth century.

At **Crowle** (SE 7713) can be seen, in the church of St Oswald, a fragment of cross-shaft of the eleventh century. It has interlace, a

man on horseback, two figures facing each other and two dragons.
It shows Danish influence. Crowle lies on the A161, about 6m
(9·7 km) S of Goole.

Four miles E of Scunthorpe on the B1207 is **Broughton**, where the
church of St Mary (SE 9608) has an interesting tower, of which the
lower part was once the main body of the church. This and the W
stair turret are still intact from the Late Saxon period. Inside, the
tower arch is more ornate in the tower than in the nave, leading to
the conclusion that the main body of the church was that exposed to
the greater decoration. There is a doorway above the tower arch.
The turret is of note since there are comparatively few in existence –
it has well-formed stone treads made separately from the newel and
is waggon-vaulted. Outside, notice the side-alternate quoins and two
small round-headed windows in the S face and one in the N. The
Saxon village name means 'farm by a fort'.

By far eclipsing these and most other ecclesiastical remains of the
period, however, is **Barton-on-Humber**'s church of St Peter
(TA 0321). This is definitely worth a detour, since it is one of the
finest and most complete Anglo-Saxon churches in the country. It is
in the care of the Department of the Environment and in 1977 was
closed for restoration, but it may be open again by now. It can be
reached by following the A1077 N from Scunthorpe since it lies 10m
(16 km) NE of that town. The church consists of a W annexe and
two lower stages of the tower which were built in the later tenth
century, and a third stage of the tower which was added in the
eleventh and has a Norman flavour. From the outside the tower has
two entrances, a N triangular-headed door and a S round-headed
door, both constructed in Escomb-fashion. Double windows are
prominent in the upper N and S faces, and the central stage of the
tower has a double window in each face (one has been disturbed by
the clock), dating from the time when this was the belfry stage. The
E window is visible from in the nave. Outside this church there is
fine decorative pilasterwork and in the uppermost stage are a further
set of three double windows.

The W annexe boasts good long-and-short work and is
narrower than the tower. There are indications of a blocked round-
headed door in the W wall and above are two circular windows. The
N and S walls both contain one round-headed window. Inside the
tower the E and W arches should be noticed for their Escomb-
fashion jambs, their through stones and well-dressed voussoirs. Both
arches have pilaster strips and hood moulds within the tower. A

door leads from the tower to the nave and another to the annexe, at first-floor level. If the E of the tower is observed from the nave, the long-and-short quoining will be seen to prove that the original chancel was narrower than what is now the tower. The gable line above belongs to an earlier extension. A carving of a man's head which might have been part of a Crucifixion scene can be seen in a panel above the E arch – it has been suggested that the entire picture was painted on this slab. This internal decoration, the decoration of the tower arches and the narrower original chancel all suggest strongly that the tower was once the main body of the church.

44 Barton-on-Humber, Saxon church

The church of St John the Baptist in **Nettleton** (TA 1100) on the A46 about 1½m (2·4 km) S of Caistor, is worth a visit for its Late Saxon tower under a fifteenth-century belfry. A string course and a mostly buried plinth, the remains of a small window in the S face and the original doorway on the W face, with a tympanum decorated with modern carvings, add to its attractions. In the upper stages on the W face is a small round-headed window, and the tower arch is notable for its unbalanced decoration.

Caistor itself has the church of St Peter and St Paul (TA 1101), in which the lower stage of the W tower and possibly the side walls of the nave are of the very latest Saxon period (within the boundaries of a Roman settlement). It is on the tower that the Saxon features can be seen; however, there are side-alternate quoins of the original nave to be seen in the E wall of the tower. The two blocked arches to W and S of the tower may be pre-Conquest. In the N face two arches of stones outline two further openings, and what appears to be a pointed window above is probably a badly weathered keyhole window.

One mile NE of Caistor on the A46 is **Cabourne** (TA 1301), where the church of St Nicholas has a pseudo-Saxon belfry built in the nineteenth century on a genuinely Late Saxon lower stage. There is a keyhole window, a W doorway and a very fine tower arch. A lovely carved font decorated with cable ornament, wheat ear and strapwork was discovered during restorations, hidden under the floor.

Rothwell (TF 1499) on a minor road 2m (3·2 km) E of Caistor has a W tower and part of the nave walls datable to the latest Saxon period, at the church of St Mary Magdalene. There are double windows in the belfry and small round-headed windows in the lower stage faces, with two in the S face. The original W door is very fine, complete with tympanum and the tower arch inside is worthy of some note. Notice, too, the good plinth, the side-alternate quoins and the string course which divides the tower under its medieval topping. The Anglo-Saxon placename means 'spring in a clearing'.

Four churches near Grimsby have similar Anglo-Saxon towers. **Clee** is virtually in Grimsby itself on the A18, and the church tower of Holy Trinity (TA 2908) is in two stages divided by a string course. Four double belfry windows light the tower and eight corbels project at random. There are two keyhole-shaped windows, a plinth, side-alternate quoins and the W doorway to look out for as proof of Saxon date. The W wall of the nave is still Saxon and can be seen as side-alternate work on the N face of the tower. Inside, the tower arch is original.

Scartho's church of St Giles (TA 2606), just outside Grimsby on the A16, has both W tower and part of the nave walls from the Late Saxon period, with similar features to Clee's. A string course, keyhole window above a blocked W door and a double plinth are easy to recognize. A second keyhole window has been defaced in the S side of the tower by a now destroyed medieval annexe. Two of the four belfry windows have elaborate capitals, and above the Saxon tower arch is a rectangular door to the tower. This is a Danish placename meaning 'hill with a gap'.

Continue along the A16 for 2m (3·2 km) southwards and the village of **Holton-le-Clay** will warrant a short visit for the much restored and patched parish church of St Peter (TA 2802), of which the lower stage of the tower is Late Saxon. Quoins, a plinth, a blocked W door and window in the the S and W faces should be noticed. Inside, the tower arch and plinth are Saxon and there is a font in the nave which is ornamental though chipped. The lower part of the nave and chancel walls may still preserve some Saxon material.

Four miles (6·4 km) S on the A16 from Scartho is **Waithe** (TA 2800). The church seems to have been completely restored in the nineteenth century but the axial tower remains intact from the very Late Saxon period. Notice the string courses, and a double belfry window in each face, which, though Saxon, has Norman-like capitals. There are no Saxon features inside.

Leaving Lincolnshire for East Anglia, Norfolk is a paradise for the seeker of Anglo-Saxon churches. Although few are of national importance, many are extremely picturesque, and boast the distinctive round towers that are also a feature of the later medieval churches of Norfolk.

North Elmham (TF 9820) has the distinction of being the site of a Saxon cathedral church, and can be reached on the B1110, 5m (8 km) N of East Dereham. The village has changed drastically since the ninth century, when Saxon houses were grouped around a hall, with a nearby cemetery. The excavated Saxon remains now lie under Elmham Park, opposite the parish church at the N end of the village. The ruined cathedral is laid out for the public to view [AM; A], just N of the present church, and is impressive as an almost complete plan of an early ecclesiastical building. The walls rise to a maximum of 8 feet, and comprise the remains of a nave, transepts, small apsidal chancel, stair turret and axial tower. Two side buildings are presumed to have been towers from the extra thickness of their walls.

The date of the cathedral has been disputed, since the presence of towers suggests its building after the ninth century when bell towers became common, but the general plan is of the eighth century. Excavations have not resolved these problems.

Notice the plinth which is decorated with four quarter shafts at the re-entrant angles of the towers and to the W of the transepts. The original stair is entered from the inside – the turret which is approachable from the outside belongs to the time when the church was used as a residence. Bishop Henry Despenser was granted licence to fortify his manor in 1387 and the additional stair turret and the demolition of the original apse probably belong to this period. The see was divided between Elmham and Dunwich in the seventh century. The buildings all lie within a moated enclosure, and are overshadowed by a tall mound in the NW angle. The earthworks are almost certainly Norman, but some parts have been claimed as Danish.

Guestwick (TG 0627) lies 9m (14·5 km) E of Fakenham, reached by minor roads off the A1067, and is served by the church of St Peter. The lower stages of the tower (which was originally axial) and parts of the NW wall of the chancel along with the NE quoin of the nave date to the Late Saxon period.

The ruined chancel is traceable from small fragments in the exterior E wall and a gable line, blocked arch and a small window high up above the N gable. The original windows remain in the first and second storeys of the tower, and the E belfry window is Saxon.

A carving of a muzzled bear or pig can be seen on the lowest voussoir of the N jamb of the blocked arch in the W face. The rounded head of a door is visible above the aisled roof. Inside the tower there is stripwork on the Saxon chancel arch.

Five miles SW of Swaffham three churches in one village of **Beachamwell** (TF 7505) have now been reduced to one. Picturesquely thatched and standing on the village green, it is dedicated to St Mary. Of this the nave, chancel, and W tower were built in the Late Saxon period. Visitors should notice the NW angle, which has the only long and short quoin left, and the four belfry windows in the round tower, as well as a small window cut through one stone as a slot in the W. There is another slot under the S belfry window. The tower arch has no distinguishing Saxon features, but there is a door between the nave and the tower above it.

Newton by Castleacre (TF 8315) has many remains of the Saxon period, and is not far from the Norman motte at Castle Acre. It is about 4m (6·4 km) N of Swaffham on the A1065. The nave, chancel, axial tower and some indications of transept make it well worth a visit.

The evidence for the transept can be seen in the S where the wall of the nave ends very badly. There are also traces of a tall narrow archway that opened from the tower. The quoins of the tower, the restored belfry windows, the window in the S face of the tower, the lines of earlier roofs over the present nave and chancel in the W and E face should all be noted. There are no windows or doors of Saxon date in nave or chancel, but a reused stone frame of an early window is now incorporated into the N wall of the chancel about 6 feet (1·83 metres) above ground. It is rebated for a shutter and has

45 Beachamwell

odd drill holes visible. Inside the church the two tower arches are interesting, though the W arch has a medieval pointed top to it.

A Late Saxon nave and chancel can be seen at the church of the Assumption of the Blessed Mary at **West Barsham** (TF 9033). This is in an attractive setting, 3m (4·8 km) N of Fakenham to the W off the B1105. The original chancel has been enlarged but much of the nave and chancel remains: the nave has three Anglo-Saxon windows (one in the S wall and two in the N) and a blocked door above the chancel arch (which is shaped like the hull of a boat).

The traveller will be delighted with **Great Dunham** (TF 8714), 5m (8 km) NE of Swaffham which can be approached directly on minor roads from Newton (see previous mention) or by minor roads off the A47 or A1065. The church of St Andrew has a Late Saxon nave and axial tower, the chancel having been rebuilt in the fifteenth century. This is particularly worth a visit on account of the unusual arcading inside. The arcading has been constructed as though the wall had been cut back leaving the pilasters and arches outstanding. The pattern is repeated every 5 feet (1·5 metres) and a length of 30 feet (9·1 metres) in the N wall has remained intact despite later alterations. The original door is proved to have been in the same

46 Newton by Castleacre

47 Great Dunham

position as the present S entrance since the arches are shorter at this point. The capitals on the arcading are carved from Barnack stone (see p. 136) and the arches are of Roman bricks. The pilasters and the wall above the arcade are of uncut flint. Also inside, the tower is connected to the nave by two arches of Roman bricks with imposts of Barnack stone. They are beautifully and simply decorated with saltires (on the W arch) and cable ornament (on the E arch). The hood moulding of the W arch has been removed, presumably to make way for a medieval rood screen of which one corbel remains. Visible only from inside the tower are the remains of doors to the original upper chambers of nave and chancel.

Outside, notice the four Saxon belfry windows and two circular windows in the E and W faces of the tower. There are two in the S face and one in the N face of similar date. Look out, too, for the long-and-short quoining. The W wall of the nave contains a blocked door which is still outlined in stripwork with an unusual notching. A seventeenth-century crest has been inserted above it, thereby somewhat confusing its appearance. One window has survived in the N wall of the nave and there are remains of another further E, and in the S wall are vestiges of two similarly placed windows.

The church of St Mary the Virgin, **Cranwich** (TL 7894) is only 4m (6·4 km) from Brandon, the flint-knapping town which grew to fame when gunflints were in big demand, and lies 10m (16 km) NW of Thetford on the A134. Within its circular churchyard the round W tower and possibly parts of the nave stand as they did nearly a thousand years ago. The tower arch is of especial note but is best seen from the W since it has been partly infilled by a later doorway. The windows that seem most certainly to be Saxon are the three circular apertures in the N, S and W, and the round-headed one in the E.

East Lexham's church of St Andrew (TF 8617) has a round tower, nave and chancel of tenth- or eleventh-century date. It lies within the grounds of a farm and is about 5m (8 km) NE of Swaffham, 1m (1·6 km) E of the A1065. The tower becomes thinner towards the top and is capped by later brickwork. The three belfry windows are all different, and inside the only Saxon remains are two blocked recesses in the belfry stage.

Weybourne (TG 1142) has only the axial tower surviving of a very Late Saxon church dedicated to All Saints. It stands near a ruined priory on the A149, 3m (4·8 km) W of Sheringham on the N coast of Norfolk. The Anglo-Saxon church was incorporated into a

48 Haddiscoe Thorpe, Saxon church

twelfth-century rebuild, and a large chancel, now ruined, was added. The tower has some interesting stripwork, and two circular double-splayed windows in the S belfry face and one in the E and W, presumably sound holes. The Saxon settlers who lived here called their village after the 'felon stream'.

The church of St Matthias at **Haddiscoe Thorpe** (TM 4398), 9m (14·5 km) SW of Great Yarmouth just N of the A143, has a Saxon W tower under a Norman belfry and the side walls of the nave are contemporaneous. It is picturesquely thatched, without aisles. The fabric of the tower makes a distinction between the four stages, and there are three original windows in the second stage – those in the S and W have a prokossos (projecting corbel) above them. The third stage is distinguished by having ten pilaster strips and four windows. Of the nave the S and N doors are of Norman form, but the W wall is certainly earlier than the late Saxon lower part of the tower. There is a circular window with double-splay in the W gable of the nave, lighting the tower.

Gissing (TM 1485), 4m (6·4 km) N of Diss, reached by minor roads, is served by the church of St Mary the Virgin with its fine Late Saxon tower near a pub. The tower is sheer from its plinth to

49 Gissing, Saxon church

its parapet with three circular windows, all double-splayed, in the N, W and S. The form of the tower arch is Saxon with mouldings that could be Norman – or just as easily nineteenth century.

Tasburgh (TM 1996) is worth a visit from those travelling along the A140, 6m (9·7 km) S of Norwich towards Ipswich – it lies about 2m (3·2 km) W of the main road, approached by side roads. The church of St Mary has a Late Saxon round tower to the W with unusual arcading. Parts of the original W wall of the nave survive, though there are few definitive Saxon features. The windows are not certainly Saxon rather than Norman, but the recesses of the arcading are very similar to those at Dunham Magna. There is little of Dark Age interest inside. The village is named after the fort of a Saxon called Taesa.

Approached by minor roads 1m or so W of the A140 about 9m (14·5 km) SW of Norwich, lies **Forncett St Peter**. The round W tower of the church of St Peter (TM 1693), the adjoining part of the W wall of the nave and possibly the S wall of the chancel date to the Late Saxon period. The churchyard is badly overgrown, and the church was almost totally obscured from the road by heavy foliage when we visited it in 1977. An avenue of trees, however, leads to its main entrance, and a school lies to the other side. Once at the church, one can see that the tower is authentic right up to the battlements and has eight circular windows at the top with four double belfry windows below. Lower still are four more windows, and three circular ones under these. A pseudo-Norman W doorway has a Saxon round-headed window above. Inside, the tower arch is impressive for its height, and the interior of the W door still dates from the Saxon period. Roman bricks appear in the arch of the window above the W door. This unusual placename is both Danish and Saxon and means 'Forni's seat, St Peter's church'.

Howe (TM 2799) lies about 6m (9·7 km) SE of Norwich reached by a minor road ½m (0·8 km) to the W of the B1332 to Bungay, and is worth a visit since the church of St Mary has a Late Saxon round W tower and nave. There are round-headed windows in the N, W and S and circular windows below them. The nave walls are datable from the original round-headed window in the N wall and the W quoins. An original W door is to be seen inside the tower and two blocked windows can be seen in the S wall of the nave. The tower arch is very fine.

Anglo-Saxon round tower, nave and chancel all survive at **Framlingham Earl** (TG 2702), reached by a side road from either the

50 Forncett St Peter, Saxon church

51 Howe, Saxon tower

A146 or the B1332, about 5m (8 km) SE of Norwich. The Saxon
quoins and pilasters are of uncut, smaller flints. There are two small
circular windows in each of the chancel side walls and Saxon
pilasters decorate the E of the chancel.

Cringleford (TG 1905) lies on the A11 about 3m (4·8 km) SW of
Norwich city centre. The church of St Peter boasts both nave and
chancel intact from the tenth or eleventh century – though only a
window in each N wall of nave and chancel remain. A few carved
stones are incorporated into the fabric inside.

Norwich (TG 2308) itself has the remains of no fewer than six
churches built in the Saxon period. None, however, are very
impressive, though they are listed in Appendix One. The best is St
Julian's which is W of King St, and has a round W tower and nave
walls of the period just before the Conquest. An air raid in 1942
almost destroyed the tower and restoration work revealed hitherto
unsuspected Saxon work in the form of three windows in the N wall
of the nave and a circular window in the S of the chancel.

The Castle Museum [10–5, Sun. 2–5] has much to offer from the
Dark Ages. It has a good collection of Anglo-Saxon antiquities from

East Anglia, with the pottery from the excavations in the Saxon town of Thetford being of particular note.

The church of St Mary at **Colney** (TG 1808) is 4m (6·4 km) W of Norwich on the B1108, and has a round tower and an aisleless nave and chancel, of which the tower and upper parts of the S nave walls are very Late Saxon. There are three blocked windows in the N, S and W faces of the tower, pilasters and vestiges of a blocked round-headed window near the S porch.

St Lawrence at **Beeston** (TG 3221) is 10m (16 km) NE of Norwich on the A1151. The church stands near a hall and a lake and has a Saxon round tower and contemporaneous N and W walls of the nave. The shorter original nave is denoted by the quoins which are not at the corners of the present church; the tower has four original windows of which those in the S and N faces are blocked – the three highest have triangular heads, the fourth is a slit.

Bessingham's church of St Mary (TG 1637) lies 4m (6·4 km) SW of Cromer and is reached by minor roads S from the A148 or W of the A140. In the very late Saxon period the round tower was erected and of the original church only the W and N walls of the nave have managed to survive the centuries of rebuilding. The windows in the tower consist of one with a round head in the first stage, four fine belfry openings and three blocked below. Inside, the tower arch and triangular-doorway above are Saxon work. Outside you should notice that the original chancel must have been narrower than the nave; the evidence for this being the position of the nave quoins.

Roughton (TG 2236) lies 4m (6·4 km) S of Cromer, on the junction of the A140 and the B1436, where the church is dedicated to St Mary. The round tower and W wall of the nave are very late Saxon, and the side walls have been raised to form a clerestory. This church has an unusually shaped tower arch. Also of note in the interior is the W door which opens into the church at a height of 16 feet (4·88 metres) above ground. However it is the windows that should preoccupy the visitor's attention. There are four to the belfry which do not have the usual mid-wall shaft. Well above eye level in the N and S are two circular windows. Three slits in the tower's second stage complete the fenestration. Those with a keen architectural sense will discern that the W responds of the N and S arcade, inside, are probably all that is left of the original walls.

After the riches of Norfolk, Suffolk has little of Dark Age interest. Nevertheless, **Sutton Hoo** (TM 287487) is certainly the most famous Dark Age site in Britain since it was here that the only intact kingly burial from the seventh century was found. The treasures are much photographed and well displayed in the British Museum. Visitors were not encouraged at the site in the summer of 1977, due to the excavations, but it can be reached by taking the A12 for 8m (12·8 km) NE of Ipswich, then turning E along the A1152. Sutton Hoo lies 1m to the W of this road on the banks of the Deben. It was here, over 1,300 years ago, that the Saxons made a great burial mound and placed in it a ship filled with treasures. Nothing now is very exciting to look at – only the remains of mounds survive and the site might not be thought worthy of a visit except for its excavation interest.

What was once a small Saxon village called the 'stream of Herela's people' is now modern **Herringfleet**, 6m (9·7 km) NW of Lowestoft on the B1074. Nothing can now be seen of the original settlement, but in the late Saxon period the villagers erected their church to St Margaret (TM 4797), of which the tower can still be seen dominating the picturesquely thatched nave. Inside there is little to note except the door to the nave, but outside the fenestration is varied. In the belfry stage the windows are decorated with stripwork carried over their heads to form tympanum. Round-headed windows in the NW and SW have midwall shutters in wood with openwork carvings.

In Cambridgeshire, linear earthworks relieve the East Anglian diet of churches. Known collectively as the Cambridge Dykes, they were built to protect the area from attack from the SW early in the Anglo-Saxon period, and lie at right angles to the Roman road known as the Icknield Way. The finest is the **Devil's Ditch** (TL 5864 and TL 6261), which runs for over 7m (11·23 km) on Newmarket Heath, running along Newmarket racecourse and ending at Reach in the NW and Wood Ditton in the SE. It can best be viewed from a lay-by on the B1102, about ¾m (1·2 km) N of Swaffham Prior, from which a footpath follows the crest of the bank in each direction. It can also be visited from the A11, which it crosses just N of its junction with the A45, about 2m (3·2 km) S of Newmarket. The bank rises above a ditch to the S. For impressiveness, it rivals if not surpasses its more famous counterparts, Offa's Dyke and Wansdyke. The other dykes are slightly less impressive (see Appendix One).

Cambridge (TL 4458), a town highly popular with foreign visitors and a cultural centre for East Anglia, is more famous for its university than for the church of St Bene't, in the street of the same name, a few hundred yards from the Guildhall. (Its name is a

52 Saxon tower of St Bene't, Cambridge

contraction of Benedict.) Although the walls of the nave above the later arcades date from after 950, the tower, of the same date, is more interesting. The tower is divided by string courses and stands on a plinth. The belfry stage has Saxon openings still visible. Originally there were three in each side – a double window flanked by two circular – but not all these are now surviving. Note the badly weathered ring-and-cable ornament on the circular windows of the S face. The tower was probably surmounted by a Germanic helm, as at Sompting, Sussex (see p. 86). The tower arch is very fine, with interesting decoration. A round-headed door above it can be seen. The church was heavily restored in the nineteenth century.

The museum is worth a visit, since it contains jewellery and other objects from nearby excavated Pagan Saxon cemeteries.

At **Great Tey** ('enclosure' in Anglo-Saxon) the church of St Barnabas (TL 8925) can be reached by side roads S from the A604 or N from the A120, about 8m (12·9 km) W of Colchester. It is only the lower three stages of the tower that are of interest to Dark Age students, for these were put up in the tenth century. Windows light the building at several levels. There are two in each face of the third stage with six recesses under them. Two further windows open into the lowest stage and the S face has a feature that must have been cut through the wall to give access from the tower to a roof space over a former transept. Inside Saxon features are almost non-existent, being confined to some pieces of stripwork.

Strethall, only 3m (4·8 km) NW of Saffron Walden and approached by several minor roads W of the A11 about 1m (1·6 km) W of the M11, has the delightful church of St Mary the Virgin. The nave is Late Saxon, with two windows set high in the W wall, one visible from the tower only, the other visible from inside the church through the rafters. These presumably indicate the original presence of an upper chamber in the W part of the nave. The W quoins are good – that in the SE was rebuilt. The church does, however, also possess a very fine attractively decorated chancel arch of the same Late date, with Escomb-fashion jambs. This church is remote from any buildings except a farm, and the approach is not to be recommended on a wet day, for the farm track is muddy and uneven.

Hadstock (TL 5544) in Essex, a pretty village 6m (9·7 km) N of Saffron Walden, on the B1052, is dominated by the Saxon church of St Botolph, on a hill. Only fragments are left of the original tenth-century buildings. Excavations have been carried out there in recent years.

Five out of the original six Saxon windows are still visible. The four in the nave still give light to present-day congregations. The fifth is blocked above the N doorway, which itself is of interest on account of its decorated imposts. The entrance has a unique Saxon battened door hung against the inner face of the wall, with hood moulding around it. It is carved with a honeysuckle motif. Only the jambs remain of the entrance to the S transept – one is on a plinth of four orders and has capitals with honeysuckle ornament. The arch in the N transept, however, is thirteenth-century on late Saxon plinths. The NW quoin of the N transept is of side-alternate construction.

Parts of the nave and the tower have survived from the Late Saxon period at the church of St Katherine, **Little Bardfield** (TL 6530), which is reached by the B1057 about 6m (9·7 km) NE of Great Dunmow and then a minor road to the NW out of Great Bardfield, not far from Finchingfield, 'the prettiest village in England'. The Saxon fabric is remarkable for the use of flint even at the windows, doors and string courses. Of the nave, only parts of the walls are proved Saxon, but the window in the W of the S wall and another, visible only from inside, in the E of the N wall, which has been blocked, are of this date. A plinth, too, indicates the workmanship since it runs round the N and W of the tower and extends along the N wall of the nave. The tower itself has several definitive features: the second stage has two round-headed windows in the S, N and W faces, a double window in each face above this level and two round-headed windows further up still. The slight remains of a blocked W door can still be seen.

A straightforward Saxon church can be seen at **Inworth** (TL 8717) on the B1023 about 1m (1·6 km) S of the A12 and 2m (3·2 km) from Kelvedon. Some later alterations to the nave and chancel have left the eleventh-century work clearly visible. The original quoins of the nave at the E and the E quoins of the chancel can be seen. The latter are visible about 6 feet (1·83 metres) from the modern, lengthened, chancel end. Two double-splayed windows in the N and S walls of the chancel are original, and the chancel arch, although not certainly, is probably Saxon.

Colchester (TL 9925), a town with ancient origins (the first real town in Britain, founded by the Romans soon after their conquest as a show place and colony for ex-legionaries) contains the Anglo-Saxon church of Holy Trinity. This lies 200 yards (183 metres) S of the High St, and both the W tower and W wall of the nave are probably tenth or eleventh century. Roman Colchester has been robbed in order to put up much of this edifice, and Roman tiles are readily visible in the quoins and facings. The triangular-headed W doorway with pilasters and hood mouldings owes its material to Roman tile furnaces. In the N and S walls round-headed windows light the lower level. In the W, a string course of tiles is interrupted by an upper doorway with round head and a blocked round-headed window to each side. In the N and S faces are ornamental recesses.

Two series of belfry windows remain from Saxon times. The lower set of windows is decorated by an arcade. Inside, the tower arch is round and constructed from Roman bricks.

In the heart of London commuterland is one church, unique in Britain, which reminds us instantly that Saxon architecture was not normally in stone, even though most timber remains have perished long ago. The church at **Greensted**, Essex (TL 5303), some 5m E of Epping on a minor road 1½m (2·4 km) W of Chipping Ongar, dates from after 950 but nevertheless contains original timber walling around the nave. The effect is somewhat marred by the Victorian brick plinth upon which it stands, since it is reputed to have been in need of restoration, but the construction is interesting (fig. 53). The

53 Greensted, NW corner of Saxon church

oak sill, for instance, which now sits on the plinth was apparently an original feature, and the only extant corner is interesting since it is the only one in existence in wood. No long-and-short work or side-alternate quoining was possible – the corner was finished off by using one log with a quadrant removed. Excavations at this remarkable church dedicated to St Andrew have shown that there was originally a small chancel built of upright logs without the sill. This was replaced in Saxon times by a larger chancel with a wooden sill, suggesting that the oak sill was in fact an important preservative feature. The church is mentioned by a thirteenth-century writer and may have housed the body of King Edmund when it was taken from London to Bury St Edmunds in 1013. The king was shot to death with arrows in the Danish invasion of 870 when he would not renounce his Christian beliefs.

Also very outstanding and one of the finest and most complete churches in the country is that at **Bradwell-on-Sea** (TM 0308). St Peter on the Wall is built over the W gate of the Roman fort of Othona, from which stones and building material were extensively reused. The walls of the fort are faintly visible although badly eroded. The church stands exposed and gaunt at the point where the Blackwater meets the North Sea. If visited without the crowds of summer tourists, this church is remarkable for its peace and remoteness. Only the nave now exists, though there are parts of the chancel and further remains found in excavation. Bradwell is reached by the B1021, 8m (12·9 km) N of Burnham-on-Crouch and then by a path from the village – it is about 2m (3·2 km) from the parish church.

The chapel was used as a barn until 1920 and consequently suffered damage which has now been restored. The main body of the church, however, still retains its pilasters which strengthen the walls like buttresses. These are made of Roman tiles and the quoins are megalithic in construction. Of the original windows two in the S wall and one in the N are intact, with another, mostly destroyed, in the N wall. The W door is square-headed and there are vestiges of a porch around it. The original apsidal E end, too, is visible on the ground and by the projecting walls. The E wall also shows clearly (in the outline of Roman tiles) that the entrance from chancel to nave was originally a triple arch as at Reculver, Kent. The church is known historically since St Cedd, bishop of the East Saxons, built a church at Othona (identified with Bradwell). Since the saint was active in around 653, the church is thus fairly certainly datable to the half-century or so after this date or slightly later. It is simple but well preserved considering its extreme antiquity.

In Hertfordshire is the very pretty village of **Reed** (TL 3635) in which the church of St Mary is worth a detour for its charmingly rural situation, away from the village it serves, and for its intact Saxon nave. It lies 3m (4·8 km) S of Royston, just W of the A10 and approached by side roads. The four quoins of the nave are particularly fine examples of long-and-short work, and a very late (probably eleventh century) date is proved by a blocked N door visible from the road. This is plastered over inside, but outside still displays the original rectangular opening and tympanum.

St Albans (TL 1406) is notable as a Roman city which flourished into the Dark Ages – it was still functioning in the late fifth century. The Dark Age remains, though necessarily overshadowed by the vestiges of Roman VERULAMIUM, are still interesting.

The church of St Stephen lies near the S boundary of Verulamium. The A414 and A5 run round the ruins. It is built of rubble and reused Roman tiles. However, later alterations have not

54 Reed, NW corner of Saxon church

obliterated the W quoins of the Anglo-Saxon nave and a tall, narrow, round-headed window, which was blocked in the twelfth century. In 1934 it was uncovered, and displays marks of a wooden frame in which the mortar was set, on the inside of the head.

The cathedral church of St Alban is known historically, and was put up to honour the martyred saint who died in the persecutions of the early third century, and Offa of Mercia is also supposed to have put up a church in 793. But nothing now exists of these churches: in the Norman abbey church are a series of baluster shafts of Barnack stone (see p. 136), which seem to be Saxon rather than Norman, and might be all that is left of them.

The church of St Michael is a much restored Anglo-Saxon building which stands in the centre of the Roman town. Since the nave and chancel were lengthened, only parts of the side walls of both still date from the tenth century – the E quoins of the original aisleless nave are clearly visible outside. Inside, there are four out of the original eight windows and a round-headed door in the N wall of the chancel seems to date from the ninth century and may have been built by Abbot Wulfsin.

Three miles (4·8 km) N of St Neots on the B1043 to Huntingdon lies the church of the Holy Trinity, **Great Paxton** (TL 2164). The latest phase of Saxon building, during the early eleventh century, saw the erection of this aisled, cruciform church with a clerestory of which the nave and crossing still exist. The gable of the N transept is visible. It is probably reasonable to infer that the church was put up during the reign of Edward the Confessor since the Domesday Book records that there was a priest at Great Paxton and that Edward held the manor before the Conquest. There are two clerestory windows in each of the N and S walls, 24 feet (7·5 metres) above ground level, and a further outline of a blocked window against the tower which proves that the nave has been shortened in the W. A string course still exists in the nave and, inside, the N round arch of the original crossing as well as the jambs of the chancel arch (which was remodelled in the Middle Ages) still exist.

Peterborough (TL 1998) cathedral has Anglo-Saxon origins, and foundations of a wall of this date exist below floor level. This is of little interest to the casual visitor, however, and the Dark Age **Hedda Stone** is more remarkable. This curious example of Anglo-Saxon sculpture is a rectangular block-shaped shrine, carved from a solid stone, 3½ feet (1·06 metres) long and 2½ feet (0·76 metres) high. In the long faces the arcades contain figures of the apostles. The

coped top or 'roof' has panels with symmetrical designs, of which
the most notable are a pair of animals. Although a Mercian work,
the Hedda Stone shows Northumbrian influence, and can be
compared with the figural ornament on the Rothbury Cross. It dates
from the ninth century.

Wales

Apart from memorial stones and sculptures, Wales has surprisingly few Dark Age remains. On the whole, those in the north are more varied than those in the south. One of the problems of Welsh Dark Age archaeology is the general lack of remains later than the sixth century. Before around 700 the early Welsh inhabited hillforts, but after that period hillforts were abandoned and almost nothing is known about the settlements that replaced them – presumably open farmsteads that have not been discovered. The dearth of remains in the field also applies to finds in museums, which are remarkably few in number. Unlike the Irish or Picts, the Welsh do not seem to have developed ornamental metalworking, nor are they known to have produced any manuscript art of note. The Dark Age remains of Wales, then, comprise mainly some hillforts with evidence of post-Roman occupation, a few hut groups, a couple of ecclesiastical sites with few visible remains of any note prior to the twelfth century, and a varied assortment of stones. There are over four hundred of these, and a selection of the best are listed in Appendix One.

The Lleyn peninsula of Gwynedd was probably extensively settled in the Dark Ages: its landscape is in many respects similar to that of Cornwall, being more open than the mountainous regions to the east, and now criss-crossed with a network of small winding roads, often single-tracked, that present hazards to the incoming motorist. Even here, however, the mountains provide a backdrop, and Lleyn itself is dominated by the Rivals (Yr Eifl), three peaks of which one is crowned by one of the most impressive iron age hillforts in Britain, Tre'er Ceiri. The dramatic coastal scenery projecting into the Irish Sea provided an ideal landing place for Dark Age traders and settlers from Ireland. It is therefore not surprising that it has produced a concentration of ogham inscriptions (an Irish type of writing, see p. 44), though only that at Brynkir is still visible *in situ*.

A well-preserved stone inscribed in Latin can be seen at **Llangian** (SH 2929), which is reached by taking a minor road to the NW off the A499 from Abersoch, for just over a mile. A notice in Llangian proclaims it to have been the best-kept village in Wales in 1964, and it is still picturesque. The stone can be seen in the churchyard of the old church, which stands opposite a chapel in the centre of the village. Follow the path from the lych-gate to the church, and turn to your right. The monolithic pillar can be seen very near the church wall. The clearly legible inscription reads

MELI MEDICI FILI MARTINI I(a)CIT
(*The stone of Melus the Doctor, son of Martinus*)

This is the only doctor's tombstone to have survived from Dark Age Britain, and one of the very few tombstones to mention the profession of the deceased. It dates from the late fifth century. At some stage it has been converted for use as a sundial – it was perhaps the predecessor of the sundial still to be seen in the churchyard. The churchyard is circular, like many in this part of Wales, the shape probably reflecting an Early Christian period origin, and one boundary is demarcated by a stream.

Two interesting memorial stones can be seen at **Llanaelhaearn** church (SH 3945) on the A499, just over 6m (9·7 km) N of Pwllheli. The church is fairly central to the village, and there is ample parking space by the lych-gate. The first stone is sheltered by a bush to the right of the path from this gate. It is a pillar inscribed with the letters MELITV ('Melitus lies here'). The style of the lettering indicates a fifth- or sixth-century date. The second stone is now set on a wall of the N transept. It carries an inscription

55 Llangian, 5th century tombstone

ALIORTVS ELMETIACO(S)
HIC IACET
(*Aliortus the Elmetian lies here*)

This is one of the few inscriptions with a correct Latin 'iacet' instead
of 'iacit'. It refers to Elmet, the kingdom in West Yorkshire!
Presumably Aliortus came from Yorkshire to settle in Wales. This is
further evidence of the links between the men of Wales and the Gwr
y Gogledd, the 'Men of the North'. It dates from the sixth century.

Garn Boduan (SH 3139), one of the Rivals, towers over the
junction of the B4354 and A497, about 4m (6·4 km) NW of Pwllheli.
This is one of the three major stone-walled forts of Lleyn, the other
two, Garn Fadrun and Tre'er Ceiri, being exclusively of iron age
date, though it is possible that the small fort on the summit of Carn
Fadrun is Dark Age – in local tradition it was the castle of the sons
of Owain, in the twelfth century. The majority of the remains at
Garn Boduan belong to the iron age – two phases have been
recognized, associated with round stone huts, of which about a
hundred and seventy are visible. A smaller fort was built within the
iron age defences, partly utilizing them, and has produced finds of
the second to seventh century. It is traditionally associated with
Buan, a noble of the early seventh century, and recalls the citadels of
the Scottish nuclear forts.

The ecclesiastical site of **Llangybi** (SH 4341) [AM; A] (see p. 181)
is worth visiting as one of the few church sites with surviving
remains that are possibly earlier than the twelfth century. The
village is about 5m (8 km) NE of Pwllheli – a side road E leads off
the A499, Pwllheli to Caernarvon, just N of the junction with the
B4354. The church is in the middle of the village, and has a circular
graveyard. The *llan* place-name element may be significant, for it
often denotes a Dark Age church (Llangian, Llannor, Llanaelhaearn,
etc.). A cross-incised stone of uncertain date is mounted against the
inside of the lychgate. Such cross-slabs are often assumed to date
from the seventh to ninth centuries, but Early Christian traditions
probably had a long survival and such stones may have been set
up in the late medieval or post-medieval periods. Inside the churchyard there are traces of an earlier vallum visible.

Cross the churchyard and a stile leads to a path running down
through a field. When visited after the drought of 1976 it was
comparatively dry, but on previous occasions it has been very wet
and muddy. The path ends in a roofless building, of which one part

56 Llanaelhaearn, 'Melitus Stone'

is an eighteenth-century cottage and the other a well dedicated to St Gybi, a mid-sixth-century saint who was a prominent figure in north Wales. The masonry of this building is distinguished as being more massive than that of the cottage. Near the top the walls corbel inwards, suggesting that it may have had a corbelled roof. The building around St Gybi's Well, as it is known, does not date back to the sixth century – it is not impossible, however, that the well itself was used in the Dark Ages. The corbelling has been compared with that of the corbelled beehive cells of Ireland and Scotland, such as the famous examples at Skellig Michael, Co. Kerry. However, corbelling by itself is no certain indicator of Dark Age date (it was used in Ireland for shepherds' huts in the nineteenth century) and the building, on comparison with sites like Madron well chapel in Cornwall, is most probably of eleventh to twelfth century date.

The ogham inscription we mentioned at the beginning of the chapter is at **Brynkir** (SH 4845) which lies about 7m (11·3 km) NW of Portmadoc on the A487. The stone can be seen in the yard of Llystyngwyn Farm, which entails a short walk up the farm road from the main road. The stone is to the right-hand side as you reach the farm, built into a wall with a sheltering canopy. It is bilingual, and has a Latin text which reads

ICORI (X) FILIVS/POTENT/INI
(*Icorix, son of Potentinus*)

The ogham inscription is on the side of the stone and reads in transcript ICORIGAS. It dates from the sixth century. The name of the farm is of some interest – it incorporates the element *llys* (court, estate), a term which may refer back to the lands of Icorix himself.

Central Gwynedd is dominated by the Snowdonia National Park, and its Dark Age archaeology is dominated by **Dinas Emrys** (SH 6149), probably the most famous of all Dark Age sites in Wales. Conveniently situated for the motorist to the N of the main A498 from Beddgelert to Capel Curig, just over a mile out of Beddgelert itself and 7m (11·3 km) NW of Portmadoc, it stands in romantic scenery in the heart of Snowdonia. There is a lay-by adjacent, and, after seeking permission from the nearby farm, the visitor can most easily approach the site up the NE ridge, through the trees. The original entrance, however, was through the two ramparts at the W end of the site. Dinas Emrys was first occupied in the Roman iron age – excavations in 1910 produced various finds which suggested an initial occupation in the first or second century AD, including a couple of terrets (guide rings for chariot reins) which were current in northern Britain at this time.

The Dark Age occupation at Dinas Emrys has long attracted interest because of the legends associated with the site. The historian Nennius related in the ninth century how Vortigern, the fifth-

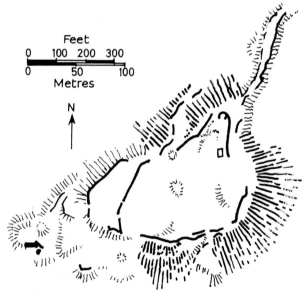

57 (a) Dinas Emrys (b) plan of Dinas Emrys

century tyrant (see p. 23) attempted to build a citadel on the site but failed because the materials were stolen overnight. To enable the building to be put up, the blood of a fatherless youth had to be sprinkled on the site. The youth who was nearly sacrificed to this end was Ambrosius, probably the Ambrosius Aurelianus who figures in the writings of Gildas as a fifth-century figure not unlike King Arthur. In the story Ambrosius revealed concentric mysteries (to the discomfort of Vortigern's magicians), the central one of which was the story of fighting dragons (symbolizing Celt and Saxon) who were buried in a cist on the hill. The mysteries are all contained in a pool, which still exists on the summit as a hollow, and which was the focus of the excavations in 1954–6. This seems to have been a cistern to water stock, but the evidence is confused.

The existing remains are slight and difficult to distinguish. The visitor should climb to the summit of the hill to begin a tour of the site, for here it is possible to distinguish the ruined drystone rampart, 8 to 10 feet (2·4 to 3 metres) thick, which links up outcrops and encloses a 'citadel' of about $2\frac{1}{2}$ acres (1 hectare). Within this enclosure lies the 'Pool'. On the highest point of the rock are the foundations of the tower, believed by the 1910 excavators to be that built by Vortigern but now identified as a Norman keep, similar to those at Dolwyddelan and Dolbadarn. On the W side of the citadel a steep and winding path leads through a gap in the rampart, over an outcrop and past a second section of rampart, until almost at the bottom of the hill it reaches the lowest rampart with a massive, obliquely inturned entrance. Elsewhere on the hill are enigmatic sections of ruined walling, which are probably either medieval field revetments or modern sheep walls.

The sequence of events at Dinas Emrys seems to have been as follows. A late Roman or early Dark Age small settlement with a timber structure, perhaps a hut or granary, was defended by an insubstantial palisade. In the post-Roman period a native type of stone-walled homestead with circular huts and outbuildings was constructed, iron and bronze was worked, and cultivation terraces on the hill may have been farmed. At this stage the two main ramparts were built. Imported pottery (A and B wares, see p. 56) are associated with this phase, as well as a sherd from a lamp with a chi-rho (the first two letters of the Greek for Christ) monogram stamped on it. A cistern was built and later a platform was constructed to give access to the cistern.

A very important group of three Dark Age memorial stones were

until recently in the picturesque village of **Penmachno** (SH 7951).
They were on display in the church, but due to renovation of the
church they have (September 1976) been taken to Bangor for safe
keeping. It is hoped that they will be returned to the church when
renovation is completed, and so may once again be on display when
this book appears in print. Penmachno lies at the end of the B4406,
and is signposted to the S from the A5 1½m (2·4 km) S of Betws y
Coed. This is the heart of Snowdonia National Park, and
throughout the summer Betws y Coed is thronged with visitors to
the famous Swallow Falls. Penmachno is worth a visit for the scenic
value of its setting (it also has a Welsh woollen mill), and boasts a
very attractive bridge. The stones were in the church between the
square and the bridge. The three pillars are as follows:
Penmachno 1 is notable for the chi-rho over the inscription which
reads

CARAVSIVS HIC IACIT IN HOC CONGERIES LAPIDVM
(*Carausius lies here in this heap of stones*)

Carausius is an uncommon name and may have been fashionable in
the late third century when an emperor of that name ruled Britain as
a breakaway state from Rome. The emperor Carausius had special
prominence in Wales – hoards containing his coins are very
common in the Principality – and he may have had some special link
with Wales. The stone dates from the fifth century.
Penmachno 2 has an inscription reading

CANTIORI(X) HIC IACIT (V)ENEDOTIS CIVE(S) FVIT (C)ONSOBRINO(S)
MA(G)LI MAGISTRAT . . .
(*Cantiorix lies here. He was a citizen of Venedos, cousin of Maglos
the Magistrate*)

The term *Venedos* is the Celtic form of Gwynedd: this shows that
Gwynedd was already recognizable as a region in the fifth century
when the stone was set up. The use of the very Roman terms *civis*
and *magistratus* which occur nowhere else in Britain in a Christian
inscription, implies that a formal Roman system of government
operated in the area, and perhaps that Roman style administration
continued in fifth-century Gwynedd. It could have been based on
the Roman fort at Caernarvon, which is known to have been
occupied at this date.
Penmachno 3 is inscribed

58 Penmachno Stones (a) 1–Carausius (b) 3–Justinus

FILI AVITORI IN TE(m)PO(re) IVSTI(ni) CON [SVLI(s)]
(*The stone of — —, son of Avitorius. Set up in the time of the
consul Justinus*)

This stone is of historical importance because the consul can be
identified from inscriptions in the Lyons district of France. He held
office in 540. This suggests links between Gaul and Gwynedd in the
sixth century AD.

In the parish church of **Llanrhos** (SH 7980), 1½m (2·4 km) S of
Llandudno reached by minor roads off the A546 to Llandudno
Junction, can be seen a fine memorial stone. The church, however, is
open only on Fridays and Saturdays, 10–4. The stone is mounted on
the wall inside the church, on the left as you enter. The inscription
reads,

SANCT/INVS SACER(dos) I(n) P(ace)
(*Sanctinus the bishop lies here in peace*)

This is evidence for a diocesan structure in the fifth-century Welsh
church, and as such is very important.

Modern Gwynedd (and Dark Age Gwynedd, too) includes the old
county of Merioneth. Here at **Towyn** church (SH 5800) can be seen
one of the most interesting memorial stones in Wales. The village is
4m (6·4 km) NW of Aberdovy, on the A493 from Dolgellau, and lies
on the coast due S of Barmouth. The stone is notable for carrying
the oldest known inscription in Welsh. Welsh probably evolved out
of an older British language during the fifth and sixth centuries,
when Old Welsh took shape. The form of the letters on the Towyn
stone indicate that the inscription is not any earlier than the seventh
to ninth centuries. If it seems remarkable that it is so late, it must be
remembered that Latin was the language used for inscriptions and
one in the vernacular is very unusual at any time in the early Middle
Ages. The inscription is carried on all four faces. It reads,

CINGEN CELEN TRICET/NITANAM TENGRUIN MALTE(c) GU/ADGAN
ANTERUNC DUBUT MARCIAU
MOLT/CƆC PE/TUAR
M(c)/ARTR

There is some dispute over its exact meaning.

Anglesey, lying off the coast of Gwynedd and now reached by the
impressive Menai Bridge, designed by Thomas Telford, was
extensively settled in prehistoric and Dark Age times. Here the
neolithic farmers built tombs like Barclodiad y Gawres and Bryn

59 Llangybi (see p. 173)

Celli Ddhu, that betray their Irish connections, and here in the iron
age the druids made their offering of weapons and ornaments in the
sacred pool of Llyn Cerrig Bach, and held out against the Romans.
Not surprisingly, the Romans built two forts in Anglesey, one at
Aberffraw, of which nothing is now visible but which was refortified
in the Dark Ages and became a major stronghold of the princes of
Gwynedd, and one at Caer Gybi on Holyhead, constructed in the
fourth century to counter Irish raids and later given to St Gybi as
the site for a monastery.

   To the SE of Holyhead lies **Llangadwaladr** (SH 3869) reached by
the A4080 from Menai Bridge. It lies about 2m (3·2 km) E of
Aberffraw. Here in the church can be seen the Catamanus Stone,
one of the few Dark Age memorial stones that actually records a
personage known to history. In translation the stone records that
'King Catamanus, the wisest and most renowned of all rulers (lies
here)'. Some of the letters are distinctive, notably the *A*s and *M*s,
and can be matched in the Book of Kells and the Lindisfarne
Gospels, which bears out the ascription of the stone to the seventh-
century King Cadfan (Catamanus). Cadfan probably died around

625, and his grandson Cadwaladr traditionally founded the church in which the stone now is and gave his name to the village. The present church is probably on the site of an earlier one. The terms used to describe Cadfan are more appropriate to an eastern potentate than a Welsh chief, and perhaps are derived from Byzantium, where such superlatives were commonplace.

From Beaumaris a journey N along the B5109 and minor roads terminates at Penmon (SH 6280). The Priory, now in state care, is a medieval foundation on the site of an earlier Dark Age one, founded by St Seiriol in the sixth century. The dominant remains are those of the medieval church and the sixteenth century dovecote of the monastery, but there are two traces of the Dark Age foundation. The first is the **Deer Park Cross** (625806), one of the few surviving free-standing crosses in North Wales. It has an 'eared' disc head, squarish shaft, and stands on a decorated base. It depicts the temptation of St Anthony, with the saint flanked by animal-headed demons. The representation compares with that on Irish crosses, notably on the Castledermot cross. A panel of ring-chain of the type developed by Gaut on the Isle of Man (see p. 49) decorates the back, and there are other interlace patterns. It dates from the tenth or eleventh centuries. There is another, lesser, cross in the Priory church. **St Seiriol's Well** (632808) is in part Dark Age, and consists of the 'wishing well', a baptistry roofed in the eighteenth century, the lower portion of which may be Dark Age, and the foundations of 'St Seiriol's cell', a circular chamber built against the rock. The whole is somewhat reminiscent of St Gybi's Well at Llangybi. Although not very impressive as Dark Age remains, the site is worth a visit (as are many of the reputedly Dark Age wells and baptistries) for its romantic setting.

Beyond Penmon, off the most easterly tip of Anglesey, lies Puffin Island, known also as **Priestholm** or **Ynys Seiriol** (SH 6582). It lies ½m (0·8 km) out to sea, and permission to visit must be sought from Baron Hill Estate office. Ynys Seiriol was a small hermitage, perhaps founded by St Seiriol in the sixth century. The existing remains are not very impressive, but the island is worth a visit if you like watching puffins! The site is dominated by the twelfth-century tower of the ruined church, on the E wall of which can be seen the line of an earlier chapel, the foundations of which were found in excavation. The church stands within the cashel of the hermitage, a largely obscured low stone bank, next to which are the foundations of three or four rectangular cells, about 10 feet (3 metres) square.

The last site to visit on Anglesey is the hut-group at **Pant-y-Saer** (SH 5182). This is more a site for the enthusiast, for the much-overgrown remains are difficult to find, and are reached overland by a footpath. Follow the A5025 for about 7m (11·3 km) N of Menai Bridge. On the outskirts of Benllech, turn W just before the Llanafon Hotel, then W into Fern Hill. A footpath leads to the W, between two houses. This goes on to open moorland. Where the path reaches open ground, turn right near a metal gate, and follow the lightly worn path to the top of the hill. Here the remains of the hut-group can be found, looking out across Red Wharf bay. The remains consist of an oval stone-walled enclosure, inside which are two large circular huts, one with rectangular annexes. The site was excavated 1932–3, and finds included a silvered bronze penannular brooch of the sixth century and some coarse pottery, now in the National Museum of Wales in Cardiff. Pant-y-Saer is one of a series of 'enclosed hut groups' in North Wales, first built in the third and fourth centuries AD, perhaps with Roman encouragement.

In modern Clwyd, the old counties of Denbigh and Flint, the traveller is again confronted with a scatter of Dark Age stones. One of the most curious is at **Gwytherin** (SH 8761), where the churchyard boasts a strange line of four pillar stones, set about 10 feet (3 metres) apart. Each is about 3 feet (0·91 metres) high, and the alignment may be prehistoric in origin. Three are uninscribed, but the fourth reads,

VINNEMAGLI FILI/SENEMAGLI
(*The stone of Vinnemaglus, son of Senemaglus*)

It dates from the fifth or sixth century, and is of interest as a pagan prehistoric monument being adapted to Christian use. To reach Gwytherin, follow the B5384, which runs SW from the A544 at Llansannon. Gwytherin lies 14m (22·4 km) SW of Denbigh.

The stones to be seen in north-east Wales are for the most part later than those in the north-west. One of the most interesting is **Maen Achwyfan** (SJ 1278) [AM; A], a disc-headed cross which stands probably in its original position beside the road. It can be reached by taking the A55 from Holywell Flints, towards St Asaph, and turning NW after about 2m (3·2 km) on a minor road to Whitford. It lies outside the village at a cross-roads on the way to Sarn. This monument was accorded the distinction of being illustrated in the 1695 edition of Camden's *Britannia*, though the antiquary Edward Lhwyd who added the notes on it was at a loss with regard to its date, function, or the meaning of its name, apart from the Maen, which means 'stone' in Welsh. We can do better now, and can ascribe it to the tenth or eleventh century (confirming the seventeenth-century suspicion that it might be Danish), and can point out that it is Northumbrian in character. It is decorated mainly with interlace and square T-fret patterns, and diaper key pattern, but also boasts a small phallic figure and some animals. It shows both Viking and Celtic influence, and is probably an outlier of the Cheshire group (see p. 116).

(see p. 116)

60 Inscription, Pillar of Eliseg

Although none of its inscription can now be read, the **Pillar of Eliseg** situated in a field overlooking Valle Crucis Abbey at Llangollen (SJ 2142) is of exceptional interest. It is visible from the road just E of the A542, about 2m (3·2 km) N of Llangollen. The pillar is of Mercian 'round shaft' type, and stands on a stone base. The inscription, in 31 lines (vestiges of 15 survive) gave the genealogy of Eliseg and Concenn, members of the ruling dynasty of Powys, and seems to have been set up in the first half of the ninth century. The mound on which the cross stands was investigated in 1779, when a stone cist was found containing an inhumation burial, presumably that of Eliseg. The stone was read in 1696 by Edward Lhwyd, and translated it reads:

Concenn son of Cattell, Cattell son of Brohcmail, Brohcmail son of Eliseg, Eliseg son of Guoillauc. Concenn, who is therefore great grandson of Eliseg, erected this stone to his great-grandfather Eliseg. Eliseg annexed the inheritance of Powys . . . throughout nine (years) from the power of the English, which he made into a sword-land by fire. Whoever shall read this hand-engraved stone let him give a blessing on the soul of Eliseg. Concenn it is who . . . with his hand . . . to his own kingdom of Powys . . . and which . . . the mountain . . . the monarchy . . . Maximus . . . of Britain . . . Concenn, Pascent . . . Maun, Annan. Britu, moreover, (was) the son of Guorthigirn (ie Vortigern) whom Germanus blessed and whom Severa bore to him, the daughter of Maximus, the king, who killed the king of the Romans. Conmarch painted this inscription at the command of his king Concenn. The blessing of the Lord be upon Concenn and all members of his family, and upon the whole land of Powys until the Day of Judgement. Amen.

Much controversy has surrounded this inscription. For one thing, although the Cattell and Concenn mentioned have been identified with kings of Powys who died in 808 and 854, the type of cross is not known in its homeland of Mercia before the late tenth or even the eleventh century. For another, it was extremely unusual for a man to set up a monument honouring his great-grandfather. A third curiosity is that the stone refers to the English as the Angli – in the ninth century a Welshman would have been more likely to have called them Saxons. But if the stone does date from the early eleventh century it is still curious, for at this date a Mercian-style monument in Powys would be very surprising. Many believe that the inscription is intended to deceive, perhaps copied from earlier sources, perhaps made up entirely in the eleventh century. If this is so, the information that it provides about early Welsh history is suspect. If however it is correct, it suggests that Vortigern, who invited over Anglo-Saxons to settle in Kent in the mid-fifth century, was one of the founders of the early Welsh kingdoms and was married to the daughter of the Roman usurper Magnus Maximus, who did something for Wales – though what is not quite clear.

Central Wales has little to offer the Dark Age enthusiast: no remains which can be certainly ascribed to the Dark Ages are visible. South Wales on the other hand abounds in Early Christian stones, but little else that is Dark Age. Dyfed is by far the richest region for the Dark Age enthusiast, the greatest concentration of stones being found in the former county of Pembroke. Dyfed has much to commend itself scenically, and a search for the Early Christian stones provides the traveller with a pretext for exploring some of the gentlest and most English countryside in Wales, as well as some of the most spectacular coastal scenery. Here space permits only a selection of typical monuments to be described, but the list in Appendix One will guide you to others, many of them of equal or nearly equal merit.

An appropriate starting point is the small town named after Wales's patron saint, **St David's** (SM 7525), at the extreme tip of

Pembrokeshire. Of the Early Christian foundation nothing now remains above ground, though various stones can be seen in the cathedral attesting its importance in the Dark Ages. An ecclesiastical foundation probably grew up here in the sixth century, founded by St David, and later suffered from Viking attacks. The first main building phase of the cathedral belongs to the late twelfth century.

In the S transept of the cathedral can be seen a good example of a monogram cross slab, a type which is distinctive of Pembrokeshire, though there is an outlier from Hereford. The model is probably to be found in Merovingian Gaul, or even Coptic Egypt, though at St David's Irish influence is probably responsible for the immediate prototype. The cross slab carries a simple cross, alpha, omega, and the monograms IHS XPC (for IESOS CHRISTOS) in the angles. It dates probably from the ninth century. A more developed form of monogram cross slab can be seen at the W end of the N aisle of the nave. It carries a very ornamental wheel-headed cross of Irish type and an inscription:

A 7 ω I(h)S XPS/ GURMARC

The '7' symbol means 'and'. Gurmarc presumably set it up, in the ninth or tenth century.

One other of the stones in the cathedral is worth singling out. Unfortunately it is broken, and only the upper left hand part of what was once an extremely fine cross-slab survives, with a moulded wheel-cross of Irish type. The left-arm end has interlace terminating in a pair of animal heads grasping a human head, while a seraph floats on three (pairs of?) wings above. The six-winged seraph comes from the Vision of Isaiah, but appears sometimes in Ireland flanking the Cross. This dates from the tenth century.

Pembroke was extensively colonized by the Irish, and boasts a rich collection of ogham stones. One can be seen at **Brawdy** (SM 8524), by taking the A487 S out of St David's for about 6m (9·7 km) to Pen-y-Cwm, then turning N for about a mile (1·6 km) in the direction of Brawdy aerodrome. It can be seen along with two other early stones in the church porch, and commemorates one Vendognus. The other two are a stone with an ogham inscription only, and a Latin stone of the sixth century commemorating one Briacus.

At **Clydai** (spelt Clydey on maps) (SN 2435) there are three early stones in the church, reached by single-track roads from the A478,

B4332 or B433. It lies about 6m (9·7 km) SW of Newcastle Emlyn. All three stones have inscriptions, two of them ogham bilinguals, and all date from the sixth century. They commemorate Etternus, son of Victor, Dobitucus son of Evolengus and Solinus son of Vendonius. One has a Maltese ring-cross, added in the seventh to ninth century.

The site of **Gateholm** (SM 7707) is a tidal island, reached from Haverfordwest by the B4327 and a side-road W to Marloes, once a notorious haunt of pirates. The island is at the NW end of Marloes beach, which is reached by taking the narrow lane to the S side of the church. It is very popular in summer with tourists. The site at Gateholm is a puzzling one, with rows of rectangular stone hut foundations on either side of a central 'street'. The finds from the site have included Roman pottery and a ringed pin of the Early Christian period, and it has been suggested that it is a Roman iron age settlement with reoccupation, or a monastery of Tintagel type with residual Roman material. The former interpretation is more likely, and there is no real reason to believe it monastic.

An important group of stones can be seen at **Penally** (SS 1199) which is reached by following the A4139 S out of Tenby for 1½m (2·4 km). The stones are in the parish churchyard, about 1m (1·6 km) SW of Tenby itself. There are three: a fragmentary cross-shaft (in the churchyard to the N of the church), a free-standing cross and a further fragment of a cross-shaft inside the church. The last, which dates from the tenth century, is the least interesting. The first cross-shaft is notable for its Northumbrian-style ornament of vinescroll with yapping animals eating a pair of dragons which in turn are consuming a vine tendril. An N-shaped ribbon animal appears on another face. It dates probably from the mid-ninth century, and shows Irish as well as Northumbrian influence. The finest of the Penally stones is the free-standing cross. It has a Northumbrian type of wheel-head, and similarly shows both Northumbrian and Irish influence. The shaft is decorated with fine interlace, and very debased vinescroll. It dates from the tenth century, and stands 7 feet (2·13 metres) high.

In some ways not as fine is the famous **Carew Cross** (SN 0403) [AM; A]. This is now to be seen in a walled emplacement at the roadside adjacent to Carew Castle, and is reached by following the A477 for 5m (8 km) and then turning N along the A4075 from Pembroke Dock. The cross is on the S side of the A4075, about 1¼m (2 km) N of its junction with the A477. It stands over 13 feet (3·96 metres) high, and is covered with fret and interlace patterns. An inscription on the base at the front of the cross reads,

MARGIT/EUT·RE/X·ETG(uin)·FILIUS
(*The cross of Margiteut, son of Etguin*)

This can be identified as Maredudd ap Edwin, the descendant of Hywel Dda, who gained control of Deheubarth (ie SW Wales) in 1033 and who was killed two years later.

At **Nevern** (SN 4840), 7m (11·27 km) SW of Cardigan on the B4582, can be seen a notable series of stones. The earliest is an ogham bilingual, commemorating Maglocunus, son of Clutorius, and datable to the fifth or early sixth century, while another ogham bilingual commemorates Vitalianus Emeretos and dates from the same period. Both are to be seen in the church. The prize of the Nevern collection, however, is a free-standing cross in the churchyard, near the SE angle of the S transept. It dates from the late tenth century, and is closely related to the Carew Cross, richly decorated with interlace, diaper key pattern and other abstract ornament. There are a few letters engraved on it, of which the DNS on the back is probably an abbreviation for DOMINUS, 'Lord'.

The museum at **Carmarthen** (SN 4120) is situated in Quay St [Mon.–Fri. 10–1, 2–5; Sat. 10–12]. It boasts an important collection of six Early Christian stones. The most famous of these is the tombstone of Voteporix. The inscription reads,

MEMORIA VOTEPORIGIS PROTICTORIS
(*In memory of Vortepor the Protector*)

It was found at Castell Dwyran, and it has an ogham translation down the side. It probably alludes to 'Vorteporius, usurper in Dyfed' mentioned by Gildas (see p. 25), who seems to have been living around AD 530. In one genealogy Vortepor's ancestry is given as 'Maxen guletic map Protec map Protector' and this suggests that Maxen Wledig (ie the Roman usurper Magnus Maximus) was regarded as his ancestor. This might explain the curious title 'Protector' which is a Roman one used to describe a type of officer-cadet. By the time of Vortepor it seems to have been hereditary, and Professor Alcock has suggested that Vortepor's line may have started with a bodyguard hostage in the court of Maximus. This is one of the very rare instances where the person commemorated on a stone is known from history.

A second stone, from Cynwyl Gaeo, is also of some interest.

61 Vortepor's tombstone, Carmarthen Museum

It reads

SERVATVR FIDAEI/PATRI(a) EQ(ue) SEMPER/ AMATOR HIC PAVLINVS
IACIT CUL(t)OR PIENT(?)/(s)SIM(us aequi)
(*Preserver of the Faith, Constant lover of his country, here lies
Paulinus, the devoted champion of righteousness*)

The inscription dates from the sixth century, and is probably the
tombstone of St Paulinus, the teacher of St David. It is a metrical
epitaph, of a type known in Classical and Gaulish inscriptions.

The other stones are of less note.

The **Clawdd Mawr** (SN 3733) is one of a series of linear
earthworks to be found in South Wales. It runs for about 2m
(3·2 km), but the best stretch runs along a N–S ridge for just under a
mile alongside the A484 near Rhos, about 12m (19·3 km) N of

Carmarthen. It faces E, with an associated ditch on that side. It probably delineated the E boundary of Dyfed, and may have been built in fear of the expansion eastwards of the Welsh into areas settled by the Irish. It dates from perhaps the tenth century.

In **Swansea** Museum (SS 6592) [10–5], situated in Victoria Rd on the edge of the dock area, can be seen some Dark Age stones and the Dark Age finds from the excavation of Minchin Hole cave. The stones consist of a Roman altar from the fort at Laughor, with an ogham inscription added in one corner – evidence for the continuity of the use of Roman forts into the Dark Ages – and another stone of the sixth century with a Latin inscription commemorating Macaritinus, son of Bericius. The museum also houses two cross-shafts of the tenth or eleventh centuries, with figures of clerics.

Another small museum with a collection of stones is at **Brecon** (SO 0428), administered by the National Museum of Wales [10–5, Thurs. 10–6]. The stones, represented by the originals or casts, include a fifth-century bilingual in Latin and ogham to Maccutrenus Salicidunus, found at Trecastle, and a Latin-inscribed stone to a certain Nennius, son of Victorinus which, as it dates from the sixth century, is nearly three centuries too old to commemorate the historian! There is also a tenth-century pillar cross from Maesmynis.

Llantwit Major (SS 9668) on the B4265, about 15m (24 km) W of Cardiff, was a burying-place for Welsh kings in the ninth to eleventh centuries. It was an important monastery, on which was focused a school of sculpture, well exemplified by surviving examples in the church. Of the several stones at this site, one of the earliest is a disc-headed cross, about 6 feet (1·83 metres) high, decorated with fret and interlace patterns and carrying an inscription which reads,

NI NOMINE D(e)I PATRIS ET F(ili) / [ET S] ERETUS SANTDI (h)ANC / [CR] UCEM HOUELT PROPE / [RA] B IT PRO ANIMA RES P [A/TR] ES E(i)US (*In the name of God the Father, and of the Son and of the Holy Ghost. This cross Houelt prepared for the soul of Res his father*)

Houelt is probably Hywel ap Rhys, who ruled Glywysing (a kingdom covering parts of Glamorgan and Monmouth) in the late ninth century. The stone shows Irish influence.

Three cross-shafts are also notable. The first, of late ninth–early tenth century date, is decorated with neat interlace, and is one of the most accomplished in Wales.

A second shaft has interlace and diaper key patterns, and inscriptions which translate as, 'Samson set up this cross for his soul, for that of Illtut, of Samson the King, of Samuel, and of Ebisar.' It dates from the tenth century.

The third shaft, of the tenth or eleventh century, carries some interlace on the side and a long inscription on the front which reads, 'In the name of God Most High begins the Cross of the Saviour, which Abbot Samson prepared for his own soul and for the soul of King Juthahel and of Artmail and Tecain.'

In **Cardiff** (ST 1877) the National Museum of Wales has recently opened a new Dark Age gallery, in which many of the most important Early Christian stones from Wales are displayed, either as originals or casts [10–5; 10–6, April–September]. The display also exhibits the finds from the excavations at Dinas Powys, Glamorgan, and from Dinas Emrys, Gwynedd.

The site of **Dinas Powys** itself (ST 1472) can be reached by taking the A4055 out of Cardiff, for about 5m (8 km). In the centre of the town a road to the N leads up to the tree-covered slopes of the hillfort, which is the most important excavated Dark Age site in Wales. The remains straddle a whalebacked hill, just over $\frac{1}{4}$m (0·4 km) long, to the NW of the medieval castle. At some stage in the iron age a hill-slope fort was begun but not completed – the bank of this earthwork (Southern Bank A – see plan fig. 62) lies to the SE of the main earthworks, with a second rampart (Southern Bank B) which is probably a siege work of the medieval period. Of the multiple banks and ditches at the northern end of the hill, only one belongs to the Dark Ages. This, the most insubstantial of all those on the site (Bank II and Ditch II), enclosed traces of a drystone hall and barn, the presence of which was mainly attested in excavation by eaves-drips. A rich accumulation of midden material included imported Mediterranean pottery of Classes A–E (see p. 56) and scrap bronze from metalworking, and a lead die for making moulds for penannular brooches – testimony to the Dark Age activity on the site. The more substantial earthworks in this area belong to the Norman ringwork (Bank I and Ditch I) and the reinforcing banks and ditches added to it slightly later (Banks III and IV).

An important collection of inscribed stones can be seen in the Museum of Stones at **Margam Abbey** (SS 8087) [AM; open only on Wed., Sat., Sun. afternoons]. This is housed in the old school adjacent to the abbey. To get to Margam, follow the A48 W for nearly 20m (32·2 km) from Cowbridge through Pyle to Pound. The Abbey is reached by turning north off the main road at Pound, and

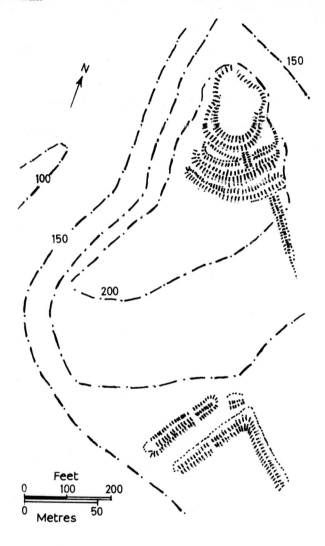

150

N

100

150

200

150

Feet
0   100   200
0   50
Metres

62 Plan of Dinas Powys

63 Margam Cross

lies about a mile SE of Margam itself. Most, but not all, of the stones have been found near the abbey. The earliest dates from the sixth century, and carries the inscription

BODVOC -HIC IACIT / FILVS CATOTIGIRNI / PROPENVS ETERNALI(S) / VEDOMAV
(*The stone of Boduocus, here he lies, the son of Catotigirnus, great-grandson of Eternalis Vedomavus*)

The finest stones are of the late ninth to eleventh centuries. The first of these is a disc-headed cross with wide splayed shaft, richly decorated with interlace and fret patterns. It carries an inscription which reads in translation, 'The Cross of Christ. Enniaun made it for the soul of Gurogoret.' The back carries a simple linear cross. Unfortunately the wheel head on this cross is partly damaged. Damage to the reverse of the wheel also detracts from the otherwise outstanding Conbelin's Cross, which stands just short of 5 feet high. The wheel has square armpits, and is decorated with interlace. The stumpy shaft is ornamented with the draped figures of St John and the Virgin (the shaft was originally taller but has been fractured at the bottom), and stands on a plinth decorated with interlace and an outstanding hunting scene with two horsemen following two dogs attacking a stag. There is also some fret pattern on the reverse of the shaft at its base. An inscription on the head records it was set up by Conbelin. Of the other stones, a small relief cross-slab with an incomplete cross of the tenth century is particularly pleasing.

The Isle of Man

The Isle of Man, lying in the middle of the Celtic 'Mediterranean', was ideally situated as a centre for activities on the adjoining coastlands of England, Wales, Scotland and Ireland. In the fifth

century the inhabitants of Man appear to have spoken a form of British, but the island was already being settled by the Irish and some memorial stones have both Irish and British names in the fifth century. By the time of the coming of the Norse, the Isle of Man was speaking Goidelic Celtic – Manx is, in fact, quite like phonetically-spelled Irish. The first Norse settlements in Man took place around 900, when the island was probably used as a base for raiding. The Norse overlay in the Isle of Man was virtually total – the present Manx parliament (the House of Keys) owes its origin to this period, while the present parish system is based on the Norse-period land divisions (treens), which in turn probably follow earlier Celtic units.

The Isle of Man and the Western Isles of Scotland were united into a confederacy under Godred Crovan (1079–95), an Arthur-like figure who appears in Manx mythology as King Orry. Constant struggles between rival factions to gain control of Man led to the collapse of Norse supremacy in 1266, when both the Western Isles of Scotland and the Isle of Man were ceded to Alexander III of Scotland in the Treaty of Perth.

The Dark Age archaeology of the Isle of Man is dominated by Manx sculpture and by the *keeills* for which the island is well known. These are small chapels, distributed each to its treen or land unit, some of which at least belong to the Early Christian period. They are extremely difficult to date in the absence of finds but it can be assumed that many of the surviving foundations date from the twelfth century or possibly even later.

There are about a hundred and seventy Dark Age sculptured stones from the Isle of Man, about one-third of which date from the Norse period, a time when Manx sculpture was to influence contemporary work on the British mainland.

The AA Atlas is inadequate for finding sites in the Isle of Man, and travellers should equip themselves with Ordnance Survey 1 inch Sheet 87.

Of all the Manx keeills, the most romantic and spectacular is **Lag ny Keeilley** (SC 2174), situated on a cliff overlooking the Irish Sea. Take the A27 S out of Dalby for about 1½m (2·4 km), till you come to the entrance to the Manx National Trust property of Eary Cushlin, on the W. A path, once a pack-horse track, leads through breathtaking scenery to the site, which involves a fairly difficult walk of about 1¼m (2 km). The keeill itself is a simple unicameral chapel, with a stone-built altar, enclosed by a low circular graveyard bank, broken by two 'entrances', one now marked by two piles of stones. To the north of the enclosure is a hermit's rectangular cell, only slightly smaller than the chapel itself. The site was excavated in 1849 and again more extensively in 1909, and finds included some simple cross-incised stones (presumably Christian symbols) and burials in long stone cists.

Almost as emotive is **Spooyt Vane** (SC 3088), known locally as Cabbal Pherick, St Patrick's Chapel. Take the A3 Peel road out of Kirk Michael for about 1¼m (2 km). To the SE of the road a wicket gate gives access to Glen Mooar, and a footpath follows a delightful stream in sylvan setting. The keeill is about ½m (0·8 km) from the main road near the path. Like Lag ny Keeilley, Spooyt Vane boasts a hermit's cell, which is built against the SE corner of the enclosing vallum of the chapel. Not far off is a waterfall, and it is easy to see why some dedicated cleric chose this idyllic spot for his retreat.

Maughold (SC 4991), on the opposite side of the island 3m (4·8 km) SE of Ramsey on the A15, is a monastic site of some distinction. The dark age site now lies in the churchyard of

64 Spooyt Vane keeill

65 Maughold churchyard keeill

Maughold village. The church itself incorporates no work earlier
than the eleventh or twelfth centuries, but probably stands on the
site of an earlier ecclesiastical building. Near the churchyard gate
under a shelter is one of the most important collections of
sculptured stones on the island. Irneit's Cross commemorates a
seventh-century bishop and has a marigold pattern on the head. The
Crux Guriat, an early ninth-century cross standing about 7 feet
(2·13 metres) high, may commemorate Gwriad, a Welsh prince who
went to Man in about AD 825. There are also a number of Norse
sculptures, including one of Roolwer, the first Manx bishop known
from historical sources (c. 1050). The decoration on the Norse
crosses includes saga illustrations, ring-chain of the type developed
by Gaut (p. 49), and runes.

Various stone foundations have been discovered in the
churchyard intermittently, and the foundations of three keeills can
be seen in the cemetery, extensively restored. Of these, the most
notable is the north keeill, which was originally surrounded by its

own cemetery. A sixth-century cross-slab was found covering one of the graves, while a fine Norse cross-slab with runic inscriptions and a depiction of a boat also came from this site.

Another notable keeill can be seen on the multi-period site at **Balladoole** (SC 2468). The site is approached off the A7 from Castletown and about $1\frac{1}{4}$m (2 km) from it. Just past Ballakeigan corner a farm road turns S to Balladoole farm. Follow this road for about $\frac{1}{4}$m (0·4 km), and just before a cottage a gate to the right gives access to the site. The site is dominated by the remains of the rampart of an iron age fort, which surrounds the oval summit of this low hill. The site was made famous by the excavations of the late Dr Gerhard Bersu, who found not only the remains of the iron age occupation, but an Early Christian lintel grave cemetery (see p. 40) disturbed by a Viking ship burial. The keeill, Keeill Vael (St Michael's Chapel) could be as late as the eleventh century, since there are traces of mortar in its construction. The Viking ship burial is visible, marked out with stones, on the eastern edge of the rampart of the fort.

On excavation, the ship burial proved to be richly furnished, and the objects had come from all over the Viking world – Carolingian, Anglo-Saxon and Scottish Celtic finds were all recovered. The finest remains were of an interlace-ornamented horse harness. A woman had been sacrificed to accompany her man to the grave, a custom found also in Scottish Viking burials. The finds are now to be seen in Douglas Museum.

Another fort, Celtic iron age in origin, probably saw reuse in the Dark Ages. This was the spectacular **Cronk Sumark** (SC 3994). The site is approached from the A3 and B8, 4m (6·4 km) W of Ramsey. It is reached by a path from the farmyard of Grangee Farm, which is reached by a private farm road. The climb to the summit is steep, and on a windy day it can be almost impossible to stand upright on the summit. The hill was defended by two outer ramparts, one of which is vitrified, with an inner citadel on the eastern peak, defended with a rock-cut ditch. In many ways it resembles the nuclear forts of Scotland or the more closely comparable 'defensive enclosure' sites like Moncrieffe Hill, Dundurn or Dumyat (see pp. 41, 255 and 262). It has never been excavated.

The remains at the **Braaid** (SC 3276) lie near the junction of the A24 and A26, just over 3m (4·8 km) W of Douglas. It can be approached by a short walk down the slope from the main road (A24). The site was first investigated in 1935–7, when it was interpreted as a bronze age stone circle with ritual alignments of stones. Dr Gerhard Bersu, who was very active in the field of Manx archaeology when he was a P.O.W. on the island, suggested that the stone alignments were the walls of a building, and reinterpreted the site as the remains of a round iron age hut and Viking long houses. To test this theory, excavation was carried out in 1962, and confirmed that two of the alignments represented the bowed-out walls of an exceptionally large (68 feet by 41 feet [20·73 by 12·5 metres]) longhouse, which lacked the short sides – these may have been of timber and turf, eroded eventually by a stream which ran (conveniently for housekeeping) through the house. The other alignments are probably also of a house, though this has not been proved.

Probably the most famous site, and certainly the most readily recognizable in the Isle of Man, is **Tynwald Hill** (SC 2681), situated on the A1 from Douglas to Peel, in St John's. It possible started its history as a prehistoric burial mound, but it has been considerably altered into a grassy stepped mound approached by a processional way. The name itself is derived from the Norse *Thing-völlr*, meaning 'assembly field', and was the site of the Norse parliamentary assembly. An open air parliament is still held there every year on 5 July (Tynwald Day), which was midsummer in the old calendar.

The Isle of Man is famous for its collections of Norse sculptures. Second only to those at Maughold, the best collection is at **Andreas** (SC 4199), where they shelter in the parish church. The stones are particularly rich in scenes from Norse mythology – the Fenris wolf devouring Odin, Gunnar in the Worm Pit, Sigurd roasting the dragon's heart and other favourite themes are depicted on these stones. Sandulf's Cross (he is named on it in runes) is intact, while Thorwald's Cross, which has Odin and the Fenris wolf on the one side, has scenes showing the coming of Christianity on the other. It dates from the tenth century. Andreas is in the north of the island, reached by the A9 about 4m (6·4 km) N of Ramsey.

A larger collection is on display in **Kirk Michael** church (SC 3190), on the W coast of the island, on the A3 6m (9·7 km) W of Peel. This splendid assemblage includes the most famous Christian stone on Man, Gaut's Cross, with its runic inscriptions announcing proudly that 'Gaut carved this and all in Man'. Presumably, since this cross was carved early in the Norse period, it was not a vain boast, and Gaut may well have carved all the crosses of the time. It is a rather touching reminder of a way of life that

66 Thorwald's Cross Slab, Andreas

supported a great craftsman whose life and achievements have been otherwise forgotten. It is distinguished by its ring-chain ornament, a type of decoration which was later made popular in Scandinavia and occurs sometimes in northern England and sometimes in Cornwall. There is some suggestion that Gaut may have come from the Hebrides, from the island of Coll. Jolaf's Cross too is worthy, with its rich interlace and detailed figural work, enclosing an extensive runic inscription – it can be claimed as one of the finest Norse sculptures in Man. The Kirk Michael collection also includes a few pre-Norse stones of lesser merit.

At **Braddan** (SC 3676), just outside Douglas on the A1, a small group of stones is preserved in the old parish church (not to be confused with its later counterpart). These display good interlace, typical Norse dragons and runic inscriptions.

Celtic sculptures can be seen in the old parish church at **Lonan** (SC 4279). This must not be confused with the new church – it is a roofless ruin. Take the A2 out of Douglas, and turn S at Ballamenaugh to the old church, which is about a mile from the main road. The finest cross has a disc head set eccentrically to its shaft, with arm-pits in the Celtic manner and decorated with late but attractive interlace. In spite of its lateness, it is impressive and evocative. The site itself is of interest to fanatics. Beneath the ruined church (parts of which may date from the twelfth century), excavations uncovered the foundations of an earlier structure beneath the west end. The mound of the earlier chapel is visible beneath the church, and traces of a vallum predating the churchyard wall can also be discerned. The name Lonan is a Manx version of Adamnan, the biographer of St Columba. The site has produced inscribed stones of the fifth or sixth century.

Between Lonan and Douglas lies **Onchan** (SC 4078), on the A2, about 1½m (2·4 km) out of the centre of Douglas. A group of Celtic-style crosses as well as one Norse example is now preserved in the parish church.

At **Peel** (SC 8424) on St Patrick's Isle can be viewed the much-altered round tower and adjacent church of St Patrick. Although it is now mainly the work of fifteenth-century renovation, the tower was originally constructed in the tenth or eleventh century, and is one of the three Irish-type round towers outside Ireland, the other two being in Scotland at Brechin and Abernethy. Round towers were constructed in Ireland during the Viking invasions. They were detached from the churches (see p. 40). St Patrick's church may date from the late eleventh century, and probably replaces an earlier structure. It seems likely that there was a Dark Age monastery on the site, but evidence for this is lacking due to extensive later rebuilding on the 7½-acre (3 hectare) island. The site is now overshadowed by the stone castle of the thirteenth to fourteenth century, and by the Gothic cathedral (mostly thirteenth-century) which served the Isle of Man until the sixteenth century.

Another rarity of Dark Age Britain is a *leacht*, a type of open-air altar which may have been built above a grave (see p. 41). The one example in the Isle of Man is known as St Patrick's Chair and is at **Marown** (SC 3177). Take the A1 out of Douglas, and turn S down the B35. Just over a mile along it, a farm track leads E to the site – the leacht stands in the middle of a field, without any trace of the accompanying cemetery or chapel which indubitably once surrounded it. Out of the square pile of irregular stones projects a fine cross-slab, possibly of the seventh or eighth century, with a smaller cross-slab of similar date. The leacht itself now stands a mere 18 inches (0·46 metre) high.

The foundations of a Norse-period house are visible at another site apart from the Braaid. At the picturesque **Cronk ny Merriu**

67 St Patrick's Chair (*leacht*)

(SC 3170), an earlier iron age promontory fort, defended by a now partly silted-up ditch and a rampart cutting off its landward site, was chosen by some Norsemen as a suitable place to build an aisled rectangular house. The site is reached by following the A25 S from Douglas and by turning off down the B25 to Port Grenaugh. Then you must walk along the clifftop for 200 yards E of the beach.

Of the several burial mounds of probable Norse date in the Isle of Man two are worth visiting on account of their proximity to other remains. **Knock y Doonee** (SC 4002), in the N of the island, is notable for being the first ship burial in Man to be excavated scientifically. It is visible from the A10, 3m (4·8 km) W of Bride on the way to Ballaugh, high on a hilltop. About ½m (0·8 km) W of Smeale cross-roads a private farm road leads to Knock y Doonee farm. The site is reached 200 yards (183 metres) SE of the farmhouse by a walk across the fields, and visitors are rewarded by a sea-view from the summit. A hollow on the mound marks the extent of the excavation of 1927, when the rivets of a boat about 30 feet (9·14 metres) long were found. A body accompanied by a sword, shield and spear had been laid to rest in the vessel. Domestic articles had been placed in the stern. A horse and possibly a dog had also been interred. An Early Christian cross slab was found nearby, but with no provable connection. Nearby, on the other side of the road, is a good example of a keeill (SC 4002). It stands in an elevated position in a field and can be seen from the burial mound. Excavation at the beginning of the century revealed that the well-preserved altar still possessed its altar slab. More significant finds, however, were the two inscribed stones. One was a simple cross slab, but the other, now in the Manx Museum, was a bilingual inscription in Roman letters and ogham. The Latin inscription reads:

AMMECAT̂
FILIVS ROCAT
HIC IACIT
(*Ammecatos son of Rocatos lies here*)

The ogham inscription is the Celtic translation. It dates probably from the fifth century. A stray pin of the fifth or sixth century was found in the field, and is now in the Manx Museum.

A second Norse burial mound can be seen in **Jurby** churchyard (SC 3498), which is reached by following the A10 4m (6·4 km) N of Ballaugh and a side road – the churchyard is about 1m (1·6 km) SW of Jurby aerodrome. The mound itself is extensively disturbed by later burials in the churchyard, and now stands only a few feet high. Jurby church houses some renowned Norse crosses, as well as a few pre-Norse ones. One particularly fine example shows Sigurd slaying the dragon.

Of the many keeills two are worth a visit, if only because they can be conveniently reached by car. Cabbal Druiaght (the Druid's Chapel) at **Glenlough** (SC 3478) is sited near the A1 about 3m (4·8 km) out of Douglas. It lies to the left of a private road S to Glenlough Farm, and in spring is picturesequely festooned with daffodils behind its protective railings.

Keeill Vreeshy at **Eyreton** (SC 3380) is similarly convenient for those who like only a short walk from a car. It lies on a sharp bend on the A23, ½m (0·8 km) NE of Crosby. The site is in a field behind some cottages on the N of the road: the authors' visit was not altogether auspicious, due to some over-boisterous bullocks, who prevented all but a very cursory examination of the site. Dedicated to St Bridget, this keeill still stands in its original oval enclosure. It is

68 Glenlough keeill

unusually well preserved, and excavators recovered a cross-slab (probably from the altar) decorated with an expanded cross of Dark Age date.

No visit to Man would be complete without some time being spent in the **Manx Museum**, Crellin's Hill, **Douglas** [10–5]. In the first of the two archaeological galleries can be seen a superb collection of Early Christian stones, including the Calf of Man Crucifixion slab, found in 1773 in a keeill on the bird sanctuary of the Calf of Man and bought by the Museum in 1956. Dating from the eighth century, it is probably from an altar frontal, and has charming figural work. This gallery also displays the bilingual stone from Knock y Doonee.

The centrepiece of the second archaeological gallery is a large-scale model of the Gokstad ship, specially made in Norway in 1939 to commemorate the Norse occupation of Man. This gallery contains the Viking and later finds from the Isle of Man, including the finds from the several burials excavated and a number of treasure hoards of silver found on the island. Latex casts of the Norse period sculptures on the island are also displayed.

Northern England

Northern England was dominated for much of the Dark Ages by
the kingdom of Northumbria, which crystallized out of the smaller
kingdoms of Bernicia and Deira when these were united by
Aethelfrith of Bernicia in the early seventh century. The whole of

north-east England was settled by the Angles. In east Yorkshire the
settlement was already under way by the mid-fifth century, but
north of the Tyne there is little evidence for Anglo-Saxons much
before the mid-sixth century. During the seventh century
Northumbria flourished as the leading kingdom in England, the
Northumbrians spreading out and dominating much of southern
Scotland in the early years of that century and colonizing
Cumberland, Westmorland and Lancashire around 650.

The Northumbrian church blossomed under royal patronage, and
in the monasteries of Monkwearmouth and Jarrow a high level of
culture was maintained. Here the Venerable Bede lived and wrote.
Later in the Dark Ages, after Northumbria had been eclipsed by
Mercia, the north of England was to enjoy a new prominence under
the Vikings, whose great city at York carried out trade far and wide
in northern Europe, rivalling some of the great Continental trading
centres. Under Viking influence, Northumbrian sculpture, which
had been outstanding in the seventh century, enjoyed a revival in the
tenth and eleventh.

The remains of this area are notably varied. There are more
Anglo-Saxon sculptures in the North than in the rest of England put
together, and there are many fine churches, including some of the
earliest in Britain.

Without a doubt the most famous and well-preserved monument
of the Dark Ages in the north is the church at **Escomb** (NZ 1930).
Dedicated to St John the Baptist it lies about 2m (3·2 km) W of
Bishop Auckland and is reached by a minor road to the N off the
B6282 out of this town. The church stands very much as it did in the
late eighth century, when it was probably built, having been used
for worship almost without a break until the nineteenth century
parish church was built. It has survived a short period without a
roof, from 1863–7, without much damage, and has plenty of
features of interest from the Saxon period. Five medieval windows
have been cut through the original simplicity, but five Saxon
windows remain. These are to be seen in the nave, with one in the W
gable. The windows should be given particular attention since it is
these that have given rise to the term 'Escomb-fashion' jambs
(p. 32), and, in addition, from the inside the jambs have grooves
which show that shutters were originally fitted.

The N wall deserves attention since it has one blocked door to the
chancel and another leads the visitor to the nave. Both are square-
headed. It is of interest that the upper stone in each jamb has been

69 Escomb, Saxon chancel arch

morticed – a woodworking technique. It is possible that the nave door was original and that to the chancel was inserted later. From the outside one of the most prominent features is the inverted V-shape of the roof of a now destroyed W annexe.

There is a sundial at Escomb which is built high into the S wall of the nave. This circular piece of stone is unique for being the oldest timepiece still in its original position in a building. It is attractively decorated with a serpent border and a plait, with an animal head above. Sculpture is otherwise absent from this church, though many stones display Roman tooling, having been reused, probably from the nearest ruined fort of the time, Binchester. The keenly observant will be able to find one stone in particular, upside down outside the E side of the N wall of the nave, which is inscribed VI LEG showing it to have been hewn by masons of the Sixth Legion. From this beginning the church has figured little in the historical records. Bede, for instance, writing from nearby Jarrow where he lived from the age of 7, makes no mention of the building. This has caused some experts to insist that the church could not have been built as early as his lifetime (c. 673–735). However, since Escomb would not have been a church of great importance there is no reason why the venerable monk should have included it in his *Ecclesiastical History of the English Nation*. The architectural details suggest a date in the earlier period of church building rather than later, so the eighth century is not an impossible date for its erection. Finally mention should be made of the chancel arch in this church. It is very fine, and has almost certainly been recut from a complete Roman arch.

Within 2m (3·2 km) of Escomb, at South Church, St Andrew, **Bishop Auckland** (NZ 2228), can be seen one of the finest Northumbrian crosses, in the church. It dates from the late eighth century, and Sir Thomas Kendrick described it as reflecting 'the hard and violent barbarism of the age'. It is decorated with vinescroll inhabited by grotesque animals, with hooked beaks and cruel claws, combined with figures which are sharply delineated and which perhaps echo distant, perhaps Syrian, models. The church lies on the A688, 2½m (4 km) NE of West Auckland and on the edge of Bishop Auckland itself.

Associated with Bede are the remains of Monkwearmouth and the companion site at Jarrow. This illustrious churchman has become famous for his historical writings which are still used today as a primary source for the period. He was born at Monkwearmouth in about 673 and became a priest at Jarrow in about 703. Although he died in Jarrow, his remains were taken to Durham in the eleventh century. The extensive excavations at these two monastic sites with their important associations have yielded much interesting information about the period. It is the church of St Peter at **Monkwearmouth** (NZ 4057) that shows the standing remains of the period, however. Between them, the W tower and the W wall of the nave span almost the entire period of Saxon church building. Originally a porch, the tower was raised in Late Saxon times to its present impressive height of nearly 60 feet (18·29 metres). It is this tower that should be given attention first – the five stages separated by string courses and the four splendid entrances (the tower entrance itself, and the entrances to the nave and to two rooms at the W of the nave). The W entrance does not seem to have had a door at any stage, but it has fine decoration of creatures not unlike birds. The E door has been mutilated and the N and S doors are similar to each other. The tower was once decorated by carved panels depicting animals in relief along the string course of the lowest stage, but these are now sadly weathered. The tower has a number of windows of note – on the highest stage the belfry has double windows in three sides. The stage below is lit by a window in the W, and below it again is a square-headed window in the S. In the third stage the W face shows very clearly the gable of the original porch, above which the tower was raised, and remains of a Rood. The only remaining openings are in the stage above the weathered decorated string course: a restored window that is only original outside, and a square-headed door in the N face that has been blocked, with the blocked remains of a square-headed window in the S face.

Inside the building the observant visitor will see the two windows in the original W wall, with the two doors – one to the tower and one above – and two windows above them. This indicates that the church was almost certainly two-storeyed. A barrel vault over the ground floor chamber of the tower was almost certainly not built at the same time as the walls at this level, but inserted when the tower was raised in the tenth century. It is possible that the church originally had side chapels, since among the large number of carved stones on display are baluster shafts which were presumably used in some sort of arching. But since the N, S, and E walls of the nave no longer survive, this cannot be proved. Two carved stones depicting lions may have been part of a bishop's throne.

It is, therefore, worth taking the A19 to the N for about 2m (3·2 km) from the centre of Sunderland to see this church that was consecrated in 674. The monastery has had a somewhat tumultuous history, having been destroyed by the forces of Malcolm, king of Scotland, in 1070. Five years later it was in operation once more, only to be abandoned in 1083 when the monks were recalled to Durham. After the Dissolution the church was used by the parish but fell into disrepair, and its antiquity was not appreciated until 1855 when the W doorway was rediscovered, having become buried. For long obscured by Sunderland slums, in recent years it has risen from its ashes and stands again in open ground, surrounded by grass.

Monkwearmouth was flourishing in the eighth century, however, for at the death of Abbot Ceolfrith in 716 there were over six hundred monks here and at **Jarrow**, 2m (3·2 km) W of South Shields (NZ 3365). It was in this monastery that the Venerable Bede lived from the age of seven, and the church of St Paul, still the parish church, preserves some early work. The nave was rebuilt in 1866 but the chancel is Saxon, possibly as early as 681; the building is unusual in that it is known to have been dedicated on 23 April 684 or 685, since the original dedication stone is still to be seen in the nave. Other features inside are of relatively little interest – the tower arches seem to be of Norman rather than Anglo-Saxon proportions. The lower part of the tower is later than the chancel, and was built to unite the main monastic church with the E chapel: the upper part of the tower is very late Saxon, as are the rest of the monastic remains. Inside, the chancel windows are visible, and a higher blocked opening and two blocked openings in the E wall of the tower seem to indicate a W gallery.

The view from the outside is much more rewarding. The chancel is separated from the nave by a Saxon tower and there is side-alternate quoining to the chancel's E quoins to prove its antiquity. The plan is interesting, since excavations indicated that the chancel was at first a separate chapel or other building, and that it had been incorporated into the church proper by the addition of the tower, possibly some time before the Danish raids, in AD 794. There is also some indication that an extension existed to the E of the chancel – two upright stones in the E wall near two buttresses would seem to suggest a door. The chancel S wall is broken by three original windows and the blocked entrances in the W wall already noted in the tower interior. The blocked door in the N wall is probably Saxon and has Roman lewis holes visible, for this, like so many Saxon churches, displays many stones with Roman tooling. The tower is of curious construction, being rectangular at the bottom but nearly square by the time the belfry is reached. Under the Norman-type belfry windows there is a triangular-headed Saxon window in the W face and a roof line on the E. At the same level on the S and N are double windows of the type usually found in Saxon belfries. On the N and S faces below this level there are two double-splayed windows, of which that in the S has been used as a door.

The monastic remains are confused by the standing walls of the later medieval monastery – the lines of some of the foundations of the original Saxon establishment are marked out in the grass beneath them. They lie to the SW of the church, adjacent to a long wall at the W end of the medieval monastic complex. This wall has two interesting doorways, one with a triangular head, which at first seem Anglo-Saxon in character but which are probably very early Norman. This wall crosses a building uncovered in excavation known as Building A – the remains of Building B lie in the same axis further E. Building A was probably a refectory. Building B was divided into three, the largest room acting as a place of assembly and writing, the smallest a private suite for the abbot or a senior monk. Between these buildings and the church lay the monastic cemetery.

To the N of the church is Jarrow Hall, an eighteenth-century house now converted into a tourist centre. Apart from the coffee room (a rare luxury on Dark Age sites!) there is an admirably laid out exhibition centre, which tells the story of the monastery and displays finds from the excavation, a tourist information centre, and a craft shop which sells the work of local artists, including objects decorated in Anglo-Saxon style.

Also approached by the A19, but much further S and virtually in Teeside itself, is **Billingham**, where the church of St Cuthbert (NZ 4522) has a tenth- or eleventh-century tower with an adjoining W nave wall at least a century earlier. The building of the tower appears to have blocked the original W entrance to the church – this is now relegated to the vestry door within the tower. There are four Late Saxon belfry windows, a W window in the first floor and a door in the S which, because of the height at which it was built, presupposes an earlier floor at this level. Billingham is known historically, since it was given by the bishop of Lindisfarne to the community of St Cuthbert in the late ninth century.

In **Durham** (NZ 2743) the magnificent Norman cathedral is the final resting place of both Bede and St Cuthbert. The Cathedral Library houses not only some important Anglo-Saxon manuscripts but the relics of St Cuthbert and a fine collection of sculptures. Of these particular note should be made of the cross-shaft from Gainsford, with its three sharply delineated figures of Late Saxon date, and the four cross heads from the Chapter House which date probably from the early eleventh century. They are extremely accomplished, and have in two cases a Lamb of God in the central roundel.

The greatest treasures, however, are the relics of St Cuthbert, found when his tomb was opened in the nineteenth century. The most interesting is his oak coffin itself, datable to 698, with its lightly incised figure of Christ on the lid and other figures round the sides, done in a style reminiscent of Merovingian France. Almost as interesting is his gold and garnet pectoral cross, simple comb, portable altar of wood (which was later encased with ornamented silverwork) and the series of tenth-century embroideries, made in

Wessex on the order of Aethelstan.

   The village of **Norton** (NZ 4422) contains the church of St Mary the Virgin and can be reached by taking the A1027 for about 4m (6·4 km) to the NE of Stockton-on-Tees. It lies within a mile or so of Billingham (mentioned earlier). It is the lower part of the central tower, the N transept, the side walls of the S transept and parts of the nave above the arcades, along with the W parts of the chancel, that are of interest in a Saxon context. These may be tenth-century. The quoins of the tower are original and each face has one triangular-headed window and two circular apertures above. The triangular-headed openings were probably doors, since they lay beneath the former gable lines visible on the tower. Inside the tower, apart from those features noted from outside, the N and S arches can be seen. The square-headed door in the S of the tower must presumably have led to the floor, indicated by the triangular-headed windows aforementioned. The evidence for the Saxon work of the nave and chancel is slight: the nave is in bond with the tower and the stumps of the chancel walls near the tower.

   A nave with slightly more definitive dating evidence can be seen at **Seaham** in the church of St Mary (NZ 4249). Take the A19 S out of Sunderland for about 4m (6·4 km) and then a B road S in Ryhope for a further 3m (4·8 km) to reach the seaside settlement. The church stands close to the cliffs that overlook the North Sea: the Saxon remains are the three windows high in the side walls of the nave. Excavation showed that there was a W annexe which along with the original chancel could have dated to the eighth century.

   Apart from those in Durham itself, the best collection of sculptures from the period in Co. Durham is in Conyers Chapel at **Sockburn** (NZ 3507). This is reached by taking the A167 S from Darlington for about 4m then turning E in Croft along a minor road. After about 4m (6·4 km), turn S in Neasham and continue to Sockburn some 2m (3·2 km) further on. Once there, there are twenty-five stones to see, of which the most important is a cross-shaft ultimately of Mercian inspiration. It displays Jellinge-style beasts combined with purely Saxon frets and cable patterns.

   The isolation of this site is rivalled by that of the church of St Andrew at **Bolam** (NZ 2023) where there is a good example of a Late Saxon tower with side-alternate quoins. It can be found by taking the A68 NW out of Darlington for about 10m (16 km) and turning W along a minor road, crossing the B6275. The tower has very tall belfry windows, lower down than usual, and a range of

Saxon windows both below and above the belfry. Only the SW quoin of the original nave is now visible from the outside. The NW quoin can be seen inside the vestry.

Bywell (NZ 0461) has the distinction of having two churches of Anglo-Saxon origin. Since it is within a short distance of Hexham and Corbridge, which are described next and are of importance, it can be used as the focus of a short itinerary of the remains near Newcastle. The village lies about 12m (19·3 km) W of the city on the A695, and near the entrance to Bywell Hall is the more impressive of the two Saxon buildings, St Andrew's church. Much early English work obscures the Late Saxon work in the tower and W parts of the nave. However, notice the fine side-alternate quoining and the Saxon window in the W face under the belfry, the belfry windows themselves and the three circular windows above them in each face. In the S face a large door with stripwork opens out under the belfry and although the W quoins of the nave are intact there is little of interest from the period inside the church.

The church of St Peter at Bywell, on the other hand, has work of at least two centuries earlier than those at St Andrew's, possibly from the eighth century. They are less extensive however – only the chancel and N walls of the nave are this old. The church stands within sight of St Andrew's. The massive side-alternate quoin in the SE (in the organ chamber) and one in the NE between the N chapel and the vestry, prove its age. Four round-headed windows in the N wall and the general proportions of the building complete the evidence for an early date. The W parts of the chancel have been shown to be Saxon, since they are bonded to the nave, and a blocked door with Escomb-fashion jambs can be seen in the N wall. Vestiges of a gable line above indicate that this almost certainly led to an annexe.

Only 4m (6·4 km) NW of Bywell, on the A69 from Hexham to Newcastle, is **Corbridge**, much more famous for its well-preserved Roman fort than for the church of St Andrew (NZ 9864) in the village centre. It was from the Roman fort that much of the building material for the church was brought – the W porch and nave walls date from the seventh or eighth century and are almost entirely composed of Roman material. It is known that the church existed in the eighth century and it may have been connected with Wilfrid's abbey at Hexham. Some centuries later the Saxons raised the porch to its present height as a tower. Fragments of walls lead off this to the W indicating the presence of buildings to this side of the original porch. An original door, now partly blocked by a later window, is to be seen in the W with an arch above it. The arch could have been used to relieve pressure when the tower was added, or it may have been decorative. About 13 feet (3·96 metres) above ground is a small round-headed window. The E side of the tower is interesting since it contains a doorway at a high level which must have led into the gabled W end of the church. Above the clock is a Saxon window. The original W wall of the nave projects each side of the tower like buttresses.

Inside the church notice the small Saxon window above the Saxon W door, and the heads of two windows above the arcade in the N of the nave. The tower arch is of exceptional interest since the stones are reused from Roman times – the N impost even retains the moulding from when it left the legionary workshop.

Corbridge church is thus well worth a visit, especially in conjunction with the abbey church of St Andrew at **Hexham** (NY 9364), a mere 3m (4·8 km) further W on the A69. This stands to the W of the market place and is indisputably connected with St Wilfrid who was abbot of Ripon from about 660 and bishop of York in 669, during which term of office he built the churches at both Hexham and Ripon. The crypts of these churches are still very similar. Wilfrid's successor Acca, bishop of Hexham, is known to have 'ennobled' the church, presumably adding embellishments and furnishings. The church is thus clearly datable to the eighth century, and from this period the crypt and a large number of fragmentary pieces of evidence remain. Many parts of the original building have been found over the years, but are not now visible. Others are still to be seen, the most outstanding feature being the crypt closely comparable to that at Ripon. A steep flight of stairs (nearly all original) leads into the barrel-vaulted room only 5 feet by 9 feet (1·52 × 2·74 metres). The main room leads off this and is 8 feet by 14 feet (2·44 × 4·24 metres), and it was in this inner area that the relic would have been housed. Originally a passage led eastwards from the ante-chapel and emerged at the top of thirteen steps which are now obscured under the NW pier of the crossing. A further passage led to a smaller chamber and eventually connected with the main body of the church. It is interesting that the walls of this, the finest Anglo-Saxon crypt in the country, are composed of Roman stones. The most notable of these are two with inscriptions. In a doorway of the passage to the right is a Roman altar inscribed to Apollo and his rare British counterpart, Maponus. The other refers to a tumultuous period of Roman history, since it is one of the inscriptions that originally contained the name of Geta, brother of Caracalla, and son of the Emperor Septimius Severus who died at York. After Geta's murder, his brother, by then Emperor, ordered that his name should be erased from every public monument in the Empire. The crypt at Hexham thus has evidence of just this act of brotherly hatred in about AD 211.

Three niches in the main room of the crypt have sunken cavities to take oil lamps; the main room has one of these as well as a ventilation shaft to the nave. In the nave itself there are some Saxon remains. Near the SE corner of the crossing are some irregularly shaped flat slabs of flooring and the southern 5 feet (1·5 metres) of the crossing step are almost certainly of the original foundation. The apse of the original church can be seen through a trap door in the floor of the present chancel, and immediately to the right is the tomb of St Acca. The west wall may be that of St Wilfrid's church – above the thirteenth-century plinth and easily distinguishable from the better dressed modern stones. These Saxon stones can be recognized by their Roman tooling since they were reused – there are twelve stones in the four bottom courses, and fifteen stones above these were probably a Saxon rebuilding of Wilfrid's church.

The N wall of the nave, too, contains early work. Outside, the bottom two courses for most of the length, and one course for the rest, can be assumed to belong to Wilfrid's church. It has been argued that the apse was not part of the original church, but a separate chapel which was eventually incorporated into the church, in a manner similar to the plan found at St Augustine's, Canterbury.

The sculptures at Hexham are of great interest – the most important in Northumberland are found here in the Abbey. The most notable is Acca's Cross, which dates from the Golden Age of Northumbria in about 740, although it is not as accomplished as the crosses at Bewcastle or Ruthwell. It has a runic inscription, but since this is now difficult to read it is not possible to say for sure whether the cross is indeed that which is recorded as being set up as a memorial to Acca. The decoration is inhabited vinescroll and although the cross was broken in the Middle Ages, it has now been restored and stands in the S transept. Two other crosses at Hexham have been claimed at one time or another as being Acca's, but they are now usually known as Hexham 2 and 3. The former has a Crucifixion panel on the central part of the shaft and the latter has a panel of vinescroll ornament. These stones represent the Hexham school of Northumbrian sculpture, which seems to have been a new school introduced to the area from the east. There is a large number of carved stones, string courses, columns and imposts, window heads, screens, pilasters and part of a Rood with a large variety of decorations which are to be seen and enjoyed in the Abbey, and from which some of the reconstructions of the original building have been deduced.

Before leaving the church notice the Frith Stool which stands just inside the choir. Although this could be as late as the ninth century, it has long been associated with St Wilfrid himself, and has been used as a Sanctuary Chair. It is a tub-shaped block with a plait on top of the arms and a Solomon's knot towards the back. It is also supposed to have been used as the coronation seat of the kings of Northumbria.

It is worth taking the A69 to reach the church of St Mary at **Ovingham** (NZ 0863), which lies just S of the main road (and should not be confused with Ovington nearby), 6m (9·7 km) E of Corbridge. Adjacent is Prudhoe Castle. Of the church, all the tower under the parapet is Saxon, and visitors should notice the Late Saxon belfry windows with tympana above. A door high up and a window on the lower face in the S, and a window in the W face are all original. It is probable that parts of the nave above the later arcades are Saxon, but the only direct evidence for this is that the original W quoins of the nave are still attached to the tower, and, since the walls continue this line, they can be assumed to be Saxon. Inside, the tower and nave are connected by a door at first-floor level.

Another good example of a Saxon tower belongs to St Michael's church, **Warden** (NY 9166), 3m (4·8 km) NW of Hexham and approached by the A69 from there and then a minor road N after about 3m (4·8 km). It is known that St John of Beverley came to Warden several centuries before this church was built in the tenth or eleventh centuries, and that he used to meditate in a building at or near the site. In the eighteenth century drastic rebuilding took place, so the belfry is not the original. The plinth around the W nave walls and parts of the N wall denote the limitations of the Saxon walls above. In the tower three windows have survived – one halfway up the W face and two in the S face. The original W wall of the nave projects about 2½ feet (0·76 metres) each side of the tower.

One of the most important pieces of sculpture in Northumbria is the Rothbury Cross, now in pieces. The head is in the Black Gate

Museum in Newcastle but a portion of the shaft is in All Saints Church **Rothbury** (NU 0602), which is reached by following the B6341 SW from Alnwick. The cross dates from around 800 and is in excellent style, only a little inferior to that at Bewcastle. Apart from the inhabited vinescroll, it has biting beasts and a lion. There is a representation of the Ascension in Carolingian style, and this is the earliest representation of this theme in English art.

For those wishing to see a fine example of a standing cross the Bewcastle Cross is a must. It stands in a churchyard in a desolate northern landscape at the W end of Hadrian's Wall. **Bewcastle** (NY 5675) is reached by hill roads from the B6318, and lies about 9m (14·5 km) due N of Brampton. In Roman times there was a fort at Bewcastle – traces of it can be seen in front of the church. This cross, despite its importance, is perhaps the most overrated monument artistically in Dark Age Britain, and its reputation rests on the fact that, along with the superior Ruthwell Cross, it represents the first flowering of Insular sculpture in the post-Roman period. It is a Northumbrian work produced in the Golden Age, in the first flush of enthusiasm for classical art that resulted from the conversion of the Northumbrians to the Roman faith and the many missions to Rome by personalities such as Benedict Biscop. It stands 14½ feet (4·42 metres) high, a headless column of sandstone decorated with panels depicting, in descending order, John the Baptist, Christ in Majesty and St John the Evangelist, and a panel of inhabited vinescroll on the back. The sides carry panels of ornament with interlace, chequer patterns and animals. Like the Ruthwell Cross, the Bewcastle Cross has extensive runic inscriptions, the interpretation of which has been the subject of some debate; it tells a poem in Northumbrian dialect, and also may refer to Alcfrith who died in 709. It has been suggested that it was erected by Wilfrid, perhaps in the 680s. It lacks the pleasing classicism of Ruthwell, and the vigour of later Northumbrian work. Like Wilfrid, it is uncompromising and uninspired.

Further to the west in Cumbria, no examples of Anglo-Saxon architecture survive, nor are there any Celtic sites visible. There are, however, a number of important sculptures.

The Gosforth Cross is one of the finest Late Saxon crosses to survive anywhere. Dating from the later tenth century, it stands nearly 15 feet (4·57 metres) high in the churchyard of St Mary in the village of **Gosforth** (NY 0703), which lies on the A595 some 9m (14·5 km) N of Ravenglass. It has a long slender shaft, round at the

70 The Bewcastle Cross

71 The Gosforth Cross

bottom, square further up, with a small ring-head. It is decorated
with figural work, including Christ with arms upstretched and two
figures below, one with a lance. Interlaced beasts and ring-chain
decorate sections of the rest of the shaft, along with other figural
work including horsemen. Some scenes may relate to Scandinavian
mythology, and the general style of the cross is Danish. The ring-
chain echoes that of Gaut in the Isle of Man. Inside the church are
two fine hog-backed tombstones, one with a battle-scene, one with a
crucifix, combined with Urnes-style ornament. A further fragment
of a cross-shaft shows a biting dragon, and there is a sculpture with
two men in a boat with fishes and three further cross heads to be
seen.

   Related to this cross are two at **Penrith** (NY 5130) in the heart of
the Lake District and reached conveniently from turn-off 40 on the
M6. The two are known as the Giant's Grave and stand near the N
wall outside the parish church in the centre of the town. The W
cross is over 11 feet (3·36 metres) high with interlace and a tiny
head. The E cross is slightly shorter and has a figure of a woman
with a serpent above and a Lamb of God. It, too, has interlace. The

72 Penrith, Giant's Grave and Giant's Thumb

extent of the deterioration of the crosses in the last half-century due
to polluted atmospheric conditions can be seen by comparing them
with the drawings on display in the church. Like the Gosforth Cross
these are distinctively Cumbrian, though the model is the 'Peak
Decorated' round shafts of Mercia. They both date from around
1000. Near them are four sides of hogback coffins. In the same
churchyard to the NW of the W tower is the Giant's Thumb, a
rather picturesquely named wheel-headed cross in Anglian tradition.

In the church of St Peter at **Heversham** (SD 4983) the late ninth-
century cross-shaft has inhabited vinescroll in a somewhat coarser
style than that encountered at Bewcastle. The church can be reached
on the A6 about 2m (3·2 km) S of Levens.

At **Irton** (SD 1000), just E of the A595 at Holmrook and about
6m (9·7 km) N of Ravenglass, the church of St Paul boasts an
exceptional cross with its head intact. It stands in the churchyard,
ten feet high. There are vinescrolls on the side panels, but on the
front and back are interlace, fret and step patterns, as well as petal-
pattern rosettes in Irish style.

Cross Canonby (NY 0739) offers a variety of sculptures. Turn N
off the A596 at Crosby, 2m (3·2 km) N of Maryport. The sculptures
are in the Norman church of St John the Evangelist. One is a section
of cross-shaft with individual biting dragons, with a Jellinge-style
dragon of the tenth century on one edge. A coffin lid with a cross
and a human figure may be Anglo-Danish. Outside the church is an
Anglo-Danish hogback.

At **Kirkby Stephen** (NY 7808) on the A685 5m (8 km) S of
Brough, the church of St Stephen has one important piece of
sculpture – part of an Anglo-Danish cross-shaft with interlace and a
bound figure, the 'Bound Devil'. It dates from the tenth century.
There are other, smaller, fragments by the tower arch, and a
hogback tombstone on the W side of the north aisle.

Dearham (NY 0736) lies S of the A596, 2m (3·2 km) E of
Maryport. The church of St Mungo is Norman, and contains a fine
collection of stones. The largest is a wheel-headed cross of tenth-
century date, decorated with interlace. Another, known as the
Kenneth Cross, has interesting figural work, comprising a mounted
horseman, a bird and man confronted and interlace. A third has a
runic inscription, rosettes, three standing figures holding hands
under arches, a quatrefoil, a cross, and a bearded head upside down
in a semicircle. Upside down below that is the name ADAM.

At attractively named **Aspatria** (NY 1542), on the A596 about 8m

(12·9 km) NE of Maryport, hogbacks and other sculptures are housed in the church of St Kentigern, who was the first bishop of Glasgow (c. 518–603), and who is also known as Mungo ('dear friend'). The stones include a section of tenth-century cross-shaft with interlace, two fragments of another, a copy of the Gosforth cross in the churchyard, and seven small fragments in the vestry and one in the exterior N wall. The most famous, however, is the hogback coffin-lid with a rich decoration of interlace and animal ornament. This coffin had a tegulated roof.

There is an important ninth-century cross at **Dacre** (NY 4626) in the church of St Andrew, lying about 4m (6·4 km) SW of Penrith; it can be reached by a minor road S of the A66. The cross shaft has a depiction of a human-faced animal. Adjacent is another, tenth-century, cross with Adam and Eve (the head is missing).

Lancashire has very few Dark Age remains. The most notable are a series of crosses from the north of the county. In the church of St Wilfred at **Halton** (SD 5065) a number of cross fragments can be seen and an outstanding reconstructed cross is in the churchyard. Halton lies about 5m (8 km) S of Carnforth, and can be reached by minor roads off the A6 or A683 and from turn-off 34 from the M6. The cross dates from the eleventh century and is in Anglo-Danish style, with Evangelists' symbols and scenes from the Sigurd cycle, as well as the Resurrection and a possible Crucifixion. It also displays interlace.

The Whalley Bridge cross is the best of three to be seen in the churchyard of St Mary's church in the village of **Whalley** (SD 7336), reached by the A59 or A671 and lying about 4m (6·4 km) S of Clitheroe. It dates from the early eleventh century and has more in common with Welsh crosses than Northumbrian.

In **Lancaster** (SD 4862) a collection of sculptures can be seen in the N chapel of the church of St Mary in the town centre. Like the other sculptures in the county they all date to late in the period. The earliest are fragments from a cross-shaft with vinescroll ornament; one shows Adam, Eve and the serpent; another is a cross-head fragment with Christ in a circle, and yet another has an inscription to someone called Hard, son of Cuthbert.

Liverpool seems an unlikely place to find Dark Age objects but the City Museum, William Brown St [10–5, Sun. 2–5] has one of the finest collections of Pagan Saxon antiquities in Britain, beautifully displayed in their new archaeological gallery. The collection comes from the excavations of the eighteenth-century antiquary, Bryan

Faussett, and was bought by the Liverpool collector Mayer in the nineteenth century. They include the Kingston Brooch (the finest gold and garnet disc brooch yet found), various other examples of Kentish polychrome jewellery, bracteates, beads and a variety of other objects. Notice, too, the gold medallion from St Martin's, Canterbury, with the name of bishop Liuhard, one of Augustine's followers.

Further north, overlooking Morecambe Bay, is **Heysham** (SD 4161) which possesses the only two Anglo-Saxon churches surviving in the county. Here on a promontory are the ruins of a small chapel built probably as early as the ninth century and traditionally associated with St Patrick. Of the original work the side-alternate quoins, part of a southern window and a rather crudely decorated south doorway are to be seen. Rock cut graves W of the ruins add to the rather mysterious atmosphere of the place

73 Kingston Brooch

74 St Patrick's Chapel, Heysham, Saxon arch

and are of uncertain date. The ruins seem to be those of a very
simple one-roomed building.

Below St Patrick's chapel is the church of St Peter, which also
dates from the eighth or ninth century in parts, despite later
extensive rebuilding. Under a buttress in the N wall of the nave,
rebuilding work discovered a blocked door which can now be seen
in the SW corner of the churchyard. The W wall is still original, as
are the ends of the S wall, and E wall above the chancel arch. The
blocked W door is the most notable feature and the W wall contains
a blocked square-headed window of uncertain date. Adjacent to the
church is a hogback tombstone and a section of a very remarkable
cross-shaft depicting a building not unlike the supposed original
appearance of St Patrick's chapel. It shows various busts in niches
and what may represent the raising of Lazarus. The rest of the
ornament is of foliage scrolls and it probably dates to the ninth
century.

The area that used to be the county of Yorkshire has many
things and places of interest from the Dark Ages, ranging from
sculptures to fine churches, and thus many itineraries can be
followed in the area.

The west of the county is particularly well endowed with sculptures and among the earliest are those at **Ilkley** (SE 1147). This lies on the A65 12m (19·3 km) NW of Bradford, and in the churchyard of All Saints three major crosses were re-erected in the nineteenth century. The shortest dates from about 800 and has a half-length figure of an angel and beasts in panels. The head now with it does not belong to it. The next dates from about 850, with pairs of intertwining beasts in panels and vinescroll ornament. The tallest and most important is also datable to about 850. It has Christ above beasts on the front, and the four evangelists' symbols on the back. The sides are adorned with vinescrolls. Further fragments can be seen in Ilkley museum.

The Anglo-Saxon nave of St Oswald's church at **Collingham** (SE 3946) was so heavily restored in the nineteenth century that it is not worth visiting for its Saxon architectural merit, but it does have two very interesting ninth-century crosses embedded in the S wall, which were found in 1840. The Apostles' Cross dates from the first half of the ninth century and has Christ and eleven apostles on it; the Aerswith Cross dates from the end of the same century and has beasts, dragons and runes on it. The church can be reached by following the A58 NE from Leeds for about 10m (16 km).

The church of All Saints, **Dewsbury** (SE 2325) shelters a variety of interesting sculptures. The finest is a ninth-century cross-shaft in three pieces. The fragments of the circular shaft show Christ seated near several other figures with IHS XRVS inscribed. A contemporaneous piece of another cross has the Virgin and Child under an arch on one side, and figural scenes illustrating the miracles on the others. Another early ninth-century fragment of a cross head is decorated with an angel. Other, later pieces have interlace, scrolls and figures. An Anglian-style hogbacked stone dates from the late ninth century.

A magnificent free-standing cross embellishes the churchyard of the parish church of **Leeds** Kirkgate (SE 3033), dedicated to St Peter. It is over 11 feet (3·35 metres) high and dates to the tenth or eleventh century. Front and back have figural work, including a depiction of Wayland Smith. The sides are ornamented with vinescroll.

An attractive though rather coarse and primitive little cross is displayed at St Peter's **Addingham** (SE 0749) on the A65 about 3m (4·8 km) W of Ilkley. Hewn in about the eleventh century, it is not without artistic merit. It shows two figures below a cross in a circle.

A bishop and a horned figure upside down were chosen by the

mason who carved a cross, now fragmentary, which is to be seen in the N transept of the church of All Saints at **Crofton** (SE 3817), about 3m (4·8 km) E of Wakefield on the B6378. This cross was carved in the eleventh century, possibly two centuries after the second cross fragment to be seen in the church, which has a more common decoration in the form of scrolls, interlace and two intertwined beasts.

At the intersection of the A660 and the A659 about 10m (16 km) NW of Leeds is the village of **Otley** (SE 2045) with a fine collection of seventeen pieces of Anglo-Saxon sculpture in All Saints' church. A very splendid ninth-century monument, with rich decoration of tiers of busts under arches and fine inhabited vinescroll in the best Northumbrian tradition, is now represented only by three sections of shaft and one piece of cross head. A section of another cross of the same period has a dragon in a panel with part of a figure under an arch beneath. The remaining fragments belong to the tenth or eleventh centuries and include cross heads and shafts with interlace. There is too a grave-slab of the eleventh century decorated with Viking-inspired Ringerike-style ornament.

About 6m W of Skipton, the church of St Peter at **West Marton** (SD 8950) on the A59 displays an exceptional cross fragment found at Scriven Park, with human figures and animals intertwined in interlace of Viking-derived type.

At **Thornhill** (SE 2518) there is a collection of ten cross fragments of the mid-ninth century. Four carry runic inscriptions naming the people who set them up. They are to be seen in St Michael's church, and Thornhill can be reached by the B6117 about a mile S of Dewsbury.

This collection of sculptures is completed by those at **Walton Cross** (SE 1822) which lies 4m (6·4 km) NW of Hartshead, to the W of the road near a farm and is visible from the road. Hartshead is reached by taking turn-off 25 from the M62, since it lies about 1m (1·6 km) E of the motorway and is connected to it by minor roads. The cross itself has not survived, but the base is exceptionally large and fine, with interlace, animals and plant ornament of the eleventh century.

The west of Yorkshire also boasts a number of structures well worth a visit. The most outstanding is that at **Ripon** (SE 3171), where the cathedral of St Peter possesses an eighth-century crypt, one of the finest in Britain and closely comparable to that at Hexham, since it too was built by St Wilfrid. It was at Ripon that

Wilfrid established his first monastery, and here that his body was brought first and buried south of the altar. Had the Scottish monks at Ripon not left rather than observe the Roman method of calculating Easter, Wilfrid might not have been sent here. (This was a problem that took up a great deal of debating time in the early Saxon church.) Of the monastery only the crypt remains – it is rather more simple than that at Hexham, having only two passages, one to the antechamber and one to the main room. As at Hexham, the walls have little recesses to take lamps. Ripon lies about 13m (20·8 km) N of Harrogate on the A61.

Bardsey (SE 3643) is a village 8m (12·9 km) NE of Leeds city centre, on the A58 to Wetherby, and is worth a visit to see the church of All Hallows which has fabric dating from the ninth century. In this century the W porch, as it was then, and the nave walls were built, and about a century later the porch was raised to the present tower. Later arcading has removed much of the nave walls and the chancel has been swept away for later building. The two builds of the tower are proved by the difference in the quoining which changes very obviously. There is, too, the line of the porch gable to be seen in the W face of the tower. The double belfry windows in the second and third stage of the S face are Saxon, with single windows in the E.

Inside, the external walls of the original porch (lower part of the tower) can be seen from the aisles; two doors cut through its N and S walls with a window above each. Also to be seen from inside the church are the large side-alternate quoins of the original nave.

An almost complete nave dating from the seventh or eighth century is found in the church of All Saints, **Ledsham** (SE 4529). The lower parts of the W tower are of the same date, too, though there have been many later additions. Ledsham lies about a mile W of the A1, reached by a minor road opposite the junction with the A63, some 5m (8 km) N of Pontefract. Restoration in 1871 left the S and W walls of the nave almost intact, and all the quoins except that at the NE angle are visible to prove the antiquity of the walls between. The original windows of the nave are blocked – there four in the N wall above the arcades and one in the S wall with two partly destroyed windows in this wall, too, near the remains of a door above the medieval S door.

The tower was originally a porch that was put up slightly later than the nave – the evidence for this is a gable line in the clock room. There are two windows in the S face dating from this period, and inside a Saxon window cuts through the wall above the tower arch. The S porch is an original feature, though it has medieval alterations. The top half of the S doorway from the nave to the S porch exists – it was a remarkably tall narrow entrance – 14 feet (4·27 metres) high and only 2 feet (0·61 metres) wide.

St Wilfrid of Ripon turns up again at **Monk Fryston** (SE 5029), as the saint to whom the parish church was dedicated. If you have just been to Ledsham, only 4m (6·4 km) due W of this village, take the minor road to meet the A1, cross this and follow the A63 to Monk Fryston. Here you will see the W tower which was put up in the very latest period of building before the Norman Conquest. The belfry is post-Saxon. The Saxon parts of the tower are distinguishable by their side-alternate quoins, which are obscured in part by later buttresses. Three Saxon belfry windows are visible above the string course. There is a fourth (modified), now visible only from inside the nave.

Kirk Hammerton (SE 4655) lies just S of the A59 midway between Harrogate and York, and the church of St John the Baptist has a very early nave and chancel (possibly seventh or eighth century), with a tenth-century W tower of which the W door might be even later in the period. The walls have been removed by later work, but all six quoins of nave and chancel survive: those to the north visible in the nineteenth-century nave.

The W tower has Saxon belfry windows and is very similar to the simple towers of Lincolnshire. The only other lights are two narrow slits in the S, W and N, and a door in the W face. The more elaborate plinth that runs round the tower, in contrast to the simpler plinth of the nave, is the evidence for dating the tower later. On the exterior of the nave the S door, albeit heavily restored, is Saxon. A blocked door of uncertain function is visible to the E of this door inside.

The tower arch is an unusual horseshoe shape and has traces of a small doorway above. The chancel arch is elaborate but has been badly mutilated – during construction of the nave in the nineteenth century it was cut away on the N side and supported by a beam in 1834. It was not restored to its present position until 1891. The sole evidence for any windows inside are the faint traces of a blocked round-headed window in the S wall of the chancel, also visible from the exterior.

Further along the A59 to the E is **York** (SE 5951) itself, which, despite its important excavations that have discovered much about the Saxon and Viking town, has little to offer the visitor in the way of ruins from these periods. A fine collection of finds, however, is housed in the Yorkshire Museum [10–5, Sun. 1–5], including the Ormside bowl, a silver bowl from Westmorland with a lining of copper gilt, probably buried in a Viking grave at the end of the tenth century. The bowl itself shows Continental influence in its animal ornament. A number of interesting sculptures have been collected together in the grounds of the Yorkshire Philosophical Society in the Hospitium [Easter–Sept. only]. Other Viking grave-slabs found in recent excavations are to be put on display in the museum which is to be opened in the undercroft of York Minster. The Yorkshire Museum has recently opened a display of finds from the new excavations of the Viking remains.

One structure in York is unique in British Dark Age archaeology. This is the Anglian Tower, which can be seen on the Roman fortress wall. To reach it, walk from the Yorkshire Museum to the famous Roman Multangular Tower, and from here follow the wall past the fragmentary remains of a Roman interval tower to the Anglian Tower itself, a barrel-vaulted edifice which blocks a gap in the Roman defences. Its date is disputed, but it must be after AD 400 and before 870. The Roman defences can be seen behind it. Particular notice should be paid to the round-headed arch in the tower, constructed not with a through-stone but with individual voussoirs.

The only ecclesiastical offering of note is St Mary Bishophill Junior (SE 6051) where the west tower is very Late Saxon. This church is found on the corner of Bishophill near Priory Street. As might be expected, since York was a principal Roman fortress, many Roman bricks and tiles can be seen in the fabric of this building. The quoins are side-alternate and the four double belfry windows are outlined in stripwork – a feature of more northerly churches (the window itself in the W side has been replaced later). The masonry changes at the medieval parapet. The best feature of this tower is the internal arch which is exceptionally fine.

The best sculpture in this part of Yorkshire is without doubt the **Nunburnholme** Cross (SE 8548), which is in the church of St James at Nunburnholme, reached by side roads N of the A1079, about 3m (4·8 km) E of Pocklington. Dating from around 950, it has been restored from two pieces. It appears to have been the work of two sculptors, and shows both Danish and earlier Anglian influence. The figural work includes scenes from Scandinavian mythology, including the eating of the dragon's heart by Sigurd. The figures in arches on the upper portion of the cross include a pleasing Virgin and Child.

After Nunburnholme, the remaining sculpture is relatively unimpressive. The most interesting is that at **Folkton** (TA 0679), just N of the A1039 about 5m (8 km) W of Filey. There are, in fact, several sculptures in the W wall of the tower of the church of St John Evangelist, but the best is a cross-shaft with intertwining dragons that dates from the early eleventh century and represents a development of the Nunburnholme type of beast.

At **North Frodingham** (TA 1053) on the B1249, about 5m (8 km) E of Great Driffield, a cross head can be seen in the church of St Elgin, which lies about ½m (0·8 km) W of the village. It is a wheel-headed cross, with Danish-style animal ornament related to that on the Nunburnholme cross. It dates from the tenth century.

Aldbrough (TA 2438), on the B1242 7m (11·3 km) S of Hornsea, has in the church of St Bartholomew a Saxon sundial with an interesting inscription: translated, it is a dedication to 'Ulf who ordered this church to be built for his own and Gunware's souls'. It can be seen in the N wall of the S aisle.

Unique in Dark Age Britain is the door at **Stillingfleet** (SE 5941) in the church dedicated to St Helen. It now serves as the S door of the church, and stands inside a very fine Norman arch of *c*. 1160. The door itself is, however, either earlier, or represents a long survival in this area of Danish traditions. The ironwork on the door includes a depiction of a Viking ship, which should be of the eleventh century. The N door also displays ironwork, but nothing as distinctive. Stillingfleet lies on the B1222, about 7m (11·3 km) S of York.

In east Yorkshire the village of **Wharram le Street** (SE 8665), within 1m (1·6 km) of the splendid view to be gained from Grimston Hill and situated on the B1248 about 6m (9·7 km) SE of Malton, has St Mary's church with its Late Saxon architectural features. Rebuilding in the fourteenth century has not drastically changed the church plan. The foundations of the rebuilt chancel and the standing parts of the nave (the E and W walls, and E part of the N wall) are believed to be original. The tower has four Late Saxon belfry windows and there are two other Saxon windows in the S and W. A blocked door to the nave is visible from inside the tower, above the tower arch which, like the W door, shows Norman features.

Travellers moving E along the A163 from Selby to Market Weighton will be well rewarded by turning N along a minor road about 3m (4·8 km) NE of Selby until, after another mile or so, they reach **Skipwith** (SE 6538). This village has the church of St Mary, with the lower part of its tower and W areas of the nave which could be as early as the eighth or even the seventh centuries. The tower was given an additional storey, perhaps in the eleventh century. Note the plinth and string course of the tower, and the slight indications that the upper stage of the Saxon tower had its windows blocked to strengthen the fabric before the perpendicular belfry was added later. A corbel will be seen to project under the string course in the W face and below it two courses of stones project decoratively.

There are two Saxon windows in the lowest stage of the tower and three at a higher level. Inside, the tower arch is interesting, since the gap between hood moulds and arch proper is infilled by normal walling. A blocked door can be seen above, and in the tower itself is a recessed rectangular panel of unknown function.

North Yorkshire has a number of churches of Saxon note, of which that dedicated to St Peter at **Hackness** (SE 9690) can be reached by following the A170 to the SW out of Scarborough for about 3m (4·8 km), and then turning N through the Forge Valley for a further 3m (4·8 km) along a minor road. The abbess Hilda of Whitby is recorded by Bede as having built a monastery at Hackness in 680. The nave of St Peter's, however, is rather later than this, probably of the ninth century. The monastery is now no longer standing. The most interesting Dark Age features of the church are to be found inside – two fragments of early windows are visible in the S wall above the arcade (one can be seen from the aisle). The chancel arch is an intact example of Saxon workmanship with one impost carved with a pattern of interlaced creatures. This had been dated by its style to the late eighth century, but there is no reason to date the church this early since the stone could easily have been reused. Three of the quoins of the nave survive.

75 Hackness, decorated impost on chancel arch

The church of All Saints at **Appleton le Street** (SE 7373) on the B1257 3m (4·8 km) W of Malton has a W tower and nave walls which can be dated to about the tenth or early eleventh century.

There are the W quoins of the nave to note near the tower, and side-alternate quoins of the tower itself, which is broken by string courses. In the lower stage of the tower a blocked door once led through the S face and the W door was later blocked to form a window. Square-headed windows once lit the N, W and S faces higher up, and a circular window in the E has been cut from a single stone. Four large double belfry windows light the second stage with four smaller windows above. The third stage of the tower is almost certainly very Late Saxon, though not actually post-Conquest, while the lower parts are earlier.

At **Masham** (SE 2381), on the A6108 about 8m (12·9 km) NW of Ripon, there are both sculptures and the church of St Mary itself of Saxon interest. As the sculptures suggest, the W, E and N walls of this nave could be as early as the seventh or eighth century, on the tentative ground that there is nothing in it that could not be this early. The Norman tower clearly was put up later than the rest of the nave, and there is side-alternate quoining. A string course runs along the north wall of the aisle – originally it would have been on the outside of the Saxon church. The sculptures are more interesting, perhaps, and are to be found in the churchyard. The most important is a cross-shaft probably carved in the ninth century and showing Mercian influence. It carried figures in four zones set within arcades. The bottom row of figures are animals in the Breedon tradition (p. 125), the second and third rows illustrate an unidentified legend, and in the fourth zone there are twin figures in each arcade. An interlaced cross fragment of lesser note is housed in the church.

The cross shaft at **Croft** (NZ 2909) is one of the most splendid in Yorkshire. It is displayed in the N chapel of the medieval church of St Peter, next to the River Tees and the village bridge. The village lies on the A167 3m (4·8 km) S of Darlington. The cross dates from the ninth century and can be compared with the famous Easby Cross in the Victoria and Albert Museum. It has very lively vinescroll ornament.

The church of All Saints at **Pickhill** (SE 3584) lies 1m (1·6 km) E off the A1, about 11m (17·6 km) N of Boroughbridge. In the tower there are two sculptures; the first is in Anglo-Danish style, dating from the tenth century, and depicts a dragon in an interlace pattern. The second is a hogback tombstone of the same period terminating in a boar's head, like those at Brompton, and a further fragment with a human figure on it.

Middleton (SE 7885) is about 1m (1·6 km) W of Pickering on the A170 and well worth a visit, for the church of St Andrew has a late Saxon west tower, W walls of the nave and possibly side walls, too, and the western quoins of a narrower and earlier nave still to be seen. The evidence for this is the plinth on the tower, the string course, the mutilated W doorway with Anglian cross above and two windows in the S face, two windows in the N face. The original wall of the nave projects each side of the tower. In addition, it possesses several Anglo-Danish crosses now in the church. The best are wheel-headed and date from the tenth century. One bears a figure standing facing ahead with a spear, axe, sword and shield. A second has a hunter with his dog beneath. On the back of each is a dragon and both have interlace on their sides. A further cross has a wheel head and ornament of interlace. Two further fragments are of a crude cross head and a cross-shaft with a seated figure.

At **Ellerburn** (SE 8385) in a valley which lies 1½m (2·4 km) N of Thornton Dale which itself lies 2m (3·2 km) E of Pickering on the A170, are several Anglo-Danish sculptures in the church of St Hilda. The best is a cross head and part of the shaft of a cross, decorated with a Jellinge-style dragon. Built into the porch wall is a further cross head, along with a small fragment decorated with two figures.

The sculpture at **Melsonby** (NZ 1908) can be reached by a minor road to the N off the A66 some 2m (3·2 km) W of Scotch Corner on the A1. Two pieces of grave slab are to be found in the church of St James, of which the most interesting dates to the ninth century. On one side is a human-headed animal rather like a camel, biting a serpent, with other creatures underneath. On the other are busts in oval depressions. The accomplished style is reminiscent of the sculptures at Breedon. This can be seen in the N aisle on the W side. The second sculpture is a cross fragment on the W side of the S aisle, with very fine interlace.

Kirkdale (SE 6787) can be reached from the A170, about 8m (12·9 km) W of Pickering and 4m (6·4 km) E of Helmsley, by side roads running N from the main road. The church of St Gregory is famous for its Anglo-Saxon sundial above the S doorway. The inscription in translation reads, *Orm, son of Gamal, acquired the church of St Gregory when it was tumbled and ruined, and had it rebuilt from the ground in honour of Christ and St Gregory, in the days of Edward the King and Tosti the earl.* Tosti was the brother of King Harold, and thus the date of the church can be fixed as lying between 1055 and 1065. Of the Saxon work, only the nave survives, but the early sculptures from the site now in the church bear out the tradition of an earlier church rebuilt by Tosti. The most interesting features are the W doorway, with an elaborate W face, and the chancel arch jambs. Local tradition associates the church with St Cedd, a seventh-century cleric, there is nothing to suggest quite such an early date for the building; in fact, the nave seems to date from the very latest period before the Conquest. The dating has been fixed by the sundial rather than any other features – the W quoins of the nave are side-alternate.

A number of sculptures in the church are notable. There are two decorated coffin lids, the earlier perhaps of the early eighth century and decorated with a cross and scrolls. The other, which dates from the tenth century, carries interlace. A late cross with a large crucifixion on it, another (damaged) cross with interlace, and several fragments complete the collection.

At **Kirby Hill** (SE 3968) the church of All Saints has a nave perhaps built in the ninth century. It lies just E of the B6265, about 2m (3·2 km) N of Boroughbridge. Various Dark Age stones have been built into the walls, presumably from an earlier church on the site, but perhaps brought from nearby Ripon. The most interesting feature is the S doorway, within which the later medieval door has been set. The S face of the impost of this arch has a fine interlace and it also carries vinescroll, in ninth-century style. It could, however, have been brought from Ripon and reused in the door. Notice the side-alternate quoins, and the fact that some of the building material was reused from earlier Saxon building – the upside down monolithic head of a window is to be seen in the S wall.

The church of Holy Trinity at **Stonegrave** (SE 6578) can be reached on the B1257, about 10m (16 km) NW of Malton. It displays a variety of sculptures, the most interesting being a fine tenth-century cross with interlace ornament and wheel-head. Figures

76 Kirby Hill, decorated impost of s doorway

peep out from the interlace. The stone it stands on is a thirteenth-century graveslab, but this in turn is resting on an Anglo-Danish slab with interlace and a figure shooting a dragon. Two further fragments are of a tenth-century cross-shaft; two others, one with a listening figure, may belong to the ninth. There are three fragments of hogback gravestones, which complete this interesting collection. Parts of the church are Late Saxon or Saxo-Norman.

Two miles (3·2 km) S of Stonegrave on the B1257 lies **Hovingham** (SE 6775), where the church of All Saints boasts a Late Anglo-Saxon tower and an outstanding sculptured slab. The tower of this church has escaped the restorers who left little in the nineteenth century of the nave and chancel. The tower is partly built from reused stone. (The Hovingham slab was one of these stones until it was moved earlier this century to protect it from the weather.) It is probably the work of the eleventh century, and is divided into three stages by string courses. On the W face, in the third course of stones below the first string course, there is a cross-decorated slab of the ninth century in the same style as that at Middleton. The W doorway of the tower is very sophisticated, with a rounded arch and fine moulding. The windows include tall, narrow, double belfry openings in each of the faces of the third stage of the tower; the unusually narrow heads are each cut in a separate square stone. The Hovingham stone now acts as a reredos to the altar in the S aisle, and dates probably from the eighth century. It was probably an altar frontal originally, and measures 5 feet 5 inches (1·64 metres) wide and 2 feet 1 inch (0·6 metres) high. It has eight arched panels containing nimbate figures – the first two panels represent the Annunciation. This arcade runs above a frieze of inhabited vinescroll. It is similar in many ways to the Hedda stone in Peterborough, and to some of the Breedon carvings.

Brompton by Northallerton (SE 3896) lies about a mile N of Northallerton, just off the A684. It is famous for its amazing collection of hogback tombstones, which can be seen (excluding those now in the Durham Cathedral library) in the church of St Thomas. Three are extremely well-preserved, and terminate in bears sitting up facing one another, grasping the tombstone between their paws. Apart from these, which date from the tenth century, there is an Anglo-Danish cross, complete with head, and a further, similar, cross-shaft in the nave, along with a ninth-century cross-shaft with figures, scroll, cocks and beetle-like men. Adjacent are three wheel-heads from crosses.

A very important cross is now divided between two churches on either side of the boundary between the North and West Ridings. The larger portion is at **Cundall** (SE 4273), reached by side-roads from the A1 or A168 and lying about 7m (11·3 km) due E of Ripon. The cross-shaft stands under the tower of the church of St Mary and All Saints. It dates from around 800, and has Breedon-style fret patterns and long-legged beasts as well as vinescroll ornament. It shows Wessex influence, and can be compared with the Masham pillar. It also displays figural work. The other portion is at **Aldborough** (SE 4166), about ½m (0·8 km) out of Boroughbridge travelling S on a side road. It is in the church, which itself lies inside the Roman town of Isurium.

The seventeen stones at **Kirk Leavington** (NZ 4309) can all be seen in the porch of St Martin's church, and are remarkable for their diversity. All date probably from the Anglo-Danish period. Note particularly the little figure with a kilt and helmet standing between two birds, and the two beast-headed men. Kirk Leavington can be reached on the A19, about 7m (11·3 km) S of Stockton-on-Tees. (It is also called Kirklevington on maps.)

Scotland

Southern Scotland, which was occupied by Britons and later Angles, has most of its Dark Age remains concentrated in the fertile lands of Dumfries, Galloway and the Lothians. Much of the Southern Uplands must have been as unattractive to settlers in the Dark Ages as at other periods, and the more suitable areas for settlement, such as the Firth of Clyde, have lost all traces of their Dark Age occupants beneath urban development in Glasgow, Paisley Motherwell and Airdrie. In the south-east, the Cheviots were an obstacle to intensive settlement, though some Dark Age remains are to be found in the Tweed valley. The main monuments of the period in southern Scotland comprise hillforts with evidence of Dark Age occupation, and an assortment of sculptures, both Celtic and Anglian.

North of the Forth–Clyde line, the distribution of Dark Age remains is again dictated in some measure by geographical considerations. The areas richest in visible remains are the low-lying and comparatively fertile areas, notably Fife, Angus and parts of Perthshire on the one hand and the lower-lying parts of Aberdeenshire, Elgin and Nairn on the other. The Grampians and the North-West Highland range barred extensive settlement – they were even more densely forested in the Dark Ages – though Argyll and the Western Isles were more suited for settlement on account of their waterways. The monuments of northern Scotland are those of the Picts and the Scots, and comprise various types of forts and the rich series of Pictish sculptures. Ecclesiastical sites are scattered through both Lowland and Highland Scotland, but few can boast very impressive remains.

Starting in the south-west, picturesque and gentle Galloway has several sites of interest to the visitor.

Whithorn (NX 4440) [AM; S] is one of the most famous ecclesiastical sites in Scotland, though the ruins of the present priory are the work of the Premonstratensians in the thirteenth century. The Dark Age remains are associated with St Ninian, who according to the Venerable Bede built his *candida casa* there in the fifth century and was thus the first Christian to begin the conversion of the peoples of Scotland. Whithorn can be reached on the A746, 11m S of Wigtown.

A great deal of controversy has surrounded Ninian and Whithorn, but current opinion holds that he went to an already Christian community from the area round Carlisle. Excavations in 1965 found burials at the E end of the priory church that could date

from the time of Ninian, and in the same area in 1949 a roughly
built stone structure was uncovered which could have been built as
early as the eighth century.

Whithorn has produced a number of sculptured stones, which are
housed in the museum which stands on the road to the priory ('the
Pend') just before the entrance to the church.

One group of stones dates from the time of Ninian or slightly
later. The earliest is the Latinus Stone, which dates from the mid-
fifth century and has an inscription in twelve lines, reading,

TE DOMINU(m) LAVDAMVS LATINVS ANNORV(m) XXXV ET FILIA SVA
ANN(orum) IV (h)IC SI(g)NVM FECERUT NEPVS BARROVA DI
(*We praise thee Lord Latinus, of 35 years and his daughter of four
years. The grandson of Barrovadus set this up.*)

Adjacent to this is the Peter Stone, which, like the Latinus stone,
is a plain standing slab. It has an inscription reading,

(L)OCI PETRI APVSTOLI
(*The Place of Peter the Apostle*)

There is a wheel cross above, its arms made from the arcs of circles,
on a stem. This probably represents a *flabellum*, or processional
standard. It formerly stood by the side of the road near Whithorn,
and may have marked a chapel or graveyard dedicated to St Peter.
It dates perhaps from the seventh century, and the lettering implies
contact with Merovingian Gaul. It also suggests that by the seventh
century Whithorn had acquired some important relic of the saint.

A collection of cross-incised stones in the Whithorn museum
come from St Ninian's cave at Physgill (see p. 244). Such stones are
notoriously difficult to date, but they seem to range from the seventh
century to the later Middle Ages.

When Galloway was taken over by the Angles of Northumbria
around the middle of the seventh century the monastery was
reorganized under its new bishop, Pecthelm. The Whithorn museum
collection includes two cross shafts of this (Northumbrian) period,
decorated with interlace and dating from the ninth century.

The extensive influence of the Norse apparently left the monastery
unaffected, since it appears to have flourished, giving rise to an
important local school of sculpture, the Whithorn school (see
p. 47). The only complete example of the style in the collection is
that known as No. 7, which consists of a flat slab with disc head, the
arms of the cross being indicated by cut-out round holes. The

central boss and the shaft are decorated with rather monotonous interlace.

St Ninian's Cave (NX 4236) [AM;A] leads off the beach at Physgill, near Glasserton 2m (3·2 km) SW of Whithorn. It is reached by a side road from the A747, which goes as far as Physgill House; from there a walk of under a mile leads to the shore, where the site lies to the S. In 1871 the discovery of an early type of incised cross near the entrance to the cave on the rock face seemed to confirm the traditional association with Ninian. Excavations carried out in 1884 found a succession of floors in the cave as well as crosses on boulders and on the cave walls. All the occupation levels, however, post-dated Ninian, and the original Ninianic occupation, if there ever was one, had been destroyed by later activity. Some crosses executed with pecking can be seen behind grilles in the cave, and most date from the Dark Ages.

The extremely picturesque Luce Bay, pounded by northern rollers and backed by sand dunes, is the setting for the Dark Age monument of **Chapel Finian** (NX 2748) [AM;A], which lies on the A747, about 7m (11·3 km) N of Port William. The chapel overlooks the beach and lies sheltered by a hill, from which vantage point the ruins can be clearly viewed. The present ruined foundations of a rectangular stone chapel have buttresses which recall the *antae* of some Irish churches. The chapel is enclosed by a drystone wall running in an oval. There is a well, associated with the chapel, just inside the gate. The chapel was dedicated to St Findbar, and was probably an Irish foundation of the tenth or eleventh century.

At **Kirkmadrine** (NX 0848) [AM;A] a very important group of early inscribed stones are preserved in a glass fronted recess in the outside wall of the church, reached by the A716 and a side road running W from it ½m (0·8 km) S of Sandhead. Three of the Kirkmadrine stones date from the fifth century. The first is a gravemarker, inscribed in good Roman lettering

HIC IACENT S(an)C(t)I ET PRAECIPVI SACERDOTES IDES VIVENTIVS ET MAVORIVS
(*Here lie the holy and principal priests, Ides, Viventius and Mavorius*)

Above the inscription is an expanded arm cross in a circle, the top of which has a hook, which converts it into a chi-rho. The term *praecipui sacerdotes* means 'bishops' and implies a diocesan organization for the fifth-century church in Galloway.

The second stone is generally similar, but the inscription is now incomplete. It reads,

. . . S ET FLORENTIUS

The third stone has a thicker encircled cross and the inscription

INITIVM ET FINIS
(*The beginning and the end*)

This refers to Revelation, XXII, 13. It dates from around 600.

Dumfries and Galloway are proud possessors of several Dark Age citadels.

The **Mote of Mark** (NX 8454) at Rockcliffe on the Urr estuary is worth visiting. Take the A710 S of Dalbeattie for 5m (8 km), then turn down the side road to the coast from Lochend. The Mote of Mark is best approached through the fields by a path opposite the entrance to the Scots Baronial Baron's Craig Hotel. The site lies in National Trust land and is a part of Dalbeattie Forest. Round the summit there are traces of the much denuded rampart, and in the sheltered and much overgrown centre occupation was concentrated in the Dark Ages. The view from the summit is very worth the

77 The Mote of Mark

climb, with the bird sanctuary of Heston Isle and the Cumbrian hills in the distance.

The fort was excavated in 1913 and 1973. The re-excavation showed that its defences were entirely post-Roman. A timber-laced rampart was built, probably in the fifth century, with a gateway facing the estuary and opening on to the hollow, and with a postern on the W. The central hollow was cobbled over, the stones running up to a revetment on the rock – some of these can be seen exposed.

In this area metalworkers toiled, making objects in iron, bronze and brass – lead and gold may also have been worked. The most important finds were a series of clay moulds for making richly decorated bronze mounts with interlace and other patterns. Other finds included Dark Age imported pottery and glass of Germanic origin.

At some stage the fort was fired, causing the rampart to vitrify. The most recent Dark Age finds from the site were two Anglian inscriptions in runes, one on bone and one on stone, and some other objects of Anglian character datable to the seventh century.

Even more enigmatic than the Mote of Mark is the nearby stone-walled fort at **Castle Haven** (NX 5948), which can be reached by the B727 W from Kirkcudbright, and side roads from Borgue towards Kirkandrews. At Corseyard the site is visible from the road, and here it is necessary to leave the road and walk down to it on the foreshore. It was excavated in 1905 and was consolidated, the walls being partly rebuilt, but it is now heavily overgrown and it is not possible to see what is original and what is reconstruction. It shows features of many Highland duns – it is a D-shaped stone fort. A second D-shaped wall runs up to the dun on the N and W sides. The dun is of hollow-walled construction, with intra-mural galleries and two entrances. Near the main entrance stone slabs set on the inside wall probably served as stairs to the wall head. A secondary entrance gives access to steps down a natural cleft to the beach. There can be little doubt this is an iron age dun, reoccupied in the Dark Ages. Most of the finds were iron age in character, but a blue glass bead and a penannular brooch attest post-Roman occupation. The outer enclosure may be a stock compound of Dark Age date.

Very near Castle Haven is the ecclesiastical complex at **Ardwall Isle** (NX 5749). From Castle Haven the road should be followed to Knockbrex, where a side road leads down to the shore. The island can be reached easily on foot for a few hours at low tide, but do take care. Little can now be seen of the Early Christian site, which was excavated 1964–5. The main visible Dark Age remains consist of the vallum, a low bank with stone revetment which encloses an oval area on the shore of the island immediately facing the mainland, though much of its E part is now incorporated in a sheep wall. The remains are obscured by a medieval hall house and late eighteenth-century tavern on top of the ruins of the medieval church. Excavation showed the site was used as early as the sixth century AD, when a cemetery and possibly a shrine were associated with a timber oratory. This was replaced by a stone chapel around the eighth century, which was ruined by 1000, but the foundations of which were incorporated into the medieval building. The excavation was not backfilled, and several stones from the site can be seen in Dumfries Museum (see p. 249).

Ardwall is important as it is the only site in Scotland in which it is possible to demonstrate that a timber chapel was built before the construction of stone churches, and where the development of a shrine can be traced.

Trusty's Hill (NX 5856) lies on the W side of the Fleet estuary, about 1m (1·6 km) W of Gatehouse of Fleet on a side road off the A75 at Anwoth. The site can be reached by a footpath E of the cross-roads at Anwoth. Like the Mote of Mark, it is a small vitrified fort, fortified on the S and NE sides. In the iron age a wall was built on the hilltop with a bank and ditch cutting off the NE approach and a guard hut. Later, probably in the Dark Ages, a series of outlying ramparts were built and the original fort entrance was extended with out-turned banks. These later works, with outer revetment and rubble behind, are typical of Dark Age dump ramparts. Near the entrance Pictish symbols – a double dix and Z-rod and a unique circle with human face and curved horns as well as a Pictish beast – have been carved. These can be seen on the S of two outcrops forming the entrance. They may have been carved by a Pictish raiding party.

In Dumfriesshire, there are several reminders of the time when this part of Scotland was under Anglian domination. At **Thornhill** (NX 8695) turn W on the A702 towards Moniave, and just under a mile along it a free-standing Anglian cross can be seen, in a field adjacent to the Nith Bridge (hence its name, the Nith Bridge Cross) to the S of the road. The stone is somewhat obscured by lichen, but its main decorative elements can be discerned. It dates from the late ninth century, and shows connections with stones from Hoddom and W Yorkshire. The shaft is decorated with panels of interlacing

78 Nith Bridge Cross

creatures. There is a rosette in the centre of the head.

If the A702 is followed in the direction of Moniave, the second side-road N past Penpont passes the hillfort of **Tynron Doon** on its way to Tynron. It can be seen to the N of the road, and can be approached over the fields, but is a fairly formidable climb (NX 8294). Essentially it is a multivallate iron age hillfort, with the addition of a courtyard on the NE side which is probably Dark Age and which was later converted to a motte. A midden on the steep S

79 Tynron Doon

side produced various finds of Dark Age date, including bone pins, a blue glass bead and decorated bone. A gold ornament, decorated with filigree of seventh-century date, was found on the site in 1927. It is certainly Anglian.

Dumfries Museum [10–1, 2–5; Sun. April–Sept. 2–5], charmingly housed in the Old Observatory in Dumfries (which has a Camera Obscura), cares for many of the finds from SW Scotland. Here can be seen the finds from Trusty's Hill, the Mote of Mark, Anglo-Saxon coins from Luce Sands and other objects. The main Dark Age attraction, however, is the fine collection of stones in the basement of the museum. These include a series of stones from Hoddom, notably an eighth- to ninth-century richly ornamented wheel cross head, a standing wheel-headed cross of the ninth to tenth century and a cross-shaft of the tenth or eleventh century. There is also a fine tenth-century cross with dragon-head pattern from Glencairn, an outstanding cross from Closeburn with interlace and animals of the tenth century, an interlaced grave slab, also from Closeburn, a cross head from Durrisdeer, and a fluted pillar from Ruthwell which suggests it may have been a major Anglian church, as might be expected from the Ruthwell Cross. A number of other Dark Age stones are also on display there.

The prize of Dark Age southern Scotland is the **Ruthwell Cross** (NY 1068) [AM; A], located 1m (1·6 km) N of Ruthwell and reached by the B724 5m (8 km) W of Annan. Entrance should be sought from the key-keeper, at Kirkyett Cottage, Ruthwell. The Ruthwell Cross has been described as one of the major monuments of Dark Age Europe, and along with the almost as fine Bewcastle Cross (see p. 219) marks the greatest achievement of Northumbrian sculpture of the Golden Age. It stands in a well which was built to hold it in the church, and is lit by spotlights which can be turned on by visitors. The cross dates from the late seventh century, and it has been slightly restored, due to the fact that it was broken in two and one panel defaced in 1640 on the order of the General Assembly of the Church of Scotland. The pieces, which were buried beneath the floor of the church, were dug up again in the late eighteenth century, further fragments having been broken off. As it stands today, the side arms of the cross are modern but the top arm is original. Panels of figural work combined with inscriptions ornament front and back, and vinescroll ornament inhabited by birds and beasts decorates the sides. Anglian runes border it, with a text of the Old English poem, the *Dream of the Rood*, perhaps by Caedmon. Much

80 Ruthwell Cross

debate has surrounded the date and exact interpretation of the cross, which was probably set up soon after the Synod of Whitby in 664. The most important scenes depict St John with his symbol (the eagle), John the Baptist with his lamb, Christ in Glory, with his feet on two animals, the hermit saints Paul and Anthony, the flight into Egypt, the Visitation of Mary, Christ with Mary Magdalene washing his feet, Christ healing the blind man and the Annunciation. There is also a badly defaced sculpture of the Crucifixion and an archer. A notable feature of the iconography of the cross is its allusions to the desert fathers, suggestive of contacts with the Eastern hermits in this remote spot.

Further early Anglian sculptures can be seen in the site museum at **Jedburgh** (NT 6520), on the A68 in Roxburghshire. It lies 9m (14·5 km) NE of Hawick. This museum is part of the Augustinian monastery of Jedburgh Abbey [AM;S] which is worth a visit in itself as one of the finest medieval abbeys in Britain. The Dark Age stones in the museum include the end panel from a slab shrine which may have contained the relics of St Boisil, the friend of St Cuthbert and abbot of Old Melrose nearby, from which the stone has probably come. Part of the head of an Anglian cross of the ninth century and some other fragments can also be seen in the museum.

Travelling north, the hillfort of **Traprain Law** (NT 5874) in East Lothian is one of the most famous in Scottish archaeology. It is reached by following the A1 for 5m (8 km) to East Linton, from Dunbar, then side roads S from East Linton. At Traprain the side road forks, but you carry on to the next turning W which goes up to the hill. It is now a quarry, and the remains of the fort have been extensively destroyed. It is a multi-period site, with occupation beginning in the bronze age. A series of ramparts belong to different phases – from a 20-acre (8 hectares) enclosure it was progressively enlarged to enclose 40 acres (about 16 hectares), probably in the first century AD. Inside this were thatched or stone-walled huts, and from the finds from this period can be built up a vivid picture of life in a major tribal capital in Scotland during the Roman occupation, and lasting on into the Dark Ages. In the last main phase the fort was reduced again to 30 acres (about 12 hectares) and enclosed in a rampart consisting of stone-revetted turf, which overlies the other ramparts and is the most conspicuous feature of the fort. Some debate has surrounded the date of this final occupation. It must be later than 300 since occupation of this date was found under the rampart. There is considerable evidence that it

81 Jedburgh, stone panel

continued to be occupied into the seventh century – finds include a Pictish silver chain, penannular brooches, a mould for a hand-pin (a distinctive type of dress-fastener of the seventh century) and other objects.

Not far from Traprain at **Morham** (NT 5572) part of an Anglian cross-shaft with interlace can be seen built into the wall of the parish church. Although fragmentary, it is one of the few traces of the Anglian occupation of the Lothians. Morham is reached by side-roads from Traprain, about 1½m (2·4 km) to the SW.

The nuclear fort of **Dalmahoy** (NT 1366) lies 1½m (2·4 km) W of Balerno to the N of the A70, and 10m (16 km) SW of Edinburgh. This is a classic site, the 'type site' for nuclear forts (see p. 41), and can be compared with Dunadd in Argyll (see p. 272) though it is much less craggy and has more spread ramparts. The remains consist of a central citadel, 85 feet by 140 feet (25·9 × 42·6 metres), and a series of outworks constructed by linking rock outcrops with stretches of walling. The citadel has produced a gold stud cap and pieces of clay mould of Dark Age date.

Other Northumbrian crosses are to be found in the Lothians. The best collection is at **Abercorn** (NT 0879), on the A904 about 2m (3·2 km) W of Queensferry (but unmarked on the AA Atlas and many other maps). The picturesque church is of Romanesque origin, and retains a Romanesque doorway. Within the churchyard can be discerned the *vallum* of the Early Christian monastery – now barely a few inches in height. Outside the churchyard, among the trees, excavations were carried out in the 1960s, and a trench cut across the vallum inside the churchyard showed it to have been a stone-faced rampart, like that at Iona. The monastery probably began as a Celtic establishment: it was taken over by Bishop Trumwine around 680 and is mentioned by Bede as *Aebbercurnig*. The Abercorn stones, now in the church, consist of a very fine cross-shaft, now at the head of the stairs leading to the gallery, and other fragments in the vestry, including a couple of hogbacked stones. The main shaft has fine interlace and inhabited vinescroll ornament.

In **Edinburgh**, the National Museum of Antiquities of Scotland in Queen St must be visited [10–5; Sun. 2–5]. This neo-Gothic building is a curiosity in its own right, and houses one of the finest collections of Dark Age remains in Britain. On the ground floor can be seen a fine collection of Early Christian inscribed stones and sculptures, along with casts of others; up the main stairs yet other stones and casts can be studied. A case near the sculptures on the ground floor holds the *Monymusk Reliquary*, a small house-shaped shrine which perhaps once held a relic of St Columba. It dates from the seventh century. Adjacent to it are the Irish Shannon shrine and the Hoddom Crozier shrine of later Dark Age date.

Most of the Dark Age objects are displayed on the first floor, adjacent to the prehistoric collections. Notice particularly the St Ninian's Isle Treasure in its own case, a hoard of Pictish silverwork buried around 800 (see p. 57) and found in 1958 in Shetland, the magnificent silver Hunterston Brooch from Ayrshire datable to the eighth century, the hoard of Pictish silverwork from Norrie's Law (Fife) and the series of Pictish silver chains. Adjacent are cases of Viking treasure hoards, of which the finest is that from Skaill, Orkney, and finds from Viking burials. Cases round the walls display finds from Dunadd, Buston Crannog and Mote of Mark. The finds from Jarlshof are some distance away, among the prehistoric collections.

In Edinburgh, too, the remains in Holyrood Park are worth exploring. They are reached through the gates behind the brewery at the foot of the Canongate (The Royal Mile), whence a road winds up under Salisbury Crags to Arthur's Seat. The name **Arthur's Seat** (NT 2772) is one of the few well-authenticated placenames in Britain associated with King Arthur. The road round Arthur's Seat runs up to Dunsapie Loch, which is dominated by a small fort of uncertain date. From here the cultivation terraces can be climbed to the summit of the hill, which commands breathtaking views of the surrounding countryside. Some of the cultivation terraces are medieval, but some may belong to the Anglian occupation of the Lothians. The fort on the summit shows features of nuclear forts, and perhaps should be regarded as Dark Age for this reason alone.

On the opposite side of the Forth–Clyde isthmus a cluster of Dark Age remains can be found round Glasgow. At **Govan**, which is on the A8 in a suburb about 4m (6·5 km) W of the city centre and which can be reached by Glasgow's underground railway which stops there, a rather depressing grey church houses an outstanding collection of no less than twenty-four Dark Age sculptured stones. (The church is open weekdays 9–12.30 and 2–5; mornings only Sat.) Until recently there were seventeen more stones along the E wall of the churchyard, but some were damaged in 1973 and they have been removed to Kelvingrove Museum. It is not possible here to list all the stones, but a guide pamphlet is available in the church. The stones are the product of a local school of artwork, known from this collection as the Govan school, which flourished from the tenth to the early twelfth centuries, and which has much in common with the Whithorn school. The style is eclectic, and influences can be detected from Pictland (in the figures), from Northumbria (in the interlace) and from Scandinavia (in the use of ring-chain and in the layout). The most notable stones include the so-called Sarcophagus of St Constantine, which could have been made to contain the relics of the little-known sixth-century saint to whom the church is dedicated. A hunting scene decorates the back, and other animals enhance the front. Originally it had a gabled roof-shaped cover. There were two other such shrines at Govan in the eighteenth century, so it is by no means certain that this is the one designed to house St Constantine's relics. Nearly all the stones carry numbers which refer to Romilly Allen's list in his *Early Christian Monuments of Scotland* – this is No. 1. Other stones include a series of five hogbacked tombstones, of the tenth or eleventh centuries, two cross-shafts (No. 29 and one unnumbered), both dating from around 900, and two upright cross-slabs.

Related to the Govan stones is the **Barochan Cross** (NS 4069) [AM; A] in Renfrewshire. It towers 11 feet (3·4 metres) high on a hill 5m (8 km) NW of Paisley, and can be arrived at by taking the B789 (which joins the A737 out of Paisley) through Houston – it can be seen from the road about 1m (1·6 km) further N than Houston. It is charmingly decorated on all four faces with figural compositions, and dates from the tenth century. This is one of the very few free-standing crosses in Scotland intact from the Dark Ages, though it has been broken and badly restored with concrete.

Also related to the Govan school are the stones at **Inchinnan** (NS 4769), which now lies within Abbotsinch airport (which serves Glasgow). Take the A8 westwards from Glasgow, then take the side-road S to Inchinnan. The church is to the E of the road. The stones consist of a sarcophagus cover, with a representation of Daniel in the lion's den, dating from the early tenth century, part of a cross and a graveslab, of tenth- to eleventh-century date.

On the W bank of Loch Lomond, the celebrated beauty spot, the stones at **Luss** (NS 3692) are in the churchyard in the centre of the village, which is on the A82 about 10m (16 km) N of Dumbarton. These comprise two hogbacked tombstones (probably in their original positions), two cross-slabs and a free-standing cross, all outliers of the Govan school.

Between Forth and Clyde lies **Dumyat** (NS 8397) in Stirlingshire, 4m (6·5 km) NE of Stirling, a hillfort to be climbed only by those who are fit. It is reached by the A91 from Causewayhead. Just over ½m (0·8 km) E of Blairlogie a farm road turns N round the bottom of the hill, and from this it can be ascended. The name probably means 'the dun of the Maeatae' (the local iron age tribe) and the main ramparts probably belong to the iron age. It is enclosed by a double rampart, within which is an oval, stone-walled citadel which is a later addition. This is one of a series of 'citadel forts' in which an iron age multivallate fort has been adapted, probably in the Dark Ages, into a type of fort with an outer enclosure.

Moving NE of the Forth–Clyde line into the lands of the Picts and Scots, the new Forth road bridge takes the traveller first into Fife.

St Andrews is usually associated with golf and its long-established university, but it also has a celebrated medieval abbey which overlies the site of a Dark Age monastery (NO 5116) [AM;S]. It can be reached by a variety of A roads in Fife. It came into prominence in the eighth century when the relics of Scotland's patron saint, Andrew, were brought here by King Oengus of the Picts. Until it was taken over by the Augustinian canons in the twelfth century, the monastery was administered by the Culdees, a group of very strict Celtic monks. The only work showing pre-Norman features is the tower of St Regulus or St Rule. The church of St Regulus is usually believed to have been built by bishop Robert (1126–59), but the tower itself may have been already erected in the first half of the eleventh century, being modified in the twelfth when the nave was built on to it. It shows features in common with Wharram-le-Street in Yorkshire, and its double belfry windows are similar to those on Anglo-Saxon towers. The E and W arches of the chancel are almost certainly twelfth-century work, but may have been added to an earlier chancel. The whole church was superseded by St Andrew's Cathedral in the late twelfth century.

The cathedral complex shelters a very good site museum, within which more than fifty Early Christian stones are displayed. The most noteworthy is the Shrine of St Andrew. This was probably built in the eighth century to contain the relics of the saint. It is a corner-block shrine, now with a restored gable roof. The front panel carries a spirited scene of David and the lion, and various hunting figures, while the end panels show interlaced serpents. The style is very accomplished and naturalistic, and the whole has been described as one of the finest examples of Dark Age art in Europe. The other stones include a broken cross-shaft.

The weathered **Dogton Stone** (NT 2396) [AM;A] lies about 4½m (7·2 km) NW of the centre of Kirkcaldy, reached by the B922 and a side road to Dogton. It is a free-standing cross with animal and figure sculpture and key pattern ornament.

In Angus, the most interesting monument is Brechin Round Tower (NO 5960) [AM;A], to which has been added Brechin Cathedral. It lies in the centre of **Brechin**, reached by the A94. The

82 St Regulus Tower, St Andrews

83 Brechin, doorway of Round Tower

cathedral dates from the thirteenth century, but the round tower is
some three centuries older, though the spire was added in the
fourteenth century. As in Irish round towers, the door is set some
way off the ground, with interesting sculptured detail – on either
side is a bishop, one with the usual type of crozier, the other with an
Irish Tau (ie T-shaped) crozier. Above is a Crucifixion, while
crouching beasts flank the bottom. The interior of the tower (which
is not open to the public) has seven storeys, originally served by

wooden ladders. Inside the cathedral is a remarkable ninth-century slab in Northumbrian style, the Aldbar Stone, with the Virgin and Child in the centre and an inscription to 'St Mary, Mother of Christ'. In the background-panels were once evangelist figures, but now only St John and St Mark are represented.

Angus also boasts another of the very few surviving examples of pre-Norman architecture in Scotland, the tower of **Restenneth Priory** (NO 4851). Restenneth lies about 1½m (2·4 km) E of Forfar on the B9133. The main body of the priory dates from the twelfth century, but the tower has a round-headed S doorway defined by plain square pilaster strip work and hood moulding. It has been suggested that the lower half may be as early as the eighth century. It could have been the work of Northumbrian masons from Monkwearmouth who were brought by the Pictish king Nechtan mac Derelei to build a church in 710. If so, it represents the porticus of a larger building. The upper part of the tower may have been added by Alexander I of Scotland around 1100. It is crowned by a beautiful broach spire of the fifteenth century, a rare feature in Scotland.

84 Restenneth Priory

An excellent collection of Pictish stones can be seen in the village of **St Vigeans** (NO 6352) [AM;S, but closed Sun.], less than 1m (1·6 km) N of Arbroath on a minor road. The thirty-two stones are housed in a cottage in the village, and were found in the neighbourhood of the church. The dedication of the church (and village) is to St Fechin, an Irish saint who traditionally founded an ecclesiastical community here in the seventh century, and the churchyard can be seen opposite the museum. The key to the museum can be obtained from the keyholder nearby – a notice explains where to find it. The most important of the sculptures is the Drosten stone, famous for its inscription in Irish lettering on a panel on the side. It reads

DROSTEN
IPEUORET
ETTFOR
CUS

Drosten, Uoret and Forcus are personal names. Ipe is probably Pictish. This is one of the two Pictish inscriptions in non-ogham script that survive, the other being from the St Ninian's Isle Treasure. The stone dates from the ninth century, and is richly decorated.

Angus is very rich in Pictish sculptures. Those at **Aberlemno** (NO 5255) [AM;A] on the B9134, 5m (8 km) NE of Forfar are particularly worth visiting. Two of them stand in an enclosure to the S of the road, the one a symbol stone of Class I with a variety of very clear symbols engraved on it, the other a fine Class II cross slab, with a wheel cross flanked by angels on the front and a hunting scene with Pictish symbols on the back. The finest of the Aberlemno stones, however, is to be seen in the old churchyard, which is reached by turning down a side-road to the S of the B9134, just before the roadside stones are reached. This example is a really superb piece of Pictish art, the front decorated with a richly ornamented cross flanked by intertwining and confronted beasts, the back carved into a hunting scene, a triple disc and notched rectangle and Z-rod symbol being visible above.

St Orland's Stone (NO 4050) stands in a field near a farmhouse (Cossans) about 1½m (2·4 km) NE of Glamis railway station, reached by a farm road E off the A928. On the front is a relief cross and on the reverse a variety of figures including two pairs of horsemen and a boat. It stands nearly 8 feet (2·44 metres) high.

85 Aberlemno churchyard, Pictish cross

There are four stones at **Kirriemuir**, in the cemetery at the N end of the town (NO 3854), which is reached on the A926 5m (8 km) NW of Forfar. There are two Class II and two Class III stones, the former with human figures.

At **Eassie** (NO 3547) the church boasts a particularly fine Class II cross slab [AM; A], with a richly decorated cross with figures and animals on the front, and symbols and processional scenes on the back. Eassie is reached by turning N off the A94 between Meigle and Glamis – the village is just off the main road.

The **Glamis Manse Stone** (NO 3846) can be seen in the grounds of the Manse as the name suggests – Glamis is 5m (8 km) S of Kirriemuir on the A928. The manse is on the main road at the E end of the village, and permission should be sought from the minister to see it. Folklore explains the scene depicted on this famous monument: in the words of Thomas Pennant, writing in 1776,

> In the churchyard of Glamis is a stone similar to those at Aberlemni. This is supposed to have been erected in memory of the assassination of King Malcolm and is called his grave-stone. On one front is a cross . . . on the opposite front of the stone are represented an eel and another fish. This alludes to the fate of the murderers who, as soon as they had committed the horrid act, fled. The roads were at that time covered with snow; they lost the path, and went on to the lake of Forfar, which happened at that time to be frozen over, but not sufficiently strong to bear their weight; the ice broke, and they all perished miserably.

So much for the interpretation of Pictish symbols! The stone is nearly 9 feet (2·74 metres) high, and a curious feature of the triple-disc symbol on this stone is that it is used in conjunction with a symbol of a cauldron supported on a bar by two ring handles – from it two legs protrude. If the triple-disc is a cauldron symbol, why use it twice on the same stone?

The round tower at **Abernethy** (NO 1916) in Perthshire is in many ways more impressive than that at Brechin, because it remains free-standing in a corner of the churchyard. Abernethy is 6m (9·7 km) SE of Perth and is reached by the A913 to Newburgh; the churchyard fronts the village square. The round tower may have had two periods of construction – the bottom courses are different from the rest, which may have been rebuilt in the eleventh century. The doorway has a throughstone arch reminiscent of Anglo-Saxon architecture, though the windows are more Norman in character. Inside there are scarcement ledges for six floors.

To one side of the gate on the outside of the churchyard, near the tower, can be seen a Class I Pictish symbol stone.

Moncrieffe Hill (NO 1320) can be reached from the A90, 2m (3·22 km) S of Perth, and then a side road to the E. Moncrieffe was probably the *Monad Croib* mentioned as the scene of a battle in 729. It is a citadel fort, with a stone citadel about 160 feet by 120 feet (48·8 × 36·6 metres) built within the rampart of an earlier iron age fort, which consists of a stone wall following the edge of the hill.

The nuclear fort at **Dundurn** (NN 7023) is reached on the A85 10m (16 km) W of Crieff. It can be reached by a side road S to a farm, just before St Fillans. Dundurn is probably the *Duinduirn*

86 Abernethy Round Tower

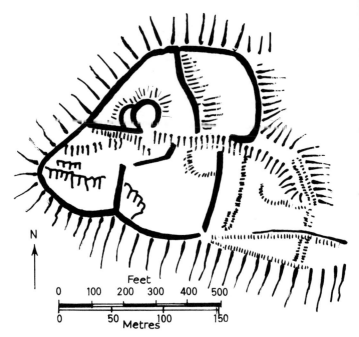

87 Plan of Dundurn

mentioned in the *Annals of Ulster* as having stood siege in 683, and may have been the capital of the Picts of Fortrenn. Like Dunadd, it has a citadel 70 feet (21·3 metres) in diameter within a series of outer defences which make use of the natural outcrop. Excavations began here in 1976, and suggest that the citadel had a timber-framed rampart and that the whole fort is of Dark Age date.

An important collection of Pictish stones will delight at **Meigle** (NN 2844) [AM;S], 6m (9·7 km) NE of Coupar Angus, on the A94 to Forfar. Most of the twenty-five were found in the vicinity of the parish church. The Meigle Museum was once a schoolhouse, but was converted to shelter the stones when the museum was taken over by the then Ministry of Works in 1949. Meigle No. 2 should be singled out – it is a huge cross-slab in the late 'boss style' of ornament (see p. 47), with Daniel in the lion's den and a cavalcade of horsemen on the back. Meigle No. 3 displays a charming horseman, while Meigle No. 1 appears to be a reused stone, since it has bronze age cup marks on the underside. Taken as a whole, the collection is one of the most outstanding in Europe.

At the W end of the nave of the thirteenth-century **Dunblane Cathedral** (NN 7801) [AM;S, but 2–5.30 Sun. in summer], on the A9 5m (8 km) N of Stirling, two Class III stones can be sought out.

At **Fowlis Wester** (NN 9224) [AM;A] 4m (6·5 km) NE of Crieff, 1m (1·6 km) N of the A85 to Perth, a 10-ft (3 metres) high cross-slab decorated with Pictish symbols towers over the village square. Notice the unusual feature on this weathered slab – the arms of the cross project beyond the slab itself. The back of the slab has, apart from typical symbols, a horseman, a hound, two horsemen (one with a hawk), a belled cow led by a man and followed by six further men, a bird and a beast eating a man. A better-preserved cross–slab now embedded in the N wall of the church was found in 1931.

The **Dunfallandy Stone** (NN 9456) [AM;A] is a Class II slab, which can be found by taking the A827 NE out of Aberfeldy for about 6m (9·7 km), then turning N along a minor road to Dunfallandy. The stone is just outside the churchyard near Dunfallandy Hotel, though it originally came from a churchyard near Killiecrankie. It has a cross, animals and angels on one side, and seated figures, a horseman and Pictish symbols on the other.

In Aberdeenshire two Pictish sculptures are of particular interest because they have ogham inscriptions. The first, at **Aboyne Castle** (NO 5299), is a cross-slab with a mirror symbol and two lines of ogham. It stands in the castle grounds, between the drive and the walled garden, not far from the W gate. The castle, which is in private ownership, can be reached by taking the B9094 in Aboyne, then turning E on a side road.

The **Brandsbutt Stone** (NJ 7622) [AM;A], which is signposted, can be seen by taking the A96 NW from Inverurie, then following a farm road about 1m (1·6 km) along it. It is a large boulder, reconstructed from broken fragments which were built into a field wall; it is a Class I monument, with the addition, probably later, of an ogham inscription which transliterates as,

IRATADDOARENS

It is supposed to have come from a circle of stones, suggesting that it is one of the stones of a prehistoric recumbant circle (a type of local bronze age monument) reused by the Picts.

It is not unknown for air travellers to the Northern Isles to be grounded at **Dyce**, Aberdeen's airport, because of bad weather conditions further north. The tedium of waiting for a plane can be relieved by taking a walk to see the Dyce symbol stones (NJ 8715) [AM; A]. The airport is on the A947, and about ½m (0·8 km) along it, turn NW on the side road. The stones are at Dyce old church. One is a Class I, the other a Class II stone with a floriated cross and with crescent-and-V-rod, triple disc, and double disc-and-A-rod symbols.

A series of fascinating stones can be seen on the A96 or in its vicinity. The most famous of those in Aberdeenshire is the **Malden Stone** (NJ 7024) [AM; A], which stands in a remote setting on a side road NW off the A96, about 6m (9·7 km) NW of Inverurie, S from Mill of Carden to Chapel of Garioch. On the front are five panels of sculpture, including a representation of Jonah and the whale, and on the back are relief carvings of Pictish symbols. Local tradition says that the stone is Janet of Drumdurno, whose attempted seduction by a warlock had a dramatic end. He turned her to stone when she fled from his advances. The symbols, it is said, are the marks made upon her apron by a hot bread shovel. In spite of the fact the carvings are executed in granite, the artistry is high and the overall appearance particularly pleasing.

The intriguing **Newton Stone** (NJ 6629) can be seen in the grounds of Newton House, from which permission should be sought before visiting it. It is reached by taking the B992 E from the A96, and lies about 10m (16 km) NW of Inverurie. The stone is close to the E side of the house, and bears two inscriptions, one in Pictish ogham, the other in a script unknown elsewhere. Until a careful examination of the technique of the carving in the 1950s showed it to be genuine, it was long believed to be a nineteenth-century fake. Adjacent to it is a Class I symbol stone in similar technique.

The **Picardy Stone** (NJ 6130) [AM; A] lies 2m (3·2 km) NW of Insch, on a side road near Myreton. Insch is reached by turning W off the A96 on the B9002. It is a well-preserved Class I stone, with very clear symbols.

Further north, in Moray, can be seen **Sueno's Stone** (NJ 0459) [AM; A] which is one of the most magnificent Dark Age sculptured stones in Britain. It stands 20 feet (6·1 metres) high, and is a Class III stone, without symbols, erected after the disappearance of historical Pictland, probably in the late ninth century. It stands on the outskirts of Forres, on the B9011 to Kinloss, and is carved on all its faces. On the front is a wheel-headed cross with interlace, below which is a scene with five men, much damaged. On the reverse are

88 Maiden Stone

four panels, much weathered but still recognizable, depicting (*a*)
nine men in three rows on horseback, (*b*) footsoldiers and horsemen
in five rows, including a row of five beheaded bodies, (*c*) a canopy
over some beheaded bodies and (*d*) a procession. There is

Northumbrian-style vinescroll on the sides. It is probably a
memorial to a battle, and may well commemorate a victory over the
Norsemen, as the name itself suggests.

Of the few forts in NE Scotland with known or certain Dark Age
occupation, the most famous is **Burghead** (NJ 1169), 8m (12·9 km)
NW of Elgin, which can be reached by turning N off the A96 to
Forres, on the B9103. The double promontory fort is much
damaged, and is threatened with further destruction in the near
future, but a plan was drawn in the eighteenth century by General
Roy, the founder of the Ordnance Survey, before destruction began,
when the features of the two forts were recognized.

The upper fort was constructed perhaps in the fourth century AD,
and has produced Roman coins among the finds. The lower fort was
occupied in the Pictish period, and both continued in use until the
coming of the Norse. About twenty-five stones with Pictish bulls on
them have been found on the site: the symbol is known as the
'Burghead bull' as a result. A slab shrine has also been found there.
There is a record of 'numerous bronze spears given away to any
English tourist who happened to be passing' (could this be evidence
of bronze age use of the promontory?) and numerous other finds. In
the ninth century the fort was fired, and left unoccupied until the
twelfth or thirteenth century. Radiocarbon confirms the Dark Age

89 Burghead Bull

date, but a limited excavation in 1966 failed to find evidence for the timber lacing with nails recorded by nineteenth-century diggers. Viking metalwork has been recorded from the fort.

Among the visible remains at Burghead a wall which originally divided the interior of the promontory into the lower and upper fort runs along an open space between the town and the sea – it is still impressive, though nothing like so splendid as it must have been before the vandalism of the site in the early nineteenth century, when the magnificent outer ramparts were needlessly removed. Originally this wall was about 24 feet (7·3 metres) wide and about 17 feet (5·2 metres) high, and timber laced with iron bolts.

Within the lower fort is a well [AM; A], originally on the line of the rampart and presumably, therefore, later than it, which is rock-cut and traditionally associated with the cult of the local saint, Ethan. It is unique. It stands at the foot of a crag, and comprises a rectangular chamber, roughly 16 feet (7·31 metres) square and 12 feet (3·66 metres) high, cut out of the living rock, and giving on to a half-bowl-shaped slope some 20 feet (6·1 metres) below the present ground level. The well could be Dark Age, but equally probably it is later medieval.

The fort at **Craig Phadrig** (NH 6445) overlooks Inverness. It can be reached by following the A9 out of Inverness, then turning SW on a minor road about 1m (1·6 km) out of the city centre in the direction of Leachkin. A track leads up the tree-covered slopes to the summit, from which very fine views can be obtained. The earliest defences were constructed in the fourth century BC, when a timber-laced rampart was put up; a second rampart was constructed inside it not much later. Both were destroyed and vitrified, and the fort abandoned until the Dark Ages. Excavation in 1971–2 yielded imported pottery (Class E) and a clay mould for a hanging-bowl escutcheon of the sixth century AD. A radiocarbon date, probably too early, for this reoccupation was AD 370. Local tradition associated the site with the Pictish king, Bridei mac Maelcon, but this is probably a recent invention.

Caithness and Sutherland have little to offer in the way of Dark Age remains except a few Pictish stones.

The fine Class III monument near Bettyhill is worth a visit. It stands in **Farr** churchyard (NC 7162), outside the E end of the church, which is reached by turning N on a side road just before the A836 dips down into Bettyhill, travelling from Melvich. It is known as the Red Priest's Stone. The name is probably a confusion arising from the name of St Maelrubha, to whom dedications are found locally – the Gaelic for red is *ruadh*. It is richly decorated, the ornament including two birds with intertwined necks in Irish style.

But to turn now to north-west Scotland. There is a small island known as **Holy Island** which lies off the coast of Arran. Access to Arran itself is by the Brodick ferry, and Holy Island is accessible in the summer by boat from Lamlash or Whiting Bay. St Molaise's Cave (NS 0529) is notable, and lies on the W shore after a walk of less than a mile from the pier at which you land, along the coastal path. The cave was excavated in 1908, and contains runic inscriptions on the walls, carved by the Norse in the eleventh to thirteenth centuries.

On the island of Bute, which is reached by car-ferry from Wemyss Bay, are several Dark Age sites. The most important is the monastic complex of St Blane's, **Kingarth** (NS 0953), one of the major monastic sites in Scotland. Follow the A844 to Kingarth S from Rothesay for about 7m (11·3 km), and just to the W a side road turns S past a church to the monastic site. The ruined church is medieval – a good example of Scottish twelfth-century Romanesque work – and it stands within a graveyard with a second graveyard on the terrace below. This in turn lies within a dry-built cashel wall, cleared at the end of the nineteenth century by the Marquis of Bute; it encloses 2 or 3 acres (around a hectare) and now stands 2–3 feet (0·6–0·9 metres) high. This is probably an enclosure of the Dark Age pre-Norse monastery, which may have been founded by St Blane in the sixth century. Some walls run out from this, but are of uncertain date. Below the churchyard and within the enclosure are visible some foundations which are probably those of monastic cells belonging to the first monastery, and which could date from the eighth century. The churchyards contain recumbent grave slabs – some are decorated in the style of the twelfth to thirteenth centuries, but others may belong to the Norse period, probably the eleventh century. To the N of the cashel enclosure are the remains of a dun of probable iron age origin, which may have been used in the Dark Ages. Many sculptured stones have been found on the site, some of which can still be seen there. In addition, numerous slate trial pieces with ornament on them suggest the presence of a scriptorium or school room.

To the SW of the monastery lie the twin forts of **Dunagoil**. The larger is an iron age vitrified fort; the smaller, Little Dunagoil (NS 0853) lies on the shore 400 metres N of the main fort, and was partially investigated in the 1960s. Within the fort it is easy to distinguish the foundations of two Norse long houses, each about 38 feet by 16 feet (11·62 × 4·88 metres), one with a single row of roof supports set off centre, the other with three rows of roof supports. Finds (mainly pottery) and comparisons with the structures in the Isle of Man suggest that they were not occupied before about the twelfth century, so they are late survivals from the Dark Ages. Little Dunagoil also has earlier Dark Age occupation.

On the W coast opposite Rothesay lies **St Ninian's Isle** (NS 0361), reached by the A844 and a side road to Straad. The remains of an early chapel site occupy a spit on the W side of the island. Within a turf and stone enclosure wall lie the foundations of a small chapel of unicameral plan, with an altar with relic cavity at the E end. The orientation of burials inside the churchyard indicate that a pagan cemetery had been taken over by Christians. The stone chapel probably replaced a timber one in the ninth century.

In Argyll, the dun at **Kildonan** (NR 7827) was occupied in the Dark Ages, when various alterations were carried out. It can be seen by following the B842 S for about 6½m (10·3 km) NE of Campbeltown. The site lies to the E of the road, and about 50 metres from it. It is roughly triangular, with a main entrance with door-checks and bar hole on the W. The first structure might have been of iron age or Dark Age date, since no determinate finds have been recovered. Later, certainly in the Dark Ages, the entrance was narrowed and huts built inside the dun, and an intra-mural staircase (now exposed again) was blocked up. The finds included a penannular brooch of the seventh century and an enamelled disc of similar date, as well as more commonplace objects. Abandoned perhaps around the ninth century, it was reoccupied again in the fourteenth. The walls were consolidated after the excavation of 1936–8.

Ugadale Point (NR 7828) and its stack fort is about a mile (1·6 km) S of Kildonan, and was occupied around the same period. On a flat summit an irregular univallate rampart encloses a small, roughly rectangular, area. Finds showed the site to have been occupied in the eighth century or earlier, as well as in the post-medieval period. It can be reached from the B842.

The A816 from Oban has much to offer the archaeologist, of many periods. From Oban itself the road can be followed S to Kilmartin, from where the B8025 leads to **Keillmore** at the end of the peninsula (NR 6980). At the NE end of the medieval chapel is a

fine free-standing cross of slate, with sculptural work on one face.
Its ornament is in the same tradition as the Kilnave cross (see
p. 274) and dates from the late eighth or early ninth century. It
includes interlace and key pattern, figural work and a central boss
which declares affinities to the Iona school.

In the heart of what was once the marshland of the Crinan Moss
lies **Dunadd** (NR 8393) [AM; A], one of the most famous Dark Age
sites in Britain. It lies 1½m (2·4 km) W of Kilmichael Glassary 4m
NW of Lochgilphead, off the A816, approached by a farm road W.
Dunadd was a capital of the Dalriadic Scots, and was first occupied
by them probably in the late fifth century AD. It is a nuclear fort –
the classic example of its type – crowning the twin peaks of a craggy
rock which rises out of the surrounding flatness: once marsh
surrounded it, providing ideal defence. The present path leads
through an enclosure on a low natural terrace, up to a second
enclosure and on to the summit, which is dominated by a citadel.
The entrance to the lower enclosure is through a natural gully, and
the wall is here well preserved, of drystone masonry, linking sections
of rock outcrop. You will doubtless admire the carving of a boar
(protected by a glass frame) on the rock just below the summit, and
look out for the adjacent ogham inscription (not noticed until recent
years), a carving of a footprint and a pecked-out basin. The
footprint may have been an inauguration stone on which the Scotic

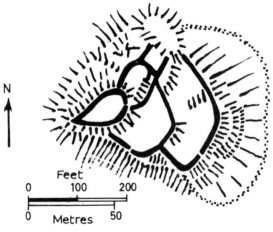

N

Feet
0   100   200

0   Metres   50

90 Dunadd (a) plan

90 Dunadd (b) inauguration footprint

kings stood to be crowned; the boar may have been carved when the site was besieged by Oengus mac Fergus of the Picts in 736. This would be borne out by the ogham inscription, which is Pictish ogham, not the Irish form as one might expect. To the NE of the main citadel a ravine can be seen in which a midden accumulated. The site was excavated in 1904 and 1929, and produced a wealth of finds, extending down to the time of the Norse settlements in the area in the ninth century. The first reliable historical reference to the site is in 683, when an Irish Annalistic entry refers to the siege of the fort.

At **Kilmartin** (NR 8398) [AM; A] a typical West Highland church on the A816, 7m (11·3 km) NW of Lochgilphead, displays a variety of sculptured stones. Many of these belong to the West Highland tradition of sculpture, in which Celtic art continued into the full Middle Ages and beyond. But alongside the later stones (which include an exceptional cross of the sixteenth century) is a slate cross of Dark Age date, to the S of the main path and decorated with interlace, key patterns and spirals. Two other early stones are nearby.

On the island of **Islay** (reached by car ferries from the W end of Loch Tarbert) there is a great profusion of early chapel sites, most of which have little visible of certain Dark Age date. There is also a rich collection of monumental sculpture related to the Iona School. The finest is the Kildalton Cross (NR 4550) [AM; A], which stands in a churchyard (signposted) beyond Ardbeg. Follow the A846 to Ardbeg, then a side road thereafter. This is one of the finest Dark Age monumental sculptures in Britain: it dates from the ninth century, and has a wheel-headed cross with open wheel. It displays a combination of figural ornament, interlace and ornamental patterns. Northumbrian influence has been suggested for some of the ornament, but the best parallels are to be found in Ireland. The treatment of the arms is similar to that on St John's Cross on Iona.

Somewhat less impressive is the Kilnave Cross (NR 2871), which stands on a side road in an old burial ground on the side of Loch Gruinart. It is reached by the B8017 and a minor road N from Aoradh up the W side of the loch. It is weathered, and dates from the mid-eighth century. It is made from a single slab of slate, and bears curvilinear ornament.

In the Firth of Lorne lie the Garvellach Islands, which can be reached by hiring a boat from the N shore of Loch Craignish, or from Cullipool on Luing, or Easdale on Seil. On one of these remote

islands, **Eileach an Naoimh** (NM 6611) [AM; A], is one of the most
remarkable monastic sites in Britain, protected by its remoteness.
The remains consist of a ruined rectangular chapel, three round
beehive-shaped cells, and a specially marked grave. The cells consist
of two double and one smaller single one – the double ones
interconnect through a doorway. The chapel has a square-headed
door at one end and a window at the other. Outside the church a
circular grave enclosure contains Eithne's Grave, which is
demarcated by two slabs at each of the E and W ends. One has a
cross incised on it. Such simple structures are very difficult to date –
Eithne's Grave could belong to the seventh century, and the other
structures to a century or so later. The site has traditional
associations with St Columba, and Eithne was said to be his mother.

Iona (NM 2824) can be reached by ferry from Oban; cars are not
allowed on the island, which is administered by the Iona
Community. There is less to see, however, of its Dark Age remains
than on Eileach an Naoimh, and the island is dominated by the
medieval monastery.

St Columba arrived in Scotland in 563, coming originally from
Ireland to minister to the Scots of Dalriada, and chose the island as
the centre for his activity. The visible remains of Columba's
monastery are those of the *vallum*, which can be seen as a low bank
and ditch running to the W of the road up to the Priory from the
pier. The Iona *vallum* is complicated by subsidiary earthworks, and
its roughly rectangular plan is only really apparent from the air – it
is one of the few early rectilinear (as opposed to curvilinear)
monastic enclosures in Britain and Ireland, and compares with
Clonmacnois in Ireland. Excavation has established that the original
vallum is pre-Viking, and has also revealed remains of timber
buildings in the SE of the enclosure.

On Tor Abb, a low hill overlooking the Priory, are the remains of
what is called St Columba's Cell, though there is no real reason for
this ascription. There is a low rectilinear foundation, and excavation
showed a rock-cut bed and the stone supports for a seat inside it. A
cross base can be seen nearby.

The Reilig Odhrain is a burial ground named after one of
Columba's followers, Oran, and lies just SW of the Priory. It is the
traditional burial ground of the early kings of Scotland. The
standing chapel is medieval.

The finest Dark Age remains on Iona are the High Crosses. There
are three, St Martin's, St Matthew's and St John's. Of these the best

91 Iona, St Martin's Cross

is the most fragmentary, St John's Cross, but a concrete replica (restored) stands just SW of the Cathedral alongside the other two. The fragments of the original are in the site museum, along with many other stones of Dark Age and medieval date from the site. St John's Cross is a composite monument carved from blocks of slate. The ornament is non-figural, but includes fine interlace and curvilinear patterns. It has the same kind of arms as the Kildalton Cross.

Of St Matthew's Cross only the lower part of the shaft survives, but the front is decorated with the figures of Adam and Eve and key-pattern ornament. Interlace adorns the back.

St Martin's Cross is almost complete – it lacks only the ends of the side arms, and is a single piece of granite with sculpture on panels on front and back. The ornament includes figural work, with the Virgin and Child on the front and Daniel at the top.

On the picturesque island of Skye a patch of bright green grass denotes the remains of the minor monastery at **Annait** (NG 272527). It lies west of the B886 and can be seen from the road. A stream must be crossed to reach it since the site lies on a spit of land between two rivers. An outer earthwork turns the site into a promontory fort, and within it is a massive stone wall with a single entrance forming the main defence. A lesser stone wall runs along the E side of the promontory, and still stands several courses high at the N end. Inside the enclosure are the ruined foundations of at least two circular cells and a rectangular chapel. The defences may be iron age, in which case this would be a reused fort converted into a monastery. The site was visited by Dr Johnson and Boswell, who thought it was a temple to an Egyptian god, Anaitis.

One of the very few Pictish stones in the Hebrides can be seen on Skye at **Clach Ard** (NG 421491), reached by the B8036 and a minor road to the W. It stands near the road about 5m (8 km) NW of Portree and is a Class I stone.

The Northern Isles

The Northern Isles have always seemed very remote and strange to the inhabitants of the rest of Britain. The 1695 edition of Camden's *Britannia* reported that,

> The air and clouds here, by the operation of the sun, do sometimes generate several things: for instance, not many years since some fishermen fishing half a league from land over-against Copinsaa (i.e. Copinsay), in a fair day there fell down from the air a stone about the bigness of a foot-ball, which fell in the midst of the boat, and sprung a leak in it, to the great hazard of the men that were in it: which could be no other but some substance generated in the clouds. The stone was like condensed or petrified clay . . . about four years ago, after a thunder in the month of June, there fell a great flake of ice more than a foot thick . . . When the winds are violent, the sea casts in pieces of trees, and sometimes hogsheads of wine and brandy, Ambergreese, exotick fowls, &c.

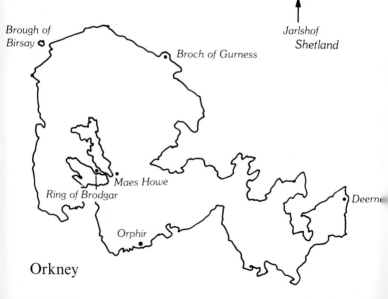

For the twentieth century traveller the Northern Isles offer fewer perils (and fewer alcoholic rewards), but their exploration can sometimes still be something of an adventure. There are Dark Age remains in very remote corners, but we have omitted them from this list. Most of those on the mainland will be fairly easy of access, but cafés are still few in number so a flask and sandwiches are useful assets in the field.

In both Orkney and Shetland the tower-like iron age brochs (see p. 43) were replaced by various types of smaller houses from the second or third centuries AD, but this change in dwelling type does not necessarily indicate any major change in the population, though obviously there were social changes. Society in the Northern Isles continued to evolve thereafter without major changes up to the coming of the Vikings. At some point Orkney and Shetland came under the domination of the Picts, and the Northern Isles were effectively Pictish when the Norse arrived in the ninth century. The native population was probably small in numbers, and seems to have coexisted peacefully with its Viking overlords. The Scandinavian occupation of the Northern Isles can be divided into two periods, Pagan, which lasts *c.* 800–1065, and Christian, from 1065 onwards – that being the probable date of the death of Earl Thorfinn the Mighty, who was responsible for setting in motion the conversion of the Isles to Christianity.

In the Orkney Isles it is very difficult to make a distinction between the remains of the late iron age and those of the Dark Ages, since there was no cultural break from the broch period to the coming of the Vikings. This social phenomenon is well typified at the **Broch of Gurness** on the Orkney Mainland, at Aikerness (HY 3826) [AM;S]. To reach this very impressive site, follow the A966; the side road which leads to the site turns off just S of the junction of the B9057 at Georth. Cars cannot be driven up to the site, but the walk out to the headland is invigorating in fine weather. The earliest remains at Aikerness are the ruins of an iron age broch and its associated defences. Outside the broch the original defences comprise a series of three stone-lined and rock-cut ditches in front of a wall. The abandonment of the broch some time in the early centuries AD might be regarded as the beginning of the Dark Ages. The new requirements dictated a new floor and slab partitions to segment the floor space in the broch. Outside the broch a complex of secondary huts were built. The outer wall of the broch defences was modified and furnished with projecting bastions. These secondary huts were probably built in the second or third centuries but continued in occupation much later, well into the Dark Ages, and their ruins are readily distinguishable by the visitor.

A number of the huts show features which are characteristic of the Pictish period in Orkney. One of these features is rectilinear planning; another is the use of the 'courtyard house' with a central courtyard from which smaller rooms led off. The post-broch finds from these structures at Aikerness include a penannular brooch of the fifth or sixth century AD.

With the coming of the Vikings the site was once more the scene of building activity. A long house was built on the line of the broch ditch (it has been rebuilt after the excavation adjacent to the site museum). The burial of a Viking woman came to light during the excavations in the 1930s – she was buried with a pair of tortoise brooches and other belongings in a stone-lined coffin.

A visit should be rounded off in the site museum which contains many finds from the 1930s excavations. The penannular brooch and the objects from the Viking burial, however, are in Tankerness House museum in Kirkwall.

Although often claimed as a 'classic' Dark Age monastery, the site of **Deerness** (HY 5908) almost certainly belongs to the twelfth century. It lies on the E side of the mainland, approached by the A960 and B9050 from Kirkwall. To get to the site, go to Skaill, then follow the uneven footpath along the cliff, through the army range

92 Broch of Gurness

(caution: there may be red flags flying). The path is dramatic, winding past the onomatopoeic Gloup, where water is sucked in and out through a natural land-bridge. The monastery lies on the Brough of Deerness, and can be reached only after an intrepid climb down the cliff on one side and up the other, the old land-bridge having collapsed. Caution and common sense must dictate whether the weather and health permit the site to be reached, but it can be viewed in safety and comparative detail from the mainland. It is worth a visit on a good day simply for the scenery. The ruins were once a small rectangular chapel and a series of rectangular cells on a headland, cut off by a stone-built *vallum*. The foundations now appear as turf-covered mounds. The site is reminiscent of Tintagel, Cornwall (see p. 64).

The classic ecclesiastical site in Orkney, both Pictish and Norse, is that at the **Brough of Birsay** (HY 2328) [AM; S], a tidal island just off the mainland, 20m (32·2 km) NW of Kirkwall on the A966. The site can be reached by the fit and firm-of-foot across a causeway, except for approximately three hours before high water until three hours after. High water is about an hour before high water at Kirkwall, and before setting out to Birsay from Kirkwall it is as well to check the time of high water in the Harbourmaster's office. [The site is closed on Mondays, October–February.]

On reaching the island, a steep path leads to the modern museum, in front of which are the main ecclesiastical remains. The most

93 Broch of Deerness

prominent remains are those of the Norse period, but the Norse occupation of the site was preceded by a Pictish cemetery and no doubt also ecclesiastical buildings, though these have not been found. The site may have been that of a monastery. The full extent of the Pictish cemetery is not known, but the line of a roughly circular wall can be observed, underlying the SE corner of the later Norse enclosure wall. What has been assumed to be part of the Pictish church associated with this cemetery underlies the south wall of the nave of the Norse church. It stands to a height of two or three courses, and was already ruinous in the eleventh century when the Norse church was built. It need not, however, predate this very greatly, and could in turn be a replacement for an even earlier timber oratory. Inside the enclosure wall, adjacent to the foundations of the church, the graves of the Pictish period are visible. The Pictish period graves are demarcated by small stumps of stone broken off (they would not have projected above ground level in the Norse period) and by the tops of slabs which formed the stone cists of the graves. The later Norse-period graves are recognizable because the marker stones stand well above the present ground level, and are mostly thick, weathered blocks of grey slate. They are confined to the area S and E of the church, in order to leave a passage to provide access to the farmstead (marked as 'bishop's palace' on published plans). When this farmstead was built, a new cemetery was added on the E side of the enclosure. Only a few slabs are visible in this added graveyard, suggesting it was not used for long.

Although nothing is now visible of the remaining Pictish occupation at Birsay, a midden was found during excavations before the Second World War, which produced extensive metalworking remains of the Pictish period. This was proof of the industry and craft carried out in this remote and weather-beaten corner of the Christian world.

Inside the graveyard, on the S side, excavators found a triple grave associated with fragments of a Pictish slab. A reconstructed cast of this stone now stands on the site, and depicts an eagle, a 'swimming elephant', a crescent and V-rod and a stemmed disc as well as naturalistic representations of three bearded figures carrying spears and square shields. This is the only known occurrence of a Pictish symbol stone being found associated with a grave.

Adjacent to the slab, but closer to the church, a row of stones about 8 feet long runs E–W, with a curved angle and a slight return

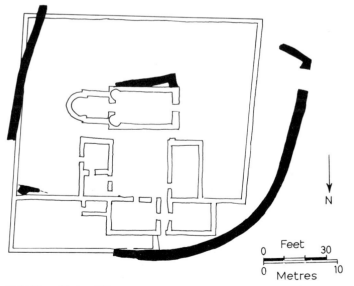

94 (a) Birsay (b) plan of Birsay

at the W end. These are all that remain of the kerb of a mound, originally about 8 feet (2·44 metres) square. This the excavator, Dr C A R Radford, interpreted as a *leacht*, like the one found at Tintagel (see p. 66) or that in the Isle of Man (see p. 203).

The foundations of the church stand within the enclosure wall of the Norse cemetery. A rectangular nave terminates in an almost square chancel with semi-circular apse. Foundations were laid for a square tower at the W end, which was apparently never completed. The construction is of lime-mortared flagstones, plastered inside and out. The chancel arch was added at a secondary stage, when two altar recesses were constructed at the E end of the nave and a screen wall built to separate the chancel apse. Near the centre of the nave some irregular flagstones can be seen which mark the position of a grave. Here the excavators found a disarticulated skeleton in a wooden coffin. This could have been the bones of Earl Thorfinn, or one of his family. Fragmentary though it is, the building bears close scrutiny, since it displays features of Anglo-Saxon architecture. A double-splay window in the chancel is of a type found in Anglo-Saxon churches and in Carolingian churches in the Rhineland. The church was built *c.* 1050, with the altar recesses and other secondary features being twelfth-century additions.

To the north of the church, astride the line of the Norse cemetery wall, is a building which has been claimed to be a bishop's palace. Three ranges edge a central courtyard: the fourth range is taken up by the church itself. The north range consisted of a hall at the E end and a screen passage separating it from an ante-chamber, warmed by large fires. Originally the building was entered through this room, but later the doorway was blocked. The west range, which is probably contemporary, was a private apartment, and the east range was perhaps store-rooms. Recently the interpretation of this as a bishop's palace has been questioned. The closest parallels to Birsay are to be found in the ecclesiastical complex at Gardar, Greenland, where the church adjoins a farm to form one monastic unit. Until more is known about this type of Norse site its interpretation as a farm or palace must be left open.

Between the ecclesiastical complex and the cliff are further foundations, still under excavation. The earliest occupation on this part of the site is represented by a Pictish midden (not now visible), into which the foundations of at least one Norse house were dug in the ninth century.

'Earl Sigurd's Hall' is on the edge of the cliff, and is partly destroyed by the sea and partly incorporated into the later 'Earl Thorfinn's Palace'. Earl Sigurd's hall had turf-cored walls, and was very similar to the hall excavated at Westness on Rousay, measuring about 100 feet (30·5 metres) long and 30 feet (9·1 metres) wide originally, with internal divisions. It dates probably from the tenth century.

Earl Sigurd's hall, and the middens of the tenth and eleventh centuries adjacent, were in use before Earl Thorfinn's palace, which partly overlay them. This is a complex structure showing many different building phases, and the sequence is extremely difficult to disentangle on the ground. Basically it consisted of a large building on the N side of an enclosure facing an open courtyard to the S. The courtyard extended to the cliff, where there was a bath-house. Finds from this complex suggest it belongs to the eleventh century.

The ruins of Earl Thorfinn's palace are obscured by the later buildings on top of it, which are the main visible remains in this area. These comprise a complex of small houses with stone and turf walls and roughly paved floors, dating from the twelfth century. They are built of beach pebbles, and many have a central fireplace made up of stone slabs set on edge.

To the S, on the cliff edge, a wide paved ramp and a slipway with roughly walled sides were used for drawing up ships.

Above the church, on the slopes of a gentle hill, is a scatter of buildings. Two of the largest were partially excavated, and can be seen by the boundary fence on the S side of the whole enclosure. Both date to the ninth or tenth century.

The northern of the two (ie the one nearest the museum) began life as a long house constructed with turf walls faced on the inside with stonework. The outer facing was of alternate courses of turf and stone. These have now mostly collapsed. The walls above the doors are rebuilt; below the doors the walling is original. The second is of similar plan. Both date from the ninth or tenth century.

The other buildings on the slope can be viewed from the other side of the demarcating fence. They include large halls with outshots, of a type found in Iceland and Greenland in the tenth or eleventh century.

The site museum displays a number of typical finds from the excavations on the site.

Birsay boasts a runic inscription, found on a stone built into the outer wall of the chancel behind the aumbry in the north wall of the church. Further runic inscriptions can be seen adorning the most famous of the prehistoric monuments on the Orkney mainland, the Ring of Brodgar and Maes Howe. The **Ring of Brodgar** (HY 2913) [AM; A] lies to the W of the B9055, about 4m (6·44 km) NE of Stromness, at the head of the isthmus separating the Lochs of Harray and Stenness. This is one of the outstanding circles of standing stones in the British Isles, a rival to Stonehenge, Avebury and Callanish. Originally there were about sixty stones, but now only twenty-seven still stand. The highest is 15 feet (4·6 metres) tall, and others are over 10 feet (3 metres) high. To find the runic inscription, count the stones clockwise from the NW entrance. No. 3 has a fine but undeciphered inscription, No. 4 has a cross, No. 8 an anvil and No. 9 an ogham inscription. With the possible exception of the ogham, which is probably Pictish work, the other carvings are probably the scribblings of Norsemen.

The finest collection of runic inscriptions is to be seen at **Maes Howe** (HY 3112) [AM; S], on the A965 about 9m (14·5 km) W of Kirkwall, just before the turning to Brodgar. The site can be seen from the road as a green mound in the fields, enclosed by a fence, and it can be entered on application to the key-keeper (who also has guide pamphlets) in the farm opposite – a torch is provided for the visitor to examine the interior. The tomb itself, which is unique in Europe and represents the triumph of neolithic funerary architecture around 2,000 BC, was broken into by Norse on several occasions in the twelfth century, and who carved a series of 24 runic inscriptions on its walls. The inscriptions include one which can be seen on the lowest stones immediately W of the chamber on the S side. It reads: 'This howe was built a long time before Lothbok's. His sons were bold; scarcely ever were there such tall men of their hands. Crusaders broke into Maes Howe. Hlif, the Earl's maidservant, carved this. Away to the north-west is a great treasure hidden. A long time ago was a great treasure hidden here. Lucky will be he who can find this great wealth. Hakon single-handed bore treasure from this howe.' Another inscription records: 'It is true what I say, that treasure was carried off in the course of three nights. Treasure was carried off before the crusaders broke into the howe.' This can be seen on the E edge of the slab that forms the S face of the NW buttress, about 2½ feet (0·76 metres) from the floor. It is continued on the W face of the NE buttress. This buttress also carries a carved figure of a dragon. Other inscriptions include an account of how Norse crusaders broke into the tomb to shelter from a storm, when one of their party went mad and rushed from the mound; a series of

personal names; graffiti extolling the charms of particular ladies; a
knot pattern and a sketch of a walrus.

A solitary twig-rune adorns the back wall of the chancel in the
ruined church at **Orphir** (HY 4112) [AM; A], on the mainland. This
ecclesiastical site is reached by taking the A964 and a side road S
from Swanbister, and lies 8m (12·9 km) SW of Kirkwall. It stands in
a churchyard, and only the small semicircular chancel and part of
the wall of the nave survive. The church is exceptional for being the
only surviving round medieval church in Scotland – a twelfth-
century example can be seen at Ludlow Castle, Salop, and there is
documentary evidence for another which once existed at Old
Roxburgh. Adjacent to it are the much overgrown foundations of
Norse period buildings. To see them, turn left just before reaching
the churchyard gate, where the Norse houses nestle in a hollow. The
thirteenth-century Icelandic *Orkneyinga Saga*, which provides most
of our information about the Northern Isles in the Norse period,
related how a 'noble church stood outside the hall door' at Orphir,
and this round church is presumably to be identified with this
description. The overgrown foundations are those of the Earl's *Bu*
(ie 'drinking hall') that is mentioned in the Saga. They were
discovered in the nineteenth century, and it is now virtually
impossible to disentangle the remains. More Norse foundations

95 Orphir, Round Church

were discovered when a new byre was built at the nearby farm, suggesting that there had once been a fairly extensive settlement. The church is known as the 'Girth House' (from the Norse for a sanctuary) and was probably built by Earl Haakon Paulsson around 1120. It is modelled on the Church of the Holy Sepulchre at Jerusalem, but was probably inspired not by the original (though Haakon had gone to Jerusalem on a pilgrimage) but by one of the many round churches copying it on the Continent.

In Shetland only one site need be singled out for a special visit, but this has some claim to being in the top rank of impressive archaeological sites in the British Isles **Jarlshof** (HU 3909) [AM; S] is situated not far from the airport on Sumburgh Head, under a mile SE of the airport buildings. It can be reached by following the A970 and the signposted road S thereafter. It stands on the shore of a bay which provided excellent harbourage, while the adjacent land provided good grazing ground and arable as well as freshwater springs.

Seven successive phases of occupation are represented in the visible remains, and an eighth (neolithic) was recognized in excavation: a late bronze age village, an early iron age village, a broch, a post-broch wheelhouse settlement, a Viking settlement, a medieval farmstead and a late sixteenth-century house – so students of the Dark Ages must disentangle these.

On entering the site the first remains that are to be seen are those of the bronze and iron age villages. From here a path leads round from the site museum to the iron age broch and late iron age and Dark Age wheelhouse complex on the edge of the sea. The sea has eroded half the broch, but the wheelhouses are exceptional.

The first of the Dark Age structures that was built inside the broch courtyard was a round house, now largely destroyed by later building but visible from the platform of the seventeenth-century laird's house which overlooks it. This was converted to an aisled wheelhouse when free-standing stone piers were constructed inside the house to replace the previous wooden posts which supported the roof. The other structures within the broch courtyard are all true wheelhouses (see p. 43). These comprise Wheelhouse 2 and Wheelhouse 3, the latter boasting a fine paved central hearth.

To the NW of the wheelhouses can be seen the Passage House, which was in use in the period immediately before the arrival of the Vikings. This comprises a sloping passage leading into three chambers, which block the original entrance of the first wheelhouse.

96 Jarlshof (a) Wheelhouse (b) Viking house

The passage, which is 25 feet (6·6 metres) long, originally had a stone staircase (later abandoned), and the Passage House appears to have been used as a dwelling. Later it was converted for use as a byre. To the E of the broch are other structures which served as storage rooms and a byre.

About 45 yards (41·2 metres) W of the Passage House the boundary wall of the post-broch settlement is reached by following the path. This runs up from the beach, and is broken by an entrance, not far from which is a cluster of stone huts which partly overlies the wall. Hut 1 is not well preserved but Hut 2 which post-dates it, is, and shows several modifications suggesting quite a long usage. On the floor of the latest entrance the excavators found an incised cross of eighth-century type on a slate slab. After this hut was abandoned, a house was built on top of it in the Viking period, though only the fireplace of this building can still be seen, the rest having been removed in excavation.

The next remains are those of the Norse occupation, which began in the ninth century. The foundations of the Norse buildings are very confusing for the visitor, as many different phases of building are all represented, spanning the period down to the thirteenth century. To disentangle the remains, visitors are best advised to buy the excellent site guidebook, though even with the aid of this and the plan it provides of the foundations, it is not very easy to work out what was what.

Begin by localizing the parent farmstead, House 1, which lies immediately to the north of the seventeenth-century Laird's House. This house went through three main phases of use, and these are reflected in the foundations. It began as a two-roomed long house, and of this first phase the kitchen end with its oven is preserved at the W end of the building, and part of the original bowed-out side walls are still visible on the S side. In the early eleventh century a byre was added to the E end with a curved passage to provide access for cattle. The W end of the house was extended, and a partition wall erected across the floor of the living-room. The byre was erected on a pile of burnt stones, thrown out from the hearth, and some of these can still be seen in the NE corner of the byre.

In the third phase a new house was built within the old, the partition wall in the living-room serving as the east gable wall of the new, smaller dwelling. This phase belongs to the twelfth and thirteenth centuries.

Immediately to the W of House 1 is a building with a well-preserved rectangular stone hearth, which probably served as the original bath house for the dwelling. To the N of House 1 are the disjointed foundations of outhouses.

During the ninth to early tenth centuries other houses (Houses 2, 3, and 4) were built adjacent to House 1, but these were built over by later buildings which complicate the understanding of their plans. The official guide book explains the remains in some detail.

A small site museum preserves typical finds from the site.

Gazetteer of visible remains not mentioned in the text

Unless otherwise stated these are parish churches, or stones in parish churches or churchyards.

Chapter 1 The South-west

Name	County	OS Grid Ref	Description
Avebury	Wilts	SU 1069	Saxon nave walls
Bremhill	Wilts	ST 9773	Saxon NW quoin of nave
Burcombe	Wilts	SU 0731	Saxon S wall of chancel
Cricklade	Wilts	SU 0993	Part of S nave wall: Saxon
Knook	Wilts	ST 9341	Saxon S door of nave
Limpley Stoke	Wilts	ST 7860	Saxon nave walls
Netheravon	Wilts	SU 1448	Saxon tower
Milborne Port	Somerset	ST 6718	Late Saxon chancel
Sidbury	Devon	SY 1391	Few walls of Saxon crypt
Stowford	Devon	SX 433870	Sixth-century stone
Tavistock	Devon	SX 481743	Sixth-century stone in vicarage garden
Winsford Hill, Exmoor	Somerset	SS 890335	Sixth-century memorial stone (Caractacus stone) perhaps *in situ*
Carnsew	Cornwall	SW 557372	Late fifth-century memorial stone
Giant's Hedge, Lerryn	Cornwall	SX 1554	Linear earthwork
Gulval, Bleu Bridge	Cornwall	SW 478318	Sixth century memorial stone, possibly *in situ*
Lewannick	Cornwall	SX 2780	Ogham bilingual stone in churchyard
Phillack	Cornwall	SW 5638	Sixth-century memorial stones and altar frontal in modern lych-gate, perhaps ninth-century

Rialton	Cornwall	SW 8561	Sixth-century memorial stone
Slaughterbridge	Cornwall	SX 1085	Sixth-century ogham stone
St Clement	Cornwall	SW 8543	Sixth-century inscription on recut ninth-century cross near church

Chapter 2 The South-East

Name	*County*	*OS Grid Ref*	*Description*
Fareham	Hants	SU 5806	Saxon E walls of Lady Chapel
Hannington	Hants	SU 5355	Saxon NE quoin of nave
Hinton Ampner	Hants	SU 5927	Saxon nave walls
Little Somborne	Hants	SU 3832	Saxon pilasters in nave
Longstock, the moat	Hants	SU 362373	Danish earthwork
Warblington	Hants	SU 7205	Saxon second storey of tower
Kilpeck	Hereford	S0 4430	NE corner of nave, Saxon
Aldington	Kent	TR 0736	Saxon N walls
Barham Down	Kent	TR 202518	Pagan Saxon barrows
Cheriton	Kent	TR 1836	Saxon W wall of nave
Coldred	Kent	TR 2747	Main fabric of Saxon church
Darenth	Kent	TQ 5671	Saxon N and W walls of nave
Derringstone Down	Kent	TR 207490	Pagan Saxon barrows
Halstow, Lower	Kent	TQ 8667	Parts of Saxon chancel
Leeds	Kent	TQ 8253	Saxon N wall above arcade
Northfleet	Kent	TQ 6274	Saxon SW quoin of nave
Orpington	Kent	TQ 4666	Saxon sundial
Peckham	Kent	TQ 6452	Saxon W tower and W wall of nave
Rochester	Kent	TQ 7468	Outline of seventh-century Saxon church on floor

Shorne	Kent	TQ 6971	Saxon nave
Stourmouth, West	Kent	TR 2562	Saxon N and possibly W wall of nave
Swanscombe	Kent	TQ 6074	Saxon lower part of tower
Whitfield	Kent	TL 3145	Seventh- to eighth-century nave, with tenth- to eleventh-century additions
Wouldham	Kent	TQ 7164	Late Saxon nave
Albury	Surrey	TQ 0647	Fragments Saxon nave and chancel, in Old Church
Cheam	Surrey	TQ 2463	Saxon chancel, now Lumley mausoleum
Elsted	Surrey	SU 8119	Saxon N and W walls of nave and chancel arch
Shoreham	Surrey	TQ 2006	Saxon parts nave walls
Singleton	Surrey	SU 8713	Lowest stage tower Saxon
Stoke D'Abernon	Surrey	TQ 1258	Main fabric Saxon
Thursley	Surrey	SU 9039	Saxon chancel and parts of nave
Botolphs	Sussex	TQ 1909	Fragments Saxon nave and chancel arch
Chithurst	Sussex	SU 8423	Slight Saxon remains
Clayton	Sussex	TQ 2913	Saxon nave and W of chancel
Hardham	Sussex	TQ 0317	Nave and chancel, very Late Saxon
Jevington	Sussex	TQ 5601	Late Saxon tower and sculpture
Lyminster	Sussex	TQ 0204	Saxon nave and part of chancel
Poling	Sussex	TQ 0404	Late Saxon nave
Rumboldswyke	Sussex	SU 8704	Main fabric of Saxon church
Stopham	Sussex	TQ 0218	Saxon nave
Woolbeding	Sussex	SU 8722	Saxon nave

Chapter 3 Central England

Name	County	OS Grid Ref	Description
Hawridge	Bucks	SP 950058	Hawridge Court Farm, Danish earthwork

Iver	Bucks	TQ 0481	Parts of nave and chancel Saxon
Norbury	Derbys	SK 1242	Mercian cross shaft
Ampney St Peter	Glos	SP 0801	Saxon nave
Ampney Crucis	Glos	SP 0601	Saxon N door of nave
Crickley Hill	Glos	SO 9216	Iron age fort with Dark Age occupation
Duntisbourne Rouse	Glos	SO 9806	Saxon nave (possible)
Dymock	Glos	SO 7031	Saxon fabric in lower parts of walls
Edgeworth	Glos	SO 9405	Parts of walls and N door Saxon
Lydney	Glos	SO 6102	Dark Age fort
Miserden	Glos	SO 9308	Saxon heads of N and S nave doors
Stanley St Leonard	Glos	SO 8003	Chapel now used as barn, Saxon
Winstone	Glos	SO 9609	Late Saxon nave
Castor	Northants	TL 1298	Mercian ninth-century sculptures
Desborough	Northants	SP 8083	Mercian sculptures
Nassington	Northants	TL 0696	Parts of nave Saxon
Carlton-in-Lindrick	Notts	SK 5883	W tower and W of nave Saxon
East Bridgeford	Notts	SK 6943	Parts of chancel Saxon
Hickling	Notts	SK 6929	Tenth-century cross
Southwell	Notts	SK 6953	Late Saxon tympanum
Caversfield	Oxford	SP 5825	Lower part W tower Saxon
Stratton Audley	Oxford	SP 625283	Stuttle's Bank, Danish earthwork
Swalcliffe	Oxford	SP 3737	Late Saxon side walls of nave
Waterperry	Oxford	SP 6206	Chancel arch Saxon
Leek	Staffs	SJ 9856	Mercian cross shaft (Peak)
Wolverhampton	Staffs	SO 9198	Mercian cross shaft

Chapter 4 Eastern England

Name	County	OS Grid Ref	Description
Bedford	Beds	TL 055494	King's Ditch, Danish earthwork

Bolnhurst	Beds	TL 084597	The Camp, Danish earthwork
Clapham	Beds	TL 029523	Danish earthwork
Renhold	Beds	TL 107513	Howbury, Danish earthwork
Sandy	Beds	TL 175479	Beeston Berrys, Danish work
Shillington	Beds	TL 119350	Danish earthwork, Church Spanel
Steppingley	Beds	TL 001351	Seymour's Mount, Danish earthwork
Tempsford	Beds	TL 161529	Gannock's Castle, Danish work
Turvey	Beds	SP 9452	Saxon parts of nave
Willington	Beds	TL 113502	The Docks, Danish earthwork
Cambridge	Cambs	TL 4459	Rebuilt arch in St Giles, Saxon
Fleam Dyke	Cambs	TL 488601 to TL 572522	Linear earthwork, Early Saxon
Shelford, Little	Cambs	TL 4551	Saxon window in chancel
Swavesey	Cambs	TL 3669	Saxon E quoins nave, S wall of chancel
Wimblington	Cambs	TL 448930	Stonea Camp, Danish earthwork
Boreham	Essex	TL 7509	Chancel probably Saxon
Chickney	Essex	TL 5728	Saxon nave and W of chancel
Hallingbury, Great	Essex	TL 5119	Saxon chancel arch and S wall of nave
Hallingbury, Little	Essex	TL 5017	Late Saxon nave
Mersea, West	Essex	TM 0012	Saxon lower part of W tower
Notley, White	Essex	TL 7818	Saxon chancel arch and side walls of nave
Prittlewell	Essex	TQ 8786	W part of N wall of chancel, Saxon
Hertford	Herts	TL 325125	Danish earthwork
Northchurch	Herts	SP 9708	W and S walls of nave, Saxon
Walkern	Herts	TL 2926	Saxon side walls of nave
West Mill	Herts	TL 3627	Saxon parts of nave

Barholm	Hunts	TF 0911	Part of S wall of nave, Saxon
Eaton Socon	Hunts	TL 174589	Danish earthwork
Fletton	Hunts	TL 2097	Ninth-century Mercian sculptures
Woodston	Hunts	TL 1897	Part of W wall, Saxon
Coleby	Lincs	SK 9760	Late Saxon tower
Great Hale	Lincs	TF 1442	Late Saxon tower
Greetwell	Lincs	TF 0171	Saxon window in S wall of nave
Harmston	Lincs	SK 9762	Late Saxon tower
Lincoln	Lincs	SK 9771	Rebuilt Saxon tower, St Benedict's
Stragglethorpe	Lincs	SK 9152	Saxon nave
Winterton	Lincs	SE 9218	Parts of nave and tower, Saxon
Aslacton	Norfolk	TM 1591	Saxon round tower
Haddiscoe	Norfolk	TM 4396	Round W tower, Saxon
Heigham	Norfolk	TG 2109	Saxon W tower and SW quoin of nave
Kirby Cane	Norfolk	TM 3794	Saxon round tower
Lopham, South	Norfolk	TM 0481	Saxon N wall of nave
Melton, Great	Norfolk	TG 1406	Parts nave and chancel Saxon
Morton on the Hill	Norfolk	TG 1215	Late Saxon nave
Norwich	Norfolk	TG 2308	W wall of cloister of Cathedral, Saxon
Norwich	Norfolk	TG 2307	St John de Sepulcre, E and W walls of transept Saxon
Norwich	Norfolk	TG 2308	St John Timberhill, E wall of chancel Saxon
Norwich	Norfolk	TG 2309	St Martin at Palace, E end of chancel Saxon
Norwich	Norfolk	TG 2209	St Mary at Coslany, Saxon round tower
Quidenham	Norfolk	TM 0287	Saxon tower and W wall of nave
Rockland	Norfolk	TL 9996	Saxon nave
Ryburgh, Gt	Norfolk	TF 9627	Saxon W tower and W wall of nave
Shereford	Norfolk	TF 8829	S wall of nave and possibly lower part of tower, Saxon

Swainsthorpe	Norfolk	TG 2100	Blocked Saxon S window
Thornage	Norfolk	TG 0436	Saxon side walls of nave and chancel
Thorpe Abbots	Norfolk	TM 1878	N wall of nave Saxon.
Walsham, North	Norfolk	TG 2830	Axial tower between W tower and N aisle of present church
Warham St Mary	Norfolk	TL 9441	Danish earthwork
Weybourne	Norfolk	TG 1143	Axial tower in parish church
Witton	Norfolk	TG 3331	W and N walls of nave, possibly lower parts of tower Saxon
Wretham, East	Norfolk	TL 909889	Danish earthwork

Chapter 5 Wales

Name	County	OS Grid Ref	Description
Caer Gybi	Anglesey	SH 2482	Roman fort with Dark Age use
Defynnog	Brecknock	SN 9227	Sixth-century memorial stone
Llanddetty	Brecknock	SO 0712	Ninth-century pillar stone
Llandyfaelog-Fach	Brecknock	SN 0332	Late tenth-century cross slab
Llanhamlach	Brecknock	SO 0926	Tenth-century slab
Llanynis	Brecknock	SN 9950	Pillar cross
Trannwng	Brecknock	SN 9629	Ogham stone
Ystradgynlais	Brecknock	SN 7810	Sixth-century stones
Capel Anelog	Caerns	SH 1527	Chapel
Carreg-y-Llam	Caerns	SH 3343	Fortified site
Segontium	Caerns	SH 4862	Roman fort with Dark Age use
Llanfaglan	Caerns	SH 4760	Sixth-century stone
Llannor	Caerns	SH 3537	Sixth-century stones
Henfynyw	Cardigan	SN 4461	Seventh- to ninth-century stone
Llanarth	Cardigan	SN 4257	Ogham and ninth- to tenth-century stone
Llanbadarn Fawr	Cardigan	SN 6081	Tenth-century cross
Llandewi-Brefi	Cardigan	SN 6655	Sixth- to tenth-century stones
Llandysul	Cardigan	SN 4140	Sixth-century stone
Cynwyl Gaeo	Carmarthen	SN 6739	Sixth-century stone

Eglwys Cymyn	Carmarthen	SN 2310	Fifth- to sixth-century stone
Laugharne	Carmarthen	SN 2910	Ninth- to tenth-century disc cross
Llandawke	Carmarthen	SN 2811	Ogham stone
Llandeilo	Carmarthen	SN 6222	Ninth- to tenth-century crosses
Llanfihangel-ar-Arth	Carmarthen	SN 4539	Sixth-century stone
Llangeler	Carmarthen	SN 4038	Ogham stone
Llansadyrin	Carmarthen	SN 2810	Sixth-century stone
Merthyr	Carmarthen	SN 3520	Fifth- to sixth-century stone
St Ishmaels	Carmarthen	SN 3808	Fifth- to sixth-century stone
Deganwy	Denbigh	SH 7879	Hillfort
Dinorben	Denbigh	SH 9675	Reoccupied hillfort
Llanrhaiadr-ym-Mochnant	Denbigh	SJ 0864	Tenth-century cross slab
Burryholms	Glamorgan	SS 4092	Ecclesiastical site
Coychurch	Glamorgan	SS 9379	Eleventh-century crosses
Llandaff	Glamorgan	ST 1578	Tenth-century cross in cathedral
Llangan	Glamorgan	SS 9577	Tenth-century cross
Llangyfelach	Glamorgan	SS 6498	Ninth-century slabs
Coygan	Glamorgan	SS 2809	Reoccupied hillfort
Llanilterne	Glamorgan	ST 0979	Sixth-century stone
Merthyr Mawr	Glamorgan	SS 8877	Collection eleventh-century stones
Pontardawe	Glamorgan	SN 7204	Ninth- to tenth-century slab
Mathrafal	Mont	MY 1310	Reoccupied hillfort
Llanaber	Merioneth	SH 6018	Sixth-century stones
Llandeilo	Pembroke	SN 0926	Ogham bilingual stone
St Nicholas	Pembroke	SM 9035	Fifth- to ninth-century stones
Mathry	Pembroke	SM 8732	Fifth- to ninth-century stones
Steynton	Pembroke	SM 9107	Ogham bilingual
St Dogmaels	Pembroke	SN 1645	Ogham bilingual
Llandysilio	Pembroke	SN 1121	Sixth- to tenth-century stones
Caldy	Pembroke	SS 1496	Ogham stone

| Llowes | Radnor | SO 1941 | Eleventh-century cross |

Chapter 6 Isle of Man

Name	*Parish*	*OS Grid Ref*	*Description*
Castleward	Braddan	SC 3778	Citadel fort
Cronk ny Arrey Llaa	Bride	SC 4599	Viking barrow
Knock y Dowan	Jurby	SC 3999	Viking barrow
St Patrick's chapel	Jurby	SC 3498	Keeill
Ballaquiney	Marown	SC 3377	Keeill
Keeill Vael	Maughold	SC 4687	Keeill
Keeill Chiggyrt	Maughold	SC 4889	Keeill

Chapter 7 Northern England

Name	*County*	*OS Grid Ref*	*Description*
Aycliffe	Durham	NZ 2822	Saxon nave walls above arcade and tenth-century cross-shaft
Sockburn	Durham	NZ 3407	Ruined Saxon seventh- to eighth-century nave
Staindrop	Durham	NZ 1320	Slight remains of Saxon nave and tower
Bamburgh	Northumb	NZ 1835	Saxon hillfort
Heddon-on-the-Wall	Northumb	NZ 1366	Part of nave Saxon
Whittingham	Northumb	NU 0611	Restored Saxon church
Warkworth	Northumb	NU 2506	Saxon Cross
Birtley	Northumb	NY 8878	Eighth-century inscribed slab
Appleby	Westmorland (Cumbria)	NY 6819	N and W walls of Saxon nave
Crosby Garrett	Westmorland	NY 7209	S walls of nave and chancel Saxon
Long Marton	Westmorland	NY 6624	Nave Saxon
Morland	Westmorland	NY 5922	Saxon tower
Plumbland	Westmorland	NY 1539	Hogback stone
Aldborough	Yorks	TA 2438	Saxon nave and sundial
Beverley	Yorks	TA 0339	Saxon abbot's chair
Bedale	Yorks	SE 2688	Parts of nave and chancel Saxon

Burghwallis	Yorks	SE 5312	Saxon nave and chancel
Collingham	Yorks	SE 3946	Restored Saxon nave, two crosses
Laughten-en-le-Marthen	Yorks	SK 5188	Parts of nave Saxon
Levisham	Yorks	SE 3891	Anglo-Danish sculpture
Terrington	Yorks	SE 6770	Saxon S nave wall
Beckermet-St-Bridget	Cumbria	NY 0506	Cross-shafts

Chapter 8 Scotland

Name	County	OS Grid Ref	Description
Broomend of Crichie	Aberdeen	NJ 7719	Pictish symbol stone
Logie Elphinstone	Aberdeen	NJ 7025	Pictish symbol stone
Tullich	Aberdeen	NO 3997	Pictish symbol stone
Migvie	Aberdeen	NJ 4306	Pictish symbol stone
Kinnellar (Kirkton)	Aberdeen	NJ 8214	Pictish symbol stone
Kintore	Aberdeen	NJ 7916	Pictish symbol stone
Balluderon	Angus	NO 3737	Pictish symbol stone
Largo	Angus	NO 4103	Pictish symbol stone
Ardestie	Angus	NO 5034	Proto-Pictish souterrain
Carlungie	Angus	NO 5135	Proto-Pictish souterrain
Ardifuir	Argyll	NR 7896	Dun with Dark Age occupation
Dunollie	Argyll	NM 8531	Dalriadic citadel (no visible Dark Age remains)
Dunaverty	Argyll	NR 6807	Fortified royal stronghold
Duncarnock	Ayrshire	NS 5055	Citadel fort
Cullykhan	Banff	NJ 6166	Iron age fort with Pictish occupation Pictish Class III slab
Reay	Caithness	NC 9665	Pictish symbol stone
Freswick	Caithness	ND 3667	Viking settlement in sand dunes (nothing visible)
Wag of Forse	Caithness	ND 2035	Post-broch settlement
Yarrows	Caithness	ND 3043	Post-broch settlement
Latheron	Caithness	ND 1933	Pictish symbol stone

Closeburn	Dumfries	NX 9092	Anglian cross shaft
Hoddom	Dumfries	NY 1672	Dark Age churchyard
Dumbarton Rock	Dunbartonshire	NS 4074	Citadel of Strathclyde. Nothing Dark Age visible
Harelaw	East Lothian	NT 5463	Reoccupied hillfort
Norman's Law	Fife	NO 3020	Citadel fort
Dunearn	Fife	NT 2187	Citadel fort
Inchcolm	Fife	NT 1982	Hogback tombstone
Clatchard's Craig	Fife	NO 2417	Hillfort, much quarried, with Pictish occupation
Denork	Fife	NO 4513	Nuclear-type fort
Castle Urquhart	Inverness	NH 5328	Iron age fort, Pictish reoccupied (no visible remains)
Dunottar	Kincardine	NO 8884	Pictish fort, traces removed by medieval castle
Castlegower	Kirkcudbright	NX 7958	Nuclear-type fort
Suie Hill	Kirkcudbright	NX 7549	Nuclear-type fort
Stroanfeggan	Kirkcudbright	NX 6392	Nuclear-type fort
Twynholm	Kirkcudbright	NX 6553	Nuclear-type fort
Elgin Cathedral	Moray	NJ 2263	Pictish symbol stone
Pabbay	Pabbay (Out. Heb)	NL 6087	Pictish symbol stone
Whiteside	Peebles	NT 1646	Citadel fort
Innerleithen	Peebles	NT 3336	Ninth-century cross-shaft
Blackford	Perthshire	NN 9209	Pictish symbol stone
St Madoes	Perthshire	NO 1921	Pictish symbol stone
Logierait	Perthshire	NO 9652	Pictish symbol stone
Struan	Perthshire	NN 8065	Pictish symbol stone
Alyth	Perthshire	NO 2448	Pictish symbol stone
Bruceton (Alyth)	Perthshire	NO 2950	Pictish symbol stone
Raasay House	Raasay (In. Heb)	NG 5436	Pictish symbol stone
Rosemarkie	Ross & Cromarty	NH 7357	Pictish symbol stone
Dingwall	Ross & Cromarty	NH 5458	Pictish symbol stone
Edderton	Ross & Cromarty	NH 7085	Pictish symbol stones
Strathpeffer	Ross & Cromarty	NH 4858	Pictish symbol stone

Hownham Rings	Roxburghshire	NT 7919	Iron age hillfort with some Dark Age occupation
Rubers Law	Roxburghshire	NT 5815	Nuclear fort
Old Melrose	Roxburghshire	NT 5434	Monastery
Borthwick Mains	Roxburghshire	NT 4314	Pictish symbol stone
Dunvegan Castle	Skye	NG 2449	Pictish symbol stone
Dunrobin	Sutherland	NC 8601	Stones in castle museum
Craigie Hill	West Lothian	NT 1575	Nuclear fort
Monreith House	Wigtown	NX 3542	Tenth-century Whithorn school cross

Chapter 9 Orkney and Shetland

Name	*County*	*OS Grid Ref*	*Description*
Corn Holm	Cornholm (Ork)	HY 6001	Hermitage
Marwick	Mainland (Ork)	HY 2224	Chapel
Broch of Burrian	N. Ronaldsay (Ork)	HY 7651	Broch with Dark Age occupation
St Tredwell's broch	Papa Westray (Ork)	HY 4950	Hermitage
Papil	Papil (Zet)	HU 3631	Monastery

Important archaeological sites with no notable visible remains

CHALTON Hants (SU 734145) Early Saxon village with rectangular houses.

CHEDDAR Somerset (ST 457531) Late Saxon palace complex of ninth to eleventh century, including timber long hall and lesser buildings. Associated with Eadmund, Eadwy and Eadgar. Excavated 1960–62.

GWITHIAN Cornwall (SW 585416) Minor settlement with round stone huts, associated with a range of finds including various classes of imported Mediterranean pottery. Important for associated fields.

KINGSTON DOWN Kent (TK 1951) Saxon cemetery, inhumations in barrows. Main excavation 1767, 1771–3 by Rev. B. Faussett. Finds included the Kingston Brooch (now in the Liverpool Museum), one of the finest pagan Saxon jewels.

LINDISFARNE Northumb (NU 128418) Early monastery associated with St Aidan, founded from Iona. Aidan abbot 635–51.

MAWGAN PORTH Cornwall (SW 852673) Small village of stone rectangular buildings with associated cemetery, dated to tenth to eleventh century.

MAXEY Northants (TF 124081) Middle Saxon village, with rectangular timber houses.

MUCKING Essex (TQ 672803) Early Saxon village, with sunken-floor huts and rectangular timber buildings, and associated cemetery. Important as one of the earliest Anglo-Saxon settlements known, occupied before 450.

OLD WINDSOR Berks (SU 991746) Middle–Late Saxon palace complex, with associated mill.

SOUTHAMPTON Hants (SU 434133) Middle and Late Saxon town (*Hamwih*) with substantial buildings, possible church, pits, wells, etc.

SUTTON COURTENAY Berks (SU 489940) Early Saxon village of sunken-floor huts, famous for being the first village to be extensively excavated (in 1923 and 1947).

THETFORD Norfolk (TL 8384) Late Saxon town, with sunken-floor huts and rectangular timber buildings, arranged in streets.

'Artisans' quarter' recognized. Given name to a type of Late
Saxon pottery, Thetford Ware.

WEST STOW Suffolk (TL 797714) Very Early Anglo-Saxon village
with sunken-floor huts and rectangular timber halls.

WHITBY Yorks (NZ 901113) Major Northumbrian monastery,
founded 657 by Abbess Hilda. Excavated 1920–25, with rich finds.

YEAVERING Northumb (NT 925305) Palace complex of King Edwin
of Northumbria. Several halls, minor buildings and 'grandstand'.

Museums with collections of Dark Age material

*This is not a complete list, and excludes museums with small collections of only local interest. Major collections are marked ***

Abingdon
Bangor
Basingstoke
*Birmingham, City Museum and Art Gallery
Brighton
Bristol, City Museum
* Cambridge, University Museum of Archaeology and Ethnology
   (see p. 163)
* Canterbury, Royal Museum
Canterbury, St Augustine's Abbey Museum
* Cardiff, National Museum of Wales (see p. 191)
Carmarthen, County Museum (see p. 188)
Cirencester, Corinium Museum
Colchester, Castle Museum
Coventry, Herbert Museum
Dartford
Derby
Devizes
Dorchester, Dorset County Museum
* Douglas, I.o.M., Manx Museum (see p. 206)
* Dumfries, Borough Museum (see p. 249)
* Edinburgh, National Museum of Antiquities (see p. 253)
Exeter, Royal Albert Museum and Art Gallery
Gloucester, City Museum
Huddersfield
Hull, Mortimer Museum
Ipswich
Leeds, City Museum
Leicester (see p. 124)
Lincoln, City and County Museum
Lindisfarne, Priory Museum
* Liverpool, City Museum (see p. 224)

* London, British Museum (see p. 96)
* London, Museum of London (see p. 96)
* London, Victoria and Albert Museum (see p. 96)
Maidstone Museum
Newark
Newbury
Newcastle, Black Gate Museum
Northampton
* Norwich, Castle Museum (see p. 159)
* Oxford, Ashmolean Museum (see p. 111)
Reading Museum
Rochester Museum
Saffron Walden Museum
St Albans, City Museum
Salisbury
Scarborough
Scunthorpe
Sheffield
Southampton, God's House Tower Museum
Southend-on-Sea, Prittlewell Priory Museum
Taunton
Thetford, The Ancient House Museum
Whitby
Whithorn, Priory Museum (see p. 243)
Winchester, City Museum
Worcester
Worthing
* York, the Yorkshire Museum (see p. 231)

Bibliography

The following bibliography is intended as no more than a guide to further reading. A single dagger (†) denotes a book suitable for the non-specialist reader.

Some general books on Dark Age Britain

Two general introductions cover both Celtic and Saxon Dark Age archaeology, as well as the prehistoric background. They are

†LAING, L *Celtic Britain* (Routledge & Kegan Paul, 1979)

†LAING, L and J *Anglo-Saxon England* (Routledge & Kegan Paul, 1979)

both are in the BRITAIN BEFORE THE CONQUEST series. For Anglo-Saxon archaeology the best introduction is still perhaps

†WILSON, D M *The Anglo-Saxons* (Penguin, 1971 [revised]; hardback, Thames & Hudson, 1960)

For the early period, the best book covering both the history and archaeology is

†ALCOCK, L *Arthur's Britain* (Penguin, 1974; hardback, Allen Lane, 1971)

Two detailed texts cover most aspects of the archaeology of the period.

LAING, L *The Archaeology of Late Celtic Britain and Ireland, c. 400–1200 AD* (Methuen, 1975, hardback and paperback)

WILSON, D M (Ed) *The Archaeology of Anglo-Saxon England* (Methuen, 1976)

The following general works may also be found useful:

Celtic

†ASHE, G *The Quest for Arthur's Britain* (Pall Mall, 1971)

†CHADWICK, N K *The Age of the Saints in the Early Celtic Church* (O.U.P., 1961)

†CHADWICK, N K *Celtic Britain* (Thames & Hudson, 1967)

HARDEN, D *Dark Age Britain* (Methuen, 1956)

†HENDERSON, I *The Picts* (Thames & Hudson, 1967)

THOMAS, C *The Early Christian Archaeology of North Britain* (O.U.P., 1971)

WAINWRIGHT, F T (Ed) *The Problem of the Picts* (Nelson, 1955)

Anglo-Saxon

Most of these are historical rather than archaeological.

†BLAIR, P H *An Introduction to Anglo-Saxon England* (C.U.P., 1956, paper, 1960)

†BLAIR, P *Northumbria in the Days of Bede* (Gollancz, 1976)

†BRITISH MUSEUM *Guide to the Anglo-Saxon Antiquities* (1923)

†JESSUP, R *Anglo-Saxon Jewellery* (Shire, paper, 1974)

†LOYN, H R *Anglo-Saxon England and the Norman Conquest* (Longmans, 1962)

STENTON, F *Anglo-Saxon England* (O.U.P., 2nd ed. 1947)

†WHITELOCK, D *The Beginnings of English Society* (Penguin, 1952)

Viking

Most of these are not specifically British.

†ARBMAN, *The Vikings* (Thames & Hudson, 1961)

†BRØNDSTED, J *The Vikings* (Penguin, rev. ed. 1965)

†KENDRICK, T *A History of the Vikings* (Methuen, 1930, recent reprint available)

†SAWYER, P H *The Age of the Vikings* (Arnold, 2nd ed. 1971)

†WILSON, D *The Vikings and Their Origins* (Thames & Hudson, 1970)

†WILSON, D and FOOTE, P *The Viking Achievement* (Sidgwick & Jackson, 1970)

Books on specific subjects

Pagan Saxons

EVISON, V *Fifth Century Invasions South of the Thames* (Athlone Press, 1965)

MEANEY, A *Gazetteer of Early Anglo-Saxon Burial Sites* (Allen & Unwin, 1964)

MYRES, J N L *Anglo-Saxon Pottery and the Settlement of England* (Oxford, 1969)

†GREEN, C *Sutton Hoo* (Merlin, paper, 2nd ed. 1968)

†BRUCE-MITFORD, R L S *The Sutton Hoo Ship Burial* (British Museum, 1968)

LEEDS, E T *The Archaeology of the Anglo-Saxon Settlements* (Oxford, 1913, reprint 1970)

LEEDS, E T *Anglo-Saxon Art and Archaeology* (Oxford, 1936, reprint 1968)

BROWN, G B *The Arts in Early England*, Vols 3–4, *Saxon Art and Industry in the Pagan Period* (John Murray, 1915)

Art and Architecture

KENDRICK, T *Anglo-Saxon Art to AD 900* (Methuen, 1938, reprint)

KENDRICK, T *Late Saxon and Viking Art* (Methuen, 1948)

†CLAPHAM, A *English Romanesque Architecture*, vol 1, *Before the Conquest* (Oxford, 1930, reprint 1969)

BROWN, G B *The Arts in Early England*, vol 2, *Ecclesiastical Architecture in England* (John Murray, 2nd ed. 1925)

BROWN, G B *The Arts in Early England*, vol 5, *Ruthwell Cross, Bewcastle Cross, Lindisfarne Gospel*, etc. (John Murray, 1921)

BROWN, G B *The Arts in Early England*, vol 6, *Sculpture* (John Murray, 1930)

TALBOT RICE, D *English Art 871–1100* (O.U.P., 1952)

†STONE, L *Sculpture in Britain: The Middle Ages* (Penguin, 1955)

WILSON, D M *Anglo-Saxon Ornamental Metalwork, 700–1100, in the British Museum* (British Museum, 1964)

†WILSON, D and KLINDT-JENSEN, O *Viking Art* (London, 1966)

Books on particular groups of monuments

TAYLOR, H M and J *Anglo-Saxon Architecture*, 3 vols (C.U.P., 1965–78)

NASH-WILLIAMS, V E *The Early Christian Monuments of Wales* (Cardiff, University of Wales Press, 1951)

FOX, C *Offa's Dyke* (British Academy, 1954)

KERMODE, P *Manx Crosses* (London, 1907)

COLLINGWOOD, W G *Northumbrian Crosses* (London, 1927)

KERMODE, P *The Manx Archaeological Survey, 1st–5th Reports* (1909–35, reprinted Manx Museum & National Trust, 1968)

BRUCE, J R *Manx Archaeological Survey, 6th Report* (Manx Museum, 1968)

ALLEN, J R and ANDERSON, J *Early Christian Monuments of Scotland* (Edinburgh, 1903)

CRUDEN, S H *The Early Christian and Pictish Monuments of Scotland* (HMSO, 1964)

Field Guides

There are numerous regional field guides to ancient monuments in Britain, most of which are confined to prehistoric and Roman remains. The volumes in the Penguin series N PEVSNER (Ed), *The*

Buildings of England are useful for sculptures and for noting Anglo-Saxon churches, but their descriptions are necessarily brief and for the churches at least the serious student should always consult TAYLOR, H M and J, in the list above, which describes all with known Saxon work. Two recent guides are excellent for Scotland and Wales, however:

MACKIE, E *Scotland: an Archaeological Guide* (Faber, 1975, hardback and paper)

HOULDER, C *Wales: an Archaeological Guide* (Faber, 1974)

Two of the Ordnance Survey historical maps will be found very useful, particularly for the lists of monuments they provide in the introductory material. They are

The Ordnance Survey Map of Britain in the Dark Ages (HMSO, 2nd ed. 1966)

The Ordnance Survey Map of Britain before the Norman Conquest (HMSO, 1974)

Index 1 – Sites

Index 2—Types of monument, art styles, inscriptions